Ethnicity
in an
International
Context

ETHNICITY
IN AN
INTERNATIONAL
CONTEXT

Edited by

Abdul Said
and
Luiz R. Simmons

Transaction Books
New Brunswick, New Jersey

Library of Congress Catalog Number: 74–20193.
ISBN:0–87855–110–7(cloth).

Printed in the United States of America.

Library of Congress Cataloging in Publication Data
Main entry under title:
Ethnicity in an international context.

    Includes bibliographical references and index.

1. Minorities. 2. Ethnicity. 3. World politics—1945-
I. Said, Abdul Aziz. II. Simmons, Luiz R.S.
JF1061.E84   301.45   74-20193
ISBN 0-87855-110-7

Contents

ACKNOWLEDGMENTS

We gratefully acknowledge the assistance of Thomas Lent in the original research for this volume. Thomas Lent gave his time and his insights unsparingly to this project from the beginning to the end.

In addition, Amaury Perez, Allen Hibbard and Dean Millot prepared the index and shared many of their thoughts on ethnicity with good cheer.

INTRODUCTION

The nation-state is no longer regarded as the paradigm of human organization. Curiously enough, while philosophers and political scientists since Bodien have pointed to the need to move beyond the nation-state into supranational legal, economic, and political organizations, it is difficult to identify an experiment, such as the European Common Market, where a supranational political consciousness has been achieved. Not only has the movement toward supranationalism been averted in environments conducive to theories of supranationalism, but also the emergence of a politics of disassociation — a disenchantment with the political institutions of the nation-state and an emphasis on ethnic, cultural, and political sovereignty — has persisted and occasionally exploded in many parts of the world.

The reasons for the conspicuous rise in ethnic politics are not always apparent. Ethnic movements have developed in environments that our theories and methodologies have told us are unlikely spawning grounds for secession and violence. Communication theory with its contribution to our perception of the processes of nation-state building has become increasingly suspect as a touchstone for interpreting the dynamics of nation building. There seems to be a normative renaissance insofar as the recognition that a nation-state is an intuitive expression of a people's perception of proper social and political organization. That such perceptions can and do change despite the social cement believed to be supplied by good communication networks and economic integration is one profitable inference to be drawn from the resurgence of ethnic activity.

The decline of geopolitics in international relations is another factor. The state, as an organizational expression of the historical preoccupation with physical security, has been progressively undermined by the development and proliferation of conventional and

nuclear weapons. The state is essentially a territorial form of organization in a century where security is no longer a function of geopolitics but of technology.

No longer the central organizing principle of physical security,
the social psychology of authority, as it manifests itself in state
patriotism, is undergoing a historical transformation. Antistatist
politics as it appears in ethnic disassociation is one expression of this
transaction.

Liberal theories of development have never embraced the idea
of ethnic diversity with intellectual enthusiasm. Diversity was seen
in terms of the coexistence of political systems, not ethnic nations.
Quite often the modus operandi of the quintessential nation builders
encouraged if not insisted on the detribalization of world politics,
which is no doubt a source of discomfort, for theories of development emphasize the necessity of rationalizing economic and political
systems to achieve economic growth.

The future of ethnic conflict is, of course, closely tied to the
future of the multiethnic state. A sample of 132 states shows that
only 12 (9.1%) can be considered ethnic-free. Twenty-five states
(18.9%) are comprised by an ethnic group that represents more than
90% of the state aggregate population, and in another 25 states
the largest ethnic group accounts for possibly 75–89% of the
population. However, in 31 states (23.5% of the total) the significant ethnic group constitutes only 50–74% of the population,
and in 39 states (29.5%) the largest group does not account for half
the state's population. It has been estimated that in 53 states (or
40.2%) the population is comprised into five or more significant
ethnic groups. In the West it is, as Raymond Aron correctly predicted, ethnic conflict that has replaced class conflict as an image
through which to understand future behavior. In Belgium, the government of Premier Aciston Eysken's fell after ten months in office.
Eysken had formed a coalition of Social Christians and Socialists
and had agreed to grant special status to approximately 5,000
French-speaking residents in the Flemish province of Limbourg.
Walloon ministers had consented to delimit the economic region
of Brussels as a gesture to relieve Flemish fears of a northward expansion of French language and culture. After a concord had been
reached to these points, the Flemish wing of the Social Christian

party escalated their demands by asking for more autonomy for a small Flemish community near Mons in Wallonia. In Spain, Basque activists are again operational in northern Spain. In Bilbao, according to the New York *Times*, "Fear and tension have risen perceptibly as young radicals, organized into a small but determined group called Basque Nation and Freedom, keep a step ahead of the police and the paramilitary Civil Guard." It is estimated that 190 Basques have been sentenced to prisons outside the Basque provinces. Basque terrorist activities have included throwing a bomb into a Civil Guard headquarters, burning the offices at the Ministry of Information and Tourism at Zarauz, and holding up a bank car for almost $192,000. According to reliable reports, a significant problem for the Spanish government is that "other regions, such as Catalonia and Galicia, might increase their agitation if it showed a more tolerant attitude toward the Basques."

In Yugoslavia, Croatian nationalists whom the government has described as "Fascist terrorists" have been identified with airline hijackings and terrorist attacks on Yugoslav diplomats. In Jasenovac, southeast of the Croatian city of Zagreb, the infamous Jasenovac camp was operated by the Ustashi, where perhaps as many as 800,000 people – primarily Jews, Serbs, and Gypsies – are thought to have been exterminated. The Yugoslav government has been careful not to press a vigorous campaign against the exiled Ustashi in apprehension of offending the four and one-half million people of Croatia, and reinvigorating enmities between Serbs and Croatians. Ethnic conflict is not confined to random or systematic acts of terrorism; it radiates in the social and cultural life of the state. The Serbian Philosophic Society's quarterly journal, *Filosogiya*, has a circulation of 1,500 copies. A Yugoslav court recently imposed a ban on an issue for making "false and alarming statements." The objections surrounded an editorial and article that the government alleged contributed to efforts to "disrupt the brotherhood and unity of the Yugoslav nationalities."

In Canada, one-fourth of the 22 million Canadians are French speaking, but most of them are in Quebec and the surrounding Eastern provinces – only three percent are west of Ontario. This distribution forms the basis for language and regional resentments. Bilingualism was an important issue in the October 1972 elections in which Trudeau's Liberals lost their majority in the House of Commons and gained only three of the forty-five seats in the prairie provinces.

In the October 1972 Parliamentary elections, Quebec and bilingualism were issues throughout the country. The issues reflect the traditional hostility between segments of Canada's French-speaking minority who feel exploited and discriminated against. Prime Minister Trudeau, who worked assiduously to upgrade the French language to be on a par with English, was an easy target for opposition party spokesmen who attacked him for deepening the divisions within the country.

In India, the fissiparous language issue remains more portentous for Indian society than her relations with China or Pakistan. Hindi is the national language as designated by the constitution, but English remains the dominant language in education, the courts, and industry. R. N. Mirdha, Minister of State for Home Affairs, has stated, "We cannot close our eyes to reality,...the bulk of the work in the central secretariat is carried on in English. Naturally we have to recruit people who have a knowledge of English." The language divisions are evident in a state where Hindi is understood by almost forty-five percent of the population and English is spoken by less than three percent and understood by almost fifteen percent. Violence has occurred in recent years in response to government efforts to press the use of Hindi.

Not all of the initiatives in the past five years have been pursued by ethnic minorities seeking to assert local patriotisms. The Soviet Union has quietly begun a controversial consolidation of its national planning regions that may ultimately erode the significance of individual Soviet ethnic republics as economic planning and management areas. This new consolidated system is being introduced despite persistent ethnic consciousness and as part of an effort to integrate the interests of ethnic republics into a more efficient economic scheme. Soviet information agencies have also been working to generate an overall "Soviet" nationalism and national pride in economic achievements to replace the fragmented ethnic loyalties across the country's hundred-odd nationalities.

In Africa, the introduction of modern technology and communication in the modernization process has not prevented what

Ali Mazrui describes as "the retribalization of politics, the resurgence of ethnic loyalties in situations of rivalry in the arena of resource allocation and domestic power politics." In Kenya, the leaders of the formidable Kikuyu people must be careful not to aggravate the sensibilities of local notables. In July 1969, President Kenyatta chose to appoint three ministers from Nyanza province in order to appease the grievances of the Luo people following the assasination of Tom Mboya. Kenya may be taken as an example of a society where interethnic conflict is managed along lines similar to conflict management among nations.

Since its independence from Britain in 1962, Uganda has been plagued by political instability created by intertribal rivalries. The struggle for power between former President Milton Obote and General Idi Amin is prefigured by shifting tribal coalitions and ethnic bargaining. Obote had alienated the formidable Buganda, whose political kingdom he abolished in 1966. The ascendancy to power of General Amin was characterized by the repression of Acholiu and Langi tribesmen within the army who continued to support Obote. Political instability in Uganda is certain to develop as Langi tribesmen and Acholi — who populate the region bordering on Sudan — accelerate their efforts against Amin.

Since ethnicism was hardly studied in the last decade, it is difficult to speculate on the depth and future of ethnic feelings or whether the ethnic group can still provide the communal satisfaction that the explosions of smaller and lesser neoethnic communities and subcultures are offering to Americans. But, during the sixties, an ethnic reformation may have been much in evidence, however much neglected. Observe that many did not conceal their envy of the black students' "peoplehood." Jewish activists, too, have acquired valuable lessons from the tactics of black ethnic politics.

This collection of essays should serve as an invitation to the student of politics to raise questions with himself and methodological questions with his discipline. Never before have issues of human rights and cultural self-determination attracted so much popularity and scholarly attention. What are the human rights of these ethnic nations? What should the position of the political scientist be in response to secessionist movements such as those that occurred in Pakistan and Nigeria? Should the prerogatives

of the sovereign state swallow the rights of the ethnic nation?
Can the two be reconciled?

Despite one's position on this dispute, the ethnic and the emerging neoethnic group will not disappear from world politics. As
emerging actors in the international system, they are indications
that our perceptions of international relations and the causes of war
and peace lag behind the consciousness of the men and nations we
study. The ethnic nation cannot yet compete with the state in
nuclear warheads and warships, but it continues to exercise formidable influence over the primary authority patterns of men.
It is from this exercise of power that revolutions are born.

The Ethnic Factor
in World Politics

Abdul A. Said and Luiz R. Simmons

The metropolis, the nation-state, the empire. . ., for men and women desperate for the health of their souls, such depersonalized collectivities have never been a place they could call home; even less so the corporation, the bureaucracy, the trade union, the party. These can only for a time put on the mask of Big Brother and counterfeit the ethos of community. Stalin and Mao may posture as heavy fathers of the nation; American corporations may pretend to be one big happy family; the fatherland may try to disguise itself as a Gothic tribe. But such deceptions soon break down under the weight of their own lies. Nothing better may replace them, only ugly, angry cynicism. But the deception is too difficult to maintain with conviction.[1]

A revived sense of ethnic identity has grown in the last few decades, and ethnic politics has emerged as a significant factor in the international political system. In recent years the antagonism of indigenous ethnic communities in Cyprus, Iraq, Malaysia, Guyana, Uganda, and Canada (to name only a few) have wrought important changes in the international relations of nation-states. There is an increasing tendency of ethnic peoples to think fundamentally in terms of the ethnic group and to demand separate political status for the group that is global in scope; and this is effectively challenging the political demography of Africa, Europe, and the Americas, as well as Asia. The ethnic conflicts of Ireland, the bloody struggle of Biafra and the secession of Bangladesh, the unsettling race riots in the United States, and the transformation of ethnic discontents into ethnic nationalism have placed their mark on the domestic and international politics of nations in persistent and conspicuous emanations.

Yet both traditionalists and behavioralists continue to rely upon the nation-state as the analytical tool for understanding international politics. According to this framework, states are political systems exhibiting community, consensus, and a monopoly on the means of violence. The incidence of war is a direct consequence of the lack of community and consensus between and among nation-states. War and the lesser tensions and hostilities are consequences of the improvident transactions of total identities, that is, nation-states. That few such total identities appear to exist in international politics has not changed the foci of analyses or perceptions of the international system.

Out of an estimated 164 disturbances of significant violence involving states between 1958 and May 1966, a mere 15 were military conflicts involving two or more states. The most significant violence after 1945 has found its *causus belli* in ethnic, tribal, and racial disputes that have often exerted a spillover effect in international politics.

The ethnology of the planet is too often a subject of inquiry limited to anthropologists and sociologists. The political scientist has not approached the study of societies to any extent because the focus of international relations since 1945 changed from nation-state to the possibilities of world federalism, regionalism, and multi-lateralism. Coincident with this development was the introduction of popular scholarly literature emphasizing the detribalization of multiracial states, the disappearance of ethnic loyalties (particularly in the postindustrial United States), and, finally, the emergence of transnational subcultures. In sum, the "vanishing ethnic" did indeed vanish, but only from the minds of students of international relations as theories of nation builders and supranationalism rose in attention and influence.

Nations vs States

Why then, statistically, has much of the present serious violence involving states been the consequence of the unresolved differences of these "vanishing ethnics"? Why do the ethnics persist? What accounts for their sensational impact on international politics in the past five years?

There are perhaps as many as 862 ethnic groups (nations) living within the nation-states of the world:

Africa (sub-Sahara)	239
Circum-Mediterranean	95
East Eurasia	93
Insular Pacific	128
North America	218
Central and South America	89[2]

What future impact will they have as and if the nation-state continues to be a declining form of economic and political association?

Raymond Aron has noted recently that ethnic conflict will replace class conflict in the latter third of the twentieth century. We believe that this is because the legitimacy of the modern state is struggling to overcome an international challenge to its supremacy rooted in the internal contradictions between the nation and the state. These contradictions become fully visible when loyalty to the state and loyalty to one's nation conflict. In this conflict are forged the incandescent passions of secession, civil war, and the unconscionable talent of some ethnic nations to completely destroy others. The state can be defined in terms of territory, population, and government, and its formation can be predicted in contemporary international relations, since it signifies the victory of positivism in the political affairs of men. One is generally recognized as a state when one exerts political control over a specific geographical area. Sovereignty is not a derivative of natural or divine law. Control is accompanied by international recognition in the transactions among nations; loss of control is invariably a precursor or loss of recognition. The state is a positivist contraption, both artifice and artificer of the nineteenth-century fruition of the positivist approach to human affairs. But the nation is a conscious expression of people's shared sense of "peoplehood," reflecting what Kurt Lewin has described as the "interdependence of fate." The political self-consciousness of nations is a product of the nineteenth century. Sir Ernest Barker stated the issue with enviable precision: "a nation must be an idea as well as a fact before it can become a dynamic force."[3]

We are entering a new era where state-nationalism as it has been known for the past few hundred years is undergoing serious, and perhaps fatal, stress. It may seem presumptuous to talk of the end of the nation-state in an era characterized by references to rising nationalism, but history is made of such contradictions. After the successful defense of monarchy, the defeated parliamentarians of the New Left were, in fact, destined to be vindicated within two generations. In our era, the secession of Bangladesh, the Kurdish independence movement, or the struggle in Northern Ireland mark a fundamental shift in international politics.

The proliferation of new states after World War II has obscured the problem of scale and underscores the absurdity of describing the People's Republic of China and the Bahamas as nation-states. The real international system consists of no more than twenty or thirty national and transnational actors who have any significant impact, and the top five actors have over half of the world's human and natural resources. The nation-state as a unit of analysis makes differences of degree so vast as to constitute differences in kind. Ethnic groups, in contrast, are more clearly defined and therefore constitute a real as opposed to a juridical construct for analysis.

The dominant causal agent behind the emerging international political system is the technological revolution in communication that permits previously isolated ethnic groups to become more visible and, in certain cases, interact across national boundaries. Perhaps mass communication, instead of unifying mankind, is paradoxically differentiating him into progressively smaller communities.

The new international system is both more parochial and simultaneously less geographic. Ethnic groups find more affinity along lines other than the national boundaries of traditional nation-states. The human need for a sense of community is gradually dissolving the bonds of geography that unite diverse groups within states. Community in this sense is of the ethnic group or of communes, citizens who find their interests coinciding outside the political context of a nation-state. What this means in practical terms is that community may rejoice at victories other than those of its state, since the defeat of its state will be a victory for its vision of community. The internal struggle within each state seeks its analogue in external politics. The domestic dispute requires the creation of a foreign-policy dispute. The case of the Kurds of Iraq serves as a good illustration. Mustafa Barazani, the Kurdish leader, rejoices at Iran's and Israel's victories, since the defeat of Arab Iraq will be a victory for the Kurdish community.

We have entered the age of ethnicity in international politics. In such an environment, where distance as a barrier to national and transnational culture groups is a diminishing consideration and relationship becomes paramount, man relies less and less upon the nation-state as an agent for fulfillment. A politics of ethnicism is beginning to dominate the behavior of divergent and anthropomorphically different cultures that will have wide impact upon their respective nation-states and demand new theoretical models explaining their respective nation-states, plus demanding new theoretical models explaining their interaction. Ethnicism confutes the viability of a national ethic and suggests the use and importance of ethnic groups to the understanding of international relations. The vitiation of concepts of national interest, such as status and faith have become dominant neologisms in explaining politics among nations.

The domestication of international politics is no doubt a disturbing trend for the decision-makers who must plot the course of the modern state. Many governments now predicate their internal legitimacy, the maintenance of which is first priority, on the performance of external policies. That is, there is an increasing trend by many governments to justify their domestic policies by reference to foreign commitments and antagonisms.

The conflict politics among states of the future will often be a response to the politics of ethnic disassociation.

The present phenomenon of ethnic conflicts cannot be adequately analyzed within the context of traditional concepts of international relations. Concepts of balance of power, bipolarity, or even polycentrism as loci of conflict obscure the fact that, as Andrew Greely has observed: "The conflicts that have occupied most men over the past two or three decades and which have led to the most horrendous outpouring of blood have had precious little to do with this ideological division. . . . In a world of the jet engine, nuclear energy, the computer, and the regionalized organization, the principal conflicts are not ideological but tribal. Those differences among men which were supposed to be swept away by science and technology and political revolution are destructive as ever."[4] The nation-state is no longer viewed as the ultimate community, nor is it even the primary source of loyalty in many instances.

Ethnicity vs Assimilation

Core cultural values persistently reject absorption into a higher level of identification. This is not to deny the role of conflict in re-tribalization. Awareness of one's ethnicity may well be, to a great degree, a function of coercive assimilation. Thus, when social groups are mobilized, congeniality and cooperation do not necessarily occur. Increased contact, exposure, and communication may exaggerate one's self-image, magnify cultural differences, produce conflict, and induce political disassociation. Additionally, economic development — an increase in material goods and services — does not immunize a society from ethnic conflict. The concomitants of economic growth — urbanization-secularization-industrialization — may lead to competition over limited opportunities and resources. Previously stable interethnic differences have fit patterns of comparative advantage or coexistence, while the industrial-technical society tends to have a commonizing effect on economic behavior and produces competitive channels of achievement.

Critics of ethnicism assert that it is dysfunctional, uneconomical, and irrational. Such criticism is hardly substantiated. Ethnic distinctions may in effect serve useful functions in cross-cultural relations. Larger states do not necessarily develop more rapidly than smaller ones. Smaller states have developed at least as rapidly as larger states since World War II (compare Taiwan, Lebanon, Cyprus, and Hong Kong to India, Indonesia, and Pakistan). Conflict is not necessarily irrational but the roots of cultural expression that produce conflict are psychosociological.[5] Cultures and ethnic groups have an inner logic that determines behavior, values, and attitudes that confound objective description or absolutism. The complexity of cultures necessitates a multidimensional appreciation of the intertwining institutions and people that synthesize a political, cultural, and collective consciousness. Concurrently, one must be sensitive to heterogeneity between and among ethnic groups.

Claude Levi-Strauss defines culture as "the complex whole which includes knowledge, belief, art, morals, custom, and other capabilities and habits by man as a member of society."[6] Levi-Strauss identifies structure to societies, diacritical features, language, conscious and unconscious levels of operation, kinship patterns, and myths. He urges the social scientist to understand the dynamics operating in the macro and micro levels of human behavior, and to relate the, "Synchronic to the Diachronic, the individual to the culture, the physiological to the psychological, the objective analysis of institutions to the subjective experience of individuals."[7] Structural anthropology aims not so much at the compartmentalization and universalization of culture and its institutions, but at the relationships between the institutions and social behavior, and the variation of customs from structures. Implicit in this notion is that culture is not only a static-structural phenomenon, but a salient one as well.

Ethnicity reveals a structure analogous to that of culture. Frederick Barth sees atomic groups "biologically self-perpetuating, their members share fundamental cultural values, realized in overt unity in cultural form; they make up a field of communication and interaction and their membership identifies itself and is identified by others."[8] An ethnic group is a culture and yet may belong to a larger culture. A static concept of ethnic groups conceives their cultural differentiation as a function of social isolation, ecological factors, adaptive measures, invention, and selective borrowing.[9] Such an approach negates the high import of cultural interaction.

Ethnic consciousness is as much an objective process of diacritical realization as it is a subjective self-ascription vis-à-vis other social groups. A complex hierarchy of potential identification exists, but Barth stresses that "ethnic identity is superordinate to most other statuses, and defines a way an individual operationalizes and externalizes his reference groups norms."[10] Adherence thus entails the analyzing of social life, and "implies a recognition of limitations or shared understanding, differences in criteria for judgment of value and performance, and a restriction of interaction to sectors of assumed common understanding and mutual interest."[11]

As structural anthropology accentuates the dynamic relationship between man and culture and its divergent consequences, social anthropology concentrates on the dynamic relationship of ethnic groups as they define social-psychological boundaries between and among themselves. Barth's insights are particularly useful here: "Boundaries persist despite a flow of personnel across them. . . categorical ethnic distinctions do not depend on an absence of mobility, contact, and information."[12] On the other hand, adds Barth, "stable interethnic relations presuppose a structure of interaction: a set of prescriptions governing situations of contact, and allowing for articulation in some sectors or domains of activity, and a set of proscriptions or social situations preventing interethnic interaction in other sectors, and thus insulating parts of the cultures from confrontation and modification."[13]

Thus begins to emerge the anthropological roots of ethnic conflict: the fluid relationships existing between ethnic groups catalyze sociopsychological identification and boundaries and do not necessarily induce conflict. Shared values are sometimes a component but not a sufficient condition of mutual understanding; the sectors of mutual activity entail competition as well as cooperation. Conflict and cooperation alike are indicators that man is living on the same plane; communication is thus predicated on a certain degree of community as illustrated in structural anthropology.

What configurations and matrixes of ethnic interaction result in conflict? Here, psychological anthropology plays an important role. It focuses on the teleological roots of ethnic conflict and the fundamental difference between ethnic groups,[14] and explores the relationship of human beings, their levels of interaction, and such crosscurrents as social change and economic development. Such currents infuse change and substance into cultural adaptation and contribute to the friction within and between cultures.

Francis Hsu's concept of psychosocial homeostasis clarifies the organic relationship between culture, ethnic contact, and the resulting phenomenon or, more specifically, ethnic contact and ensuing behavior. Hsu views psychosocial homeostasis as the level of psychic and interpersonal equilibrium within a society.[15] This tool of analysis flows from a scientific desire for a "more precise formulation of how man lives as a social and cultural being"[16] and how his cultural expressions take institutional and sociopolitical form in a disequilibriated environment.

Predictability of ethnic conflict appears to be contingent upon those levels of articulation between cultures that are affective and those that are decreasingly utilitarian, along with varying intensities. One might not expect ethnic conflict even if ethnic group A has a predominant advantage in political representation if ethnic group B is not politicized. Internecine behavior is as much a function of commonality of values as of a multiplicity of values. Thus, viewed from an ecological perspective, ethnic transactions are dependent on: (1) minimal competition for scarce resources (be they natural or occupational) where the area of articulation will be in trade; (2) territorial claims (in which articulation is politicized); (3) symbiosis and interdependence where articulation is multiple; and (4) partial competition for the same niche, where conflict is most likely.[17]

Structural and valuational motifs of interaction are integral to understanding the roots of ethnic conflict. As a corollary, the milieu of interaction is defined and redefined by sociopsychological boundaries that man involve cultural ascription, social prescription, and political proscription. Emerging from this contention is the concept of ethnopolitical culture, which reflects the structural and salient milieu as well as the values involved in interethnic communication and articulation.

Admittedly such an analysis of ethnic conflict can lead the investigator in many different paths depending on his proclivities. The rich legacy of scholarly studies on ethnicism deepens our understanding at the micro level. But, even then, what is catalytic in one conflict may be either nonexistant or peripheral in another. Thus, Catholicism in an important factor in Northern Ireland, but the Flemish and Waloons are Catholic in Belgium where language is the issue. The Copts are not proportionately represented in governmen-

tal decision making in Egypt, but no civil war has yet developed; yet
denial of constitutional rights provoked a war of secession in Pakistan.

Ethnicism and Development

Is it conflict that causes tribalism or tribalism that causes conflict? We hope to demonstrate that the biases of Western ideologies
and methodologies have consistently led us to accept the former,
while treating the latter as a casualty for the trash heap of history.
Our religious faith in progress has prevented us from recognizing
that while there is nothing inevitable about ethnic conflict, neither
is it evident that nation builders will discover the precise formula to absorb so formidable an antagonist. Thus we are compelled to
posit the ethnic nation as an irreducible dilemma for the state, one
that under the proper (or dysfunctional) conditions can emerge as
a truculent divisive force. Conflict, such as economic scarcity or
political or cultural repression, can exacerbate these tendencies, but
it is not demonstrable that an absence of these conflicts (were it
possible?) would mean the withering away of the ethnic nation.

Professor Milton Gordon has reminded us that the term *ethnic
group* has been used to embrace the unities of race, religion, and
national origin. However, the common denominator of these categories is a "common social-psychological referent," which acts to
create a consciousness of peoplehood. Thus the term *ethnic* is in-
vested with a broader significance than it has been given by some
sociologists who use the term *ethnic group* as a typology of national
origin. Obviously, the raising of such a consciousness has direct
implications in social, economic, and of course political behavior.
How difficult it must be, for example, to persuade an ethnic group
to reweave the values, attitudes, and norms that characterize a
group's authority patterns since, as Milton Gordon states:

> Common to all these objective bases, however, is the social-
> psychological element of a special sense of both ancestral and
> future-oriented identification with the group. These are the
> "people" of my ancestors, therefore they are my people, and
> they will be the people of my children and their children. . .
> in a very special way which history has decreed. I share a sense
> of indissolvable and intimate identity with *this group* and

not that one within the larger society and the world.[18]

Clifford Geertz has elaborated upon the contrast inherent in such a definition, which he refers to as *communalism*[19] In India, it is based on religious contrasts, in Malaya we are primarily attracted to racial differences, and in the Congo by tribal affiliations. Divisions based on economic, class, or political disaffection may be the harbinger for civil strife, but alienation based on culture, language, race, and nationality are elements that comprise what Professor Shils has called the *primordial* ties and are the foci of authority and patriotism *within* the state that it often seeks to replace or from which it seeks to disassociate. Geertz identifies several ascriptive characteristics around which much ethnic conflict has revolved: Assumed Blood Ties, like those that characterize the "hill tribes" of Southeast Asia and the Kurds; Race, a volatile element in the transactions between the ex-colonial powers and the ex-colonial states; Language, such as that which served as the basis for the political crisis that toppled the Belgian government and threatens the Canadian unity; Religion, of which Indian partition is an outstanding example of these divisive passions – and the turmoil in Ireland a disturbing reminder – and Custom, examples of which are the Bengalis in India and the Javanese in Indonesia.

Throughout this patchwork of social organization and behavior patterns, the ethnic group is self-consciously defined by the kind of social-political differentiation and cultural autonomy that we usually associate with candidates for statehood. Thus it would be surprising after reviewing the literature about the ethnic group as well as the literature written by ethnic spokesmen if the theorists of modernization and nation building did not dedicate themselves to constructing a viable paradigm that recognized the tenacity of these social organizations and their logical implications for theories of modernization. But curiously this has not been the case. Standard works on development have addressed themselves to analysis of the military, the bureaucracy, social classes, and urbanization. In fact, as Andrew Greeley has wryly observed regarding the United States, throughout the 1960s articles on ethnic groups and ethnic behavior were scrupulously ignored by journals of scholarship.

Perhaps the proclivities of Western scholars to treat the ethnic group and ethnic politics as a transitional social organization in the stages of political growth is rooted in the scientific rationalism of the postfeudal European period. Floyd Matson has traced the intellectual history of the application of the Newtonian model to the social sciences from the applied science of "social mathematics" invented by de Witt through the zealous initiatives of the Saint-Simonians to apply the Newtonian world view to the study and manipulation of society:

> Their vision was of a society wholly made over in the image of the new mechanics — technically rationalized in every detail, predictable in every activity, and hence brought under total scientific management. The religion of science was a faith in the existence of an objective reason, impersonal and mechanical, harmonious and determinate, existing entirely apart from individual men and indifferent to their purposes.[20]

This ideal of progress — linear, rational, and positivist — was canonized by the development of the political economy of the nation-state, which as Jacques Ellul has pointed out

> was constructed little by little, and all of its individual techniques were improved by mutual interaction. . . . Who was to coordinate this multiplicity of techniques? Who was to build the mechanism necessary to the new economic technique? Who was to make binding the decision necessary to service the machines? The individual is not by himself rational enough to accept what is necessary to the machines. He rebels too easily. He requires an agency to restrain him, and the state had to play this role. . . . To this end, the state itself must be coherent.[21]

Ellul's framework of analysis — shared to an important degree by contemporary expositors of a "counterculture" — is a stark analysis and projection of the impact of scientific rationalism on the varieties of human behavior and social organization. But the early theorists of the nation-state were not attracted by its potential to control and predict human behavior within a political and econo-

mic schemata. Thomas Hobbes is one of these writers who exerted
a great deal of influence on the development of the state. *The
Leviathan* was forged in the crucible of disorder — religious wars
and so forth — that plagued seventeenth-century Europe. As Professor Nisbet has written:

> In Hobbes's conception of the State and its law, in his treat-
> ment of the foundations of social order, and in his theory of
> internal associations, there are few if any remaining evidences
> of the medieval image of society. . . . Gone, in Hobbes, is the
> troubled affection for associations based on locality, interest,
> and faith. Gone also is the profound veneration for kinship,
> for the inviolable household, for the imprescriptible authority
> of the house-father. Neither the family, the church, nor any
> other system of authority is allowed by Hobbes to intervene
> in any significant way between the individual and the absolute
> power of the State.[22]

But we should pause to consider that for Hobbes the concentration of power was not an end in itself. It was a means to seduce
and eliminate the parochial social barriers of custom, religion, and
ethnic fratricide that he perceived to be the foremost obstacle to
human fulfillment in his century.

Whether we are dealing with the extermination of Brazilian
Indians or the contemporary ethnic conflict in Uganda, Ireland, or
Pakistan, we are naturally attracted to the anomaly of the twentieth
century — the impulse for Western modernization and the accelerating consciousness for self-determination among varieties of linguistic,
religious, and geographical ethnic groups. The questions that such a
conflict poses for a normative political scientist may be phrased in
this manner: Although I believe that states must assimilate ethnic
nations Y and Z in order to provide the modern economic, health,
and social services that they deserve as citizens of the twenty-first
century — what about the possibility that nations X and Y resist
the devaluation of sovereignty? What rights if any do they have
under my scheme for modernization? What limitations, if any,
should be placed on the central authority in their attempts to force
secessionist ethnic-nations to adapt to the political economy of the

state?

Each of us can pose a different question that places more or less emphasis on the fruits of modernization or the political or cultural exhilaration of ethnic sovereignty, but finally we must confront the root question of how we shall balance our commitment to human rights with the contemporary experience of "nation building" — often a bitter by-product of civil war. Then again, as we are rediscovering in the social sciences, our view of the controversy may be considerably influenced by the state we are living in at a particular point in history. States wracked by ethnic conflicts are probably less inclined to view secession and civil war as expressions of some transcendent human struggle than states that experience an acceptable level of ethnic conflict that does not approach disassociation. Another problem is posed when a state or international agency, attempting to intervene in behalf of a national minority, confronts the dilemma posed by Conor Cruise O'Brien:

> We tell, let us say, the Tuts that the right he fancies he possesses to dominate the Hutu is not a real right. He replies in effect that as far as his culture is concerned it *is* a right. We tell him it is not a right, because it is contrary to democracy, an ideology to which our ancestors became converted in the nineteenth century. He says his ancestors did not become so converted; are we claiming that our ancestors were superior to his? Now, that is a forked question, and we have to be very careful how we answer it. If we say, "No, no, of course not my dear fellow," he can say in reply: By what right then are we telling him that he must act according to the acquired conviction of our ancestors who are admittedly no better than his own. If, on the other hand, we say, yes, our people represent a more advanced stage of civilization than his do, he may reply that this is exactly his own position in relation to the Hutu.[23]

The response of the state to disaffected ethnic minorities has not been generous by most Western standards. The Tibetans with the Chinese, the Montagnards in South Vietnam, and the examples of Iraq, Cyprus, Rwanda, and the Sudan are indispensable reference points for predicting the state response to ethnic conflict and the politics of disassociation. Self-determination movements are invariably viewed as threats to the survival of the state. States threatened by such acts of disassociation have treated the leaders of these movements as traitors and have interned them without even the causal regard for their own concepts of due process. In Guyana, for example, a *Security Bill* was passed in 1966 by the black-controlled government to restrict the activities of East Indians. The terms of the act call for the Prime Minister to intern without trial for eighteen months anyone he believes has or *will* act in a manner that threatens public order.[24] The Sixteenth Amendment to the Indian Constitution, passed in response to the Pravidistan movement, seeks to "prevent the fissiparous, secessionist tendencies in the country engendered by regional and linguistic loyalties, and to preserve the sovereignty and territorial integrity" of the Indian state.[25]

States can usually expect to lend covert or overt assistance to other states confronting ethnic dissidents unless, of course, the dissident ethnic elements are perceived as instrumentalities in the foreign policy armamentarium of one state to disrupt the internal affairs of another state. Basque nationalism furnishes a good example of the former, Chinese foreign policy in Burma, the latter. The Basque region is on the border of Spain and France. Although the French deny providing assistance to the Spanish government, since 1970 France has increased the expulsion of Basque political refugees. Basques, on either side of the border, note that improved French-Spanish relations that culminated in the French sale of armaments to Spain have contributed to growing collaboration of the governments on the Basque problem.[26]

Ethnic-nations and Foreign Policy

While it should by now be becoming increasingly evident that ethnic conflict in Uganda can make itself felt in the diplomatic struggle in the Middle East or that Basque terrorism that ignores the French-Spanish border can pave problems between two states, there is another dimension to the study of ethnic conflict that demands a brief inquiry. The nation-state has been forced by historical circumstance to share the stage with other actors, such as multinational corporations, transnational subcultures, and, of course, ethnic nations. Quite often these ethnic nations, dissatisfied with political and social conditions at home, have begun to pirate international passenger flights, assassinate diplomats in foreign lands, and even to extort ransom from multinational giants such as Ford Motor Co. Kidnappings of businessmen and diplomats have become a familiar feature in international politics.

The mobility of ethnic nations in the international environment and the highly integrated state of our technology makes disruption of international services an easy mark. This, naturally, should and undoubtedly will call forth a response by nation-states, communist, socialist, capitalist, and so forth, manifesting itself in new conventions and bilateral treaties with procedures for extradition and perhaps even international accords. This is only one local consequence of ethnic conflict for politics among nations. Another is the manipulation of ethnic conflict in one state by another state. The Indian Parliament has acknowledged that hundreds of Nagas have been trained by the Chinese, armed and returned to northeastern India. General Ne Luin of Burma has alleged that China has furnished sanctuary to Kachin dissidents and has contributed to the credibility of reports linking China to other secessionist movements within Burma.

Concomitantly, it is, in our estimation, becoming increasingly evident that these rebellious secessionist-ethnic nations will turn to illicit trafficking in contraband in order to finance guerrilla activities or to maintain their bases of political and cultural sovereignty within a state. This raises a fundamental question about the processes through which our foreign policy takes shape. The United States still continues to pursue — with only slight deviation — practices formed in the nineteenth-century crucible of diplomacy. This procedure calls for direct transactions among governments who exercise political control over a geographical area. In an age of political consciousness characterized by retribalization and neo-ethnic behavior, this is a myopic posture. Difficult a task as it may be, foreign policy must be able to learn how to communicate with different ethnic-nations within a single state if it wishes to achieve its objectives. This will require differentiation of messages on a scale as impractical and as improvident as a century ago. It will also require political contacts with dissident ethnic-nations occasionally, at the expense of political relations with the constituted central government. Much, of course, will depend on the objectives to be achieved, and so the drawing is offered.

The United States has a major heroin-addiction problem that is the cause of significant social disorganization in its large urban centers, such as New York, Detroit, and Los Angeles. President Nixon has stated that, "If we cannot destroy the drug menace in America, then it will surely in time destroy us." Large sums of money have been appropriated by the U.S. Congress to finance the overseas activities of the Bureau of Narcotics and Dangerous Drugs, as well as Research and Rehabilitation programs at home. Through a vigorous and systematic recall of American ambassadors and personnel in designated regions of the world, the United States has raised the issue of narcotics to an issue of foreign policy. It has relied upon the traditional techniques of foreign policy in dealing with countries such as Thailand, Laos, Burma, Turkey, and Afghanistan, such as A.I.D. assistance to help farmers grow alternative crops to the poppy, technical and enforcement assistance, threats to discontinue foreign assistance, and exchanges of scientific and enforcement information. These prodigious efforts are predestined to fail for a variety of reasons that we have explored elsewhere. However, the point that concerns us here is the nature of the illicit traffic in opiates, and which groups are intimately involved in these international transactions. It is incontestable that there is a high degree of involvement in the illicit traffic by disaffected ethnic or tribal groups throughout the world. Leaving aside for the moment the powerful French-Corsicans who have dominated the Turkish-French-American axis, we find that the illicit trafficking networks are heavily influenced by regional ethnic-nations.

The major traffickers in the triborder area (China, Thailand, and Cambodia) include the K.M.T. and the Chinese irregular forces who organize mule caravans and furnish escort from Burma to Thailand. The K.M.T. are the remnants of Kuomingtang nationalist forces driven from China in 1949. They are now recruiting entirely from the local population. The Combined Forces of the K.M.T. are placed at between 4,000 and 6,000 heavily equipped men. The Fifth and Third Divisions, with an estimated manpower of 1,900 and 1,700, control eighty percent of the drug traffic in the Shan State in Burma. The K.K.Y. are former Shan State insurgents who compete

with the K.M.T. forces for control of the opium trade. The K.K.Y.
has allied with the Burmese central government against Communist
Chinese supported insurgents in return for which the government
had ignored their opium activities. The International Narcotics
Trade furnishes their interesting account of one trafficker:

> Perhaps the best illustration of the intriguing and oftentimes
> dangerous routing system is to trace a traffic pattern of one of
> the area's most notorious opium kingpins, Chan Chi-foo. Half-
> Burmese, half-Chinese, Chan is at home in the opium-growing
> sections of northwest Burma. Speaking several dialects, he
> reportedly deals as easily with bankers and businessmen in
> Bangkok as he does with mountain tribesmen in Burma. So
> extensive are his smuggling operations that Chan reportedly
> commands up to 2,000 heavily armed men as well as thou-
> sands more hill tribesmen, porters, hunters, and opium
> growers. So extensive are his caravans that legend has it that
> they may stretch for nearly a mile, and may include 400
> armed guards, a couple of hundred mules, as many porters
> and attendants, and may carry up to 20 tons of opium.[27]

Opium is smuggled into Iran from Afghanistan. Nomadic tribes
are heavily involved in this traffic. The most active tribes are the
Ghilzai, (Pathan), Baluchis, and Turkmen. The Ghilzai transport
opium from east-central Afghanistan, while the Shinwaris operate
primarily near the Pakistan border. The western sections of the Bal-
uchistan desert are staging areas for the Baluchi caravans, while the
route of the Turkmen crosses northern Afghanistan.

Afridi (Pathan) tribesmen dominate the opium traffic in Pakistan. The World Opium Survey states that, "Tribal relationships suggest that the Afridis pass their opium to the Shinwaris and Ghilzai
in Afghanistan for movement to Iran if they do not carry it through
Afghanistan themselves."[28] The decision of the Turkish government
to eliminate poppy cultivation has resulted in increasing emphasis
being placed on South and Southeast Asia as a source of opium by
international drug traffickers.

United States foreign policy will remain ineffectual with regard
to arresting the illicit traffic in narcotics as long as it continues to

negotiate with central governments who cannot control the activities of their ethnic nations. Should the U.S. negotiate with the Kabul or the Afridis? No doubt relations with the central government would be impaired, but the advantages and disadvantages of such a trade-off should be fully explored.

Neoethnic Behavior

We are in for an interlude during which an increasing number of people in urban-industrial society will take their bearings in life from the I Ching and the signs of the zodiac, from yoga and strange contemporary versions of shamanic tradition. The quest for a communal reality assumes the shape of a massive salvage operation reaching out in many unlikely directions.[29]

Is it necessary to reiterate that the ethnic group is not an anachronism of feudal and preindustrial society, but that these antagonisms of modernization dogma continue to demonstrate remarkable persistence even in *postindustrial* nations such as the United States. Odder still is that behavior (curiously resembling that which is associated with tribalism in the less developed countries) should continue to plague the states forged in the crucible of scientific rationalism and rationalist-liberal ideologies. The Marxist and Liberal ethoses have been quite insistent in their claim that the axis upon which new social confabulations shall move do not make caveats or concessions to these protagonists of an anachronistic social consciousness.

And yet despite such calumny, an ethnic revival or a rediscovery of diversity, as Andrew Greely has described it, is quite underway in a society least susceptible — in theory of course — to such blandishments. If we accept the proposition that an ethnic group is a "collectivity *based on presumed common origin*, which shapes to some extent the attitudes and behaviors of those who share that origin, and with which certain people may freely choose to identify at certain times of their lives" (emphasis added),[30] we are able to certify our understanding of behavior whose roots extend no further than the demography of the eighteenth- and nineteenth-century Europe. If we were to accept the hypothesis that to the extent that conscious self-definition permits ethnicity as a means of relating to the physical and social environment, a formula for self-definition — an "option" — then what of those who seek to experience the nexus of community but who demonstrably lack the connection of blood or land? Are those societies that have apprehended the contours of an existential visage to be afforded no options for the redefinition of community?

The social psychology of ethnicism is closely bound up with the concept of political and social community, of which Michael Oakeshotte is a notable expositor:

> Those societies which retain, in changing circumstance, a lively sense of their own identity and continuity (which are without that hatred of their own experience which makes them desire to efface it) are to be counted fortunate, not because they possess what others lack but because they have really mobilized what none is without and all, in fact, rely upon.
>
> In political activity, then, men sail a boundless and bottomless sea; there is neither harbor nor shelter nor floor for anchorage, neither starting place nor appointed destination. The enterprise is to keep afloat on an even keel; the sea is both friend and enemy; and the seamanship consists in using the resources of a traditional manner of behavior in order to make a friend of every inimical occasion.[31]

In a like fashion, Susanne Langer has observed that human associations and human values are inseparably bound up as dimensions of the same phenomenon. She writes that:

> The mind, like all other organs, can drain its sustenance only from the surrounding world; our metaphysical symbols must spring from reality. Such adaptation always requires time, habit, tradition, and intimate knowledge of a way of life. If now, the field of our conscious symbolic orientation is suddenly plowed up as tremendous changes in the external world and in the social order, we lose hold, our convictions, and there with our effectual purposes. ... All old symbols

are gone and thousands of average lives offer no new materials
to a creative imagination.[32]

Modernization has often served as the precursor to mass movements and war as men have sought to reestablish the social psychology of community in a radically altered environment. But as we
approach the twenty-first century, men seem to have wearied of
the millennial visions promised by the ideologies of the nineteenth
century. As Daniel Bell has noted:

> Thus one finds, at the end of the fifties, a disconcerting
> caesura. In the West, among the intellectuals, the old passions
> are spent. The new generation, with no meaningful memory of
> the old debates, and no secure tradition to build on, finds
> itself seeking new purposes within a framework of political
> society that has rejected, intellectually speaking, the old
> apocalyptic and visions. In the search for a "cause" there is a
> deep desperate, almost pathetic anger, . . .a restless search for
> a new intellectual radicalism. . . . The emotional energies –
> and needs – exist, and the questions of how one mobilizes
> these energies is a difficult one.[33]

We venture to suggest that no new intellectual radicalism has
risen like the phoenix from the ashes of ideological fires but that
a popular radicalism, a *neoethnic* response to the depersonalization
and rationalization of the postindustrial society and certain changes
in the traditional function of the nation-state, has diffused into
political and cultural sensibilities that assume many forms of
expression. We are not quite comfortable with the traditional con-
ceptions of Gemeinshaft and Gesellschaft. The Gemeinshaft was the
ideational model of human community, while Gesellschaft signified
the individuality and rationalistic condition of modern Western society. However, as Edward Shils has endeavored to point out,[34] the
concept of Gemeinshaft "covered a diversity of phenomena, which
truth required to be separated from each other." Professor Hermann
Scholenbach in an essay, "Die soziologische Kategorie des Bunder,"
argued that a state of intense solidarity between men and women
was possible without common territory of origin or common blood

and family ties. The elimination of these primordial elements from the concept of Gemeinshaft left society with the Bund, the league, gang, brotherhood, many of the lesser associations that mediate between man and the state, and of which de Tocqueville observed was quite prevalent in America. If this were all that was involved in the quest for community so characteristic of American society in the 1960s and early 1970s, then we would be content to leave it at that. But it strikes us as being something more than this. Neoethnicism in American life is certainly an admixture of characteristics associated with the Bund and the ethnic group. The comprehensive state of solidarity and absence of blood or land ties is evocative of the Bund — but the accompanying demands for self-determination, cultural and political sovereignty are suggestive of behavior associated with the ethnic group. The sociological landscape in the United States is prefigured by both ethnic and neoethnic behavior. Thus, we are anxious to suggest that neoethnicism is a neologism that describes both a model of social organization in postindustrial society as well as identifiable actors within it.

A politics of neoethnicism is investing itself in the styles, politics, and social organization in America that will have a wide impact on theories of national development and integration. Neoethnicism as a system is a transition from the national consciousness of the nation-state to more communal forms of identity and organization characterized by cultural patriotism, ethnic nationalism, and a revolt against anxiety. A primary agent of this transformation is the primacy of communication in the process of mobilizing unassimilated minorities and subcultures, the growth of particularistic and minority nationalism, in a redefinition of national consciousness. It has been described at its farthest points by a process of retribalization, the philosophical concession to communal imperatives characterized by the "interdependence of fate" and a proliferation of related life-styles. In its paramount expression, it is the apostasy of the nation-state, an exhaustion with the cumulative preoccupations of national and world institutions and the preference for the pursuit and study of personal and parochial problems. It is expressed in a variety of ideologies, among a variety of classes. It has assumed both subtle and overt expressions and is stimulated by structural changes in the function of the state.

Neoethnicism is not an exercise in the apocalyptic. It is an articulation of the crisis in the expectation and promise of national institutions. It confutes the viability of state institutions to respond to the social-psychological needs of community, and it has found its expression in political and cultural themes and motifs as seemingly diverse as civil disobedience, the chants of La Raza, ethnic consciousness, youth ghettos, subcultures,[35] decentralization, community control, rural and professional communes, and the growth of the modern university. It is not the expression of the disenchanted but rather it is becoming the basis for a major reorganization of American life.

The legitimacy of the postindustrial state[36] is struggling to overcome a national challenge to its supremacy as profound in its implications as were the transitions in communal psychology from the household to the polis, the rise of the territorial state, and the loss of faith of the thirties.

It has been incongruous to hear the incessant clamor for community and community control (which preoccupation we believe fair to associate with a broad spectrum of Americans) when we contemplate the original purposes of the nation-state. It was to be the "terminal community," "the remnants of former types of ethnicity," the source "of all cultural energy and economic well–being," a "community in behavior," the consummation of strange and diverse loyalties.

But what sense are theorists to make of a generation of Americans engaged in a redefinition of the "terminal community," which many expressions of college and high-school activism, ethnic resurgence, preoccupations with the occult, and the emergence of mass movements share a common theme: the transition to new phases in communal psychology.[37]

This revolt against the discontinuities of modern American life found its expression in the rich popular sociology of the fifties. The alienation of today is perhaps more pronounced among certain elements of the young, but not confined to them.

The decline of the terminal community as the focal point for diverse loyalties is manifested in the sense of "powerlessness" among those who continue to wrestle the contradiction of state institutions and nonethnic, communal aspiration, while shaping original and smaller, personal, and social institutions. This contradiction is an especially poignant preoccupation of this generation that has suffused the politics of neoethnicism and community with | spectacular vigor.

Was this an unexpected phenomenon? The dialogue of conventional politics, placing extraordinary emphasis upon political strategies, relied on a diffusion of state power through decentralization, revenue-sharing, freedom of choice, school designs, the philosophical limitation of statism inherent in "benign neglect," and a political agenda that parodies the nostalgic "power to the people" slogan of the Port Huron statement. It is so strange, for example, that the young would demand in their universities, high schools, industries, and personal ideologies a passion for reexamination, decentralization, and community.

However, the "sickness of government" is only a political symptom of the disenchantment with the disutility of the modern state.

Inquiries into the foundations of the nation-state and nationality tend to agree with the proposition that nationalism is a conscious choice where a nationality "seeks to find its expression in what it regards as the highest form of organized activity, a sovereign state."

However, the "impermeability" of the nation-state and its significance in this transformation was not wasted on the young beats for whom the cold war and new weapons had ushered in an age where "you have a sense of utter helplessness in the face of forces apparently beyond the control of man."

The intensity of neoethnic politics among the young reflects the changing sensibilities in an age of maximum weaponry where the utility of the state as a territorial instrument for preservation has lost its cogency, and where security has become a function of technology, not of geopolitics.

This reorganization of security has acted as a catalyst in the reexamination of other state institutions and functions and has revealed an extraordinary degree of weariness with the institutions of the nation-state. In such a system, where the nation-state is no longer regarded as the "highest" form of organization, interest groups — cultural and racial minorities — not receiving satisfaction from the processes of the state, are easily mobilized to pursue nonnational alternatives to political and cultural communities.

It has been observed that, "The characteristic style of industrial society is based on the principles of economics and economizing on efficiency, least cost, maximization, optimization, and functional rationality, yet it is at this point that it comes into sharpest conflict with the cultural trends of the day, for the culture emphasizes anticognition and antiintellectual currents that are rooted in a return to instinctual modes.[38]

Thus, the real generation gap of legendary parlance lies in a generation, for example, of American youth who do not demonstrate radically different values from those of their parents,[39] but who are developing a variety of nonnational institutions to enact them.

It is curious to note that expressions of tribalism and "peoplehood" among the young are found not only in the extended families of hippies, but also among young blue-collar workers in Corpus Christi, Texas.

> Everybody says, "Naw, man, I don't need anybody." There comes a time when you'll go, you need somebody bad. And like with your outlaw groups, especially with the bandits, there's just something about it that, you're brothers. Anything your brother's got you've got. And there's no no, nobody turns anybody down. Or nobody messes over anybody. You don't hurt a brother. And if, if a brother thought that it would save your life for him to die for you, he'd do it. Some people say, "Well, this is crazy. You don't do stuff like that." That's real love, and freedom, also. You're doin' your own thing and you've got somebody that you can fall back on, somebody that can fall back on you, but you're doin' something.[40]

Let us recapitulate. Ethnic behavior is rooted in the presumption of common rights. Jews, Italians, and blacks are examples of ethnics who share such an image. Neoethnic behavior is not rooted in the presumption of common origin. It resembles the social organization of the Bund, but it is distinguished by its quest for an identity that can serve as the equivalent basis of common origin. The political self-consciousness of these groups is manifested alike in demands for "community control" and in the creation of counter-cultures, and subcultures that are based upon either ascriptive characteristics (ethnic) or function, occupational, and secular characteristics (neoethnic).

The prologue of activism and the themes of community and protest in the 1960s suggest the imminence of new social forms and associations and the relocation and creation of "smaller" and original patriotisms. While legitimacy and authority have suffered the vicissitudes of ethnicism and neoethnicism, the transitory phases of mass movements, social unrest, the proliferation of radical journals, the emergence of temporary and exotic fringe cultures (such as happenings – identified with youth culture, but not confined to them); in sum, the rush to alternative forms of community prefigure the rise of an alternative, organic social order. The decline in the legitimacy of the nation-state has sponsored a revival in alternative image systems, initially described in the "forerunner" groups by the rise for the occult, mysticism, and the suprarational with its implications for the sociology of religion. It is important to recognize that, historically, mysticism has corresponded with the romantic stage of religion and a certain communal way of living and believing.

It may be the institution of ethnic quotas, the "contrameritocratic" revolt of hippies, the efforts of ethnic groups in upbuilding their neighborhoods and communal institutions, or the significance of draft evasion for the legitimacy of the state, but these expressions must be seriously contemplated as rising forms of protest to the raison d'être of the nation-state, and the revival of conflict between ethnic and neoethnic nations and the state.

It is no longer adequate to expain black nationalism as a fantasy or ethnicism as a folly, with a rising sense of community and purpose among young blacks. Exhortations to adopt a "black ideology" in toto, a path itself to blackness and nationhood, and the decision in some communities to create a greater sense of identity, unity, and spirit of nationalism augurs the rise and prominence of ethnic nationalism.[41]

A speculative essay forecasting the future of ethnic groups has observed that "culture shock" precedes the formation, organization, and emergence of immigrant self-consciousness. If this "culture shock" can be compared analytically to the disfigurations of continuity for which we are told we must prepare, then it is worthwhile to make several observations regarding the current invigoration of ethnic politics in the United States.

Ethnicism may be emerging as yet another communal response to the decline of national consciousness and the growth of neoethnicism. The explanation for its vitality can be found in the explanation for the burgeoning lesser communities and the of the young: identity and communal satisfaction.

The fulcrum of the current youth movements in the United States has been the university, and it is here that the broad scope of the politics of neoethnicism may be finally attenuated and will emerge as a national body of political doctrine.

The university occupies a prominent role with regard to the articulation of neoethnicism. What we have tended not to realize is that it is but one impressive focus of advocacy.

A distinguishing characteristic of neoethnic life is the emergence of the university life-style as an alternative life-style to the rationalization of the "technetronic" society. Analysts had become overly romantic about the role of hippies, yippies, left-wing radicals, and activists in the turmoil of the university. This but represents the fringes of a deeper and more pervasive movement. Increasing numbers of young people are expressing interests in university graduate and postgraduate instruction and administration. In fact, most reliable analysts of student protest tend to deemphasize the role of the extremist and concentrate on the role of the graduate students and young instructors, along with a high incidence of participation by older students. The events of the past decade are an extension of the politics of community and life-style, where a relatively homogeneous grouping of young men and women came to recognize through the medium and catalyst of the Vietnam war that they shared a certain inarticulate but self-conscious set of interests. In the sense of the Western experience, these communities began the arduous and often violent process of redistributing power and privilege and creating new roles and functions.

Thus, privatism, ethnicism, the occult, community-oriented protest, consumer unionism, and communes testify to the decline of the nation-state ethic and the absence of the subscription of diverse national, ethnic, neoethnic preferences to the creation of state initiatives and ideology. The deauthorization of the symbols and the ideology of the nation-state is not a temporary phenomenon, nor is it primarily a casualty of the Vietnam war. It is bound up in, although not necessarily intrinsic to, the neoethnic rage. But public temperament is in transition as well; decentralization, revenue-sharing, and community control are manifestations of this postponement of national gratification and a commitment to the development of smaller, more manageable administrative units. Some of the young have been among the first to grasp the significance of this transition and shape themes that accommodate their perspective "youth cultures." As such, these themes prefigure issues as seemingly diverse as revenue-sharing and freedom-of-choice school designs, "youth ghettos," the new sex consciousness of women, and the competition among ethnic and neoethnic groups for political and economic rewards, which had induced much of the current social conflict. One senses a crisis of expectation in the ugly sinews of distrust that gripped the United States in the past decade. No longer convinced that national or state administrative bodies were prepared or capable of developing efficient responses to local conflicts and the social-psychological needs of the individual, ethnicity and neoethnicity have become for many the prime foci of political and cultural concern and have eroded the foundations of the theories of national integration. Why this transition in collective behavior has occurred now must be a subject for further definitive inquiry, but therein lies the emphasis of the real conflict in a postindustrial society. Rationalization or community? What this will augur for the formulation of national priorities, for theories of national development, when many Americans are clearly soliciting and pushing for answers in a variety of neoethnic, ethnic institutions, is difficult to assess now. But the action has moved to another game insofar as the nation-state is concerned. Robert Nisbet has written that

> the quest for community will not be denied, for it springs
> from some of the powerful needs of human nature — needs
> for a clear sense of cultural purpose, membership, status,

and continuity. Without these, no amount of mere material welfare will serve to arrest the developing sense of alienation in our society, and the mounting preoccupation with the imperatives of community.[42]

Robert Lifton has expressed this human need in another way. Reflecting on the impact of nuclear weapons that "alter and blur the boundaries of our psychological lives, our symbolic space, and in ways crucial to our thought, feelings and action," he suggests that our sense of the continuity of life is profoundly threatened and, "They are no longer certain where anything begins or ends."[43]

Conclusion

This essay hopes to identify and explore a *trend* in international politics. It is, then, to a degree, an exercise in social forecasting and as such its hypotheses deserve to be rigorously tested by the empiricism of political transactions. These hypotheses are that:

I.   The intensification of ethnic consciousness and the subsequent fragmentation, rather than political consolidation and social integration, may well be a function of economic development and mass media exposure;

II. The concept of development, long considered to be an increase of G.N.P. and P.C.I. or a rise in production and consumption, may be redefined in terms of "liberation" from externally imposed values, socioeconomic-political inequities, or supression of cultural expressions;

III. The energies and attentions of nation-states may become absorbed by intense ethnic division resulting in less effective domestic and foreign policies;

IV. As security becomes increasingly a function of technology and the imperatives of national security are viewed less in geopolitical terms, the lack of "external" threats may catalyze ethnic consciousness and negate those forces previously contributing to social cohesion;

V. Postindustrial societies may not be immune from neoethnicism because the causes appear to be anthropologically, sociologically, and psychologically rooted and seemingly not assuaged by positivism or "progress";

VI. The nation-state may become less an entity of reference and perceived less as the primum mobile of development and sine qua non of political identification. Consequently, the concept of national interest may become more nebulous and less useful in predicting political behavior.

Notes

1. Theodore Rozak, *Where the Wasteland Ends: Politics and Transcendence in Post-Industrial Society* (Garden City, N.Y.: Anchor Books, 1973), p.392.

2. George Peter Murdock, *Ethnographic Atlas* (Pittsburgh, Pa.: University of Pittsburgh Press, 1967).

3. Ernest Barker, *National Character and the Factors in its Formation* (London: Methuen, 1927), p.173.

4. Andrew Greely, "The Rediscovery of Diversity," *The Antioch Review* (Fall 1971), p.343.

5. Nathaniel Leff, "Bengal, Biafra, and the Birness Bias," *Foreign Policy* (Spring 1972), p.130–33.

6. Claude Levi-Strauss, *Structural Anthropology* (Garden City, N.Y.: Anchor Books, 1963), p.19.

7. Ibid.

8. Fredrick Barth, ed., *Ethnic Groups and Boundaries* (Boston: Little, Brown and Co., 1969), p.10.

9. Ibid., p.11.

10. Ibid., p.17.

11. Ibid., p.15.

12. Ibid., p.9.

13. Ibid., p.16.

14. Francis Hsu, "Psychosocial Homeostasis and Jen," *American Anthropologist* (Fall 1971), p.24.

15. Ibid., p.28.

16. Ibid., pp.24–27.

17. Barth, pp.19–20.

18. Milton Gordon, *Assimilation in American Life; The Role of Race, Religion, and National Origin* (New York: Oxford University Press, 1964), p.29.

19. Clifford Geertz, "The Integration Revolution" in *Old Societies and New States*, ed. Clifford Geertz (New York: Free Press, 1963).

20. Floyd Matson, *The Broken Image* (Garden City, N.Y.: Doubleday, 1966), p.17.

21. Jacques Ellul, *The Technological Society* (New York: Vintage, 1964), p.115.

22. Robert A. Nisbet, *The Quest for Community* (New York: Oxford University Press, 1953), p.130.

23. Conor Cruise O'Brien, "On the Rights of Minorities," *Commentary* 55, no.6 (June 1973): 46.

24. The New York *Times,* 9 December 1966, p.14.

25. Cited in R.L. Hardgrave, Jr., "The D.M.K. and the Politics of Tamil Nationalism," *Pacific Affairs* 37 (Winter): 64–65.

26. The New York *Times,* 13 December 1972, p.14C.

27. *The International Narcotic Traffic* (U.S.G.P.O., 1972), p.27.

28. *The World Opium Survey,* Cabinet Committee on International Narcotics Control (U.S.G.P.O., 1972), p.33.

29. Rozak, p.241.

30. Andrew Greely, "The Rediscovery of Diversity," *Antioch Review* (Fall 1971).

31. Michael Oakeshott, *Rationalism and Politics* (New York: Basic Books, 1962).

32. Susanne Langer, *Philosophy in a New Key* (Cambridge, Mass.: Harvard University Press, 1957), p.235.

33. Daniel Bell, *The End of Ideology* (Glencoe, Illinois: The Free Press, 1960), p.374–75.

34. Edward Shils, "Primordial, Personal, Sacred, and Civil Ties," *British Journal of Sociology* (June 1957).

35. We have dealt with the phenomena of subcultures elsewhere – *see* A. A. Said, *Protagonists of Change* (Englewood Cliffs, N.J.: Prentice-Hall, 1971). We have tended to treat the subculture as a transnational parochialism and the neoethnic as a national parochialism.

36. We are content to rely on Professor Daniel Bell's analysis of postindustrial societies as ones that are characterized by a shift from manufacturing to service industries, the prominence of science-based industries in the economy, and the growth of new technical elites. *See* Bell, *The Coming of Post-Industrial Society* (New York: Basic Books, 1973).

37. *See* Luiz R. Simmons, "The Real Generation Gap," *Youth and Society* 3, no.1 (September 1971).

38. Daniel Bell, "The Cultural Contradictions of Capitalism," *Public Interest* (Fall 1970), p.73.

39.   *See* S. M. Lipset and E. Raab, "The Nongeneration Gap," *Commentary* (July–August 1970).

40.   Simmons.

41.   A short concise typology of ethnic nationalism is Louis Wirth's, "Types of Nationalism," *American Journal of Sociology* 41 (May).

42.   Nisbet, p.73.

43.   R. J. Lifton, *Boundaries* (New York: Vintage, 1970).

Ethnic Mobilization and Communication Theory

Hamid Mowlana and Ann Elizabeth Robinson

Today's popular ethnic TV idols may reflect the society but do not explain it. In the process of this communication we can identify the actors and communicators, describe the message, yet certainly know little or nothing about its effect. Is it congruent with an assimilation and nation-building process, or is it part of a reethnicization phenomenon? Certainly, something is happening and it may well be a new meaning of Americanness, but we know little about it.

An introduction to the function of mass communication in nation building and in ethnic mobilization now seems appropriate. The transmission of culture is one of the main functions of mass communication and is a basic communication activity. In the functional analysis, any communication affects one or more of four targets: society, the individual, subgroups, and the cultural system. The transmission of culture through mass media performs different functions and dysfunctions at all levels. The functions performed for society are increasing social cohesion, widening the base of common norms and experiences, reducing anomie, and continuing education by reaching adults after they have left school. The dysfunction performed is the augmenting of "mass" society. To the individual the functions of mass communication are aiding integration by exposure to mass norms, reducing idiosyncracy, and reducing anomie. The dysfunction is that it depersonalizes acts of socialization. The functions performed for the subgroups are that it extends power and acts as an agent for socialization. For the culture the function is the standardization and maintenance of cultural concensus and as a dysfunction it reduces the variety of subcultures.[1]

Functions of mass communication such as increasing social cohesion, widening the base of common norms and experiences, and acting as an agent of socialization have been frequently observed in the integration and mobilization of those states which have or are in the process of achieving national solidarity and a universalistic identity. But, as it will be argued here, mass communications can perform a dysfunction to the process of nation building as it brings to ethnic groups not only an awareness of members of their own group but also an awareness of other groups and therefore reinforces those original ethnic boundaries. Mass media, combined with the existence of parallel groups, serve to strengthen ethnic group identity at the expense of a national identity.

Social Communication and Ethnicity

Karl W. Deutsch writes of a nationality as "a people among whom there exists a significant movement toward political, economic, and cultural autonomy." The "significant movement" can be determined by investigating the overlapping clusters of interaction patterns, that is, the volume and frequency of actual communication and traffic. This communication and traffic are not limited to messages sent through the various channels of mass media, but include such factors as mobility, migration, student exchanges, newspaper readership and informal communication, and aspects of market exchanges (national currency exchanges, tariffs, quotas, exchange-control measures). Deutsch defines social mobilization as a process wherein "major clusters of old social, economic, and psychological commitments are eroded or broken and people are available for new patterns of socialization and behavior."[2] This depends in turn on the existing facilities for social communication between past and present and among contemporaries. Whenever social communication within a group breaks down due to either external forces (dissonant messages from another ethnic group or from the environment at large) or internal forces or both, mobilization is facilitated. Incompatibilities in facts or contradictions, actual or implied, among habits or values make the tension-strained individual (or group) susceptible to persuasion toward a state of consonance. What matters in ethnic mobilization, then, is the distribution of individuals and groups that can be persuaded over time ("maintained persuasion"). Deutsch states that this distribution of persuadable people is a function of the general distribution of social communication, past and present. The primary problem is the reallocation of resources, in this case the goals and values of the ethnic population to be mobilized, so that they are consonant (or at least not in conflict) with those of the dominant group.

Up to this point, we have been assuming that ethnic mobilization is in the direction of national unity, but this is not necessarily the case. An ethnic group either may be mobilized and assimilated or mobilized and differentiated. Whether the ethnic group is assimilated or not determines whether that ethnic group will end toward conflict behavior and aggression against the dominant group (a nonassimilated ethnic group, heterodox in nature) or whether it will tend toward cooperation. This is an extremely important factor in considerations of internal stability of a nation. Deutsch cites six balances important in determining the rate of assimilation: the similarity of communication habits (primarily linguistic and cultural compatibility); the teaching-learning balance (availability and quality of teaching facilities and techniques); the frequency of contact (across boundaries as compared to within the group); the balance of material rewards and punishments (employment, promotion, higher income, security, prestige – must be perceived as rewards); the balance of values and desires (common or conflicting values in the old and the new culture); balance of symbols and barriers (what are the unifying symbols and which symbols reinforce or maintain barriers?).[3] One might say that the rate of assimilation must be faster than the rate of mobilization of an ethnic group if that ethnic group is to become part of the national whole. A favorable balance must be achieved in the direction of assimilation.

Deutsch's model, based for the most part on elements of modernization and assimilation, can and has been adequately used to explain the growth of nations in many areas, but little has been said about areas where nation building is not the case but the maintenance of ethnic identity vis-à-vis national identity is apparent. An explanation of this omission may be that the psychological aspects which find the idea of ethnicity an important and serious matter in national affairs today have not been adequately taken into account.

Several scholars, among them Andrew C. Janos, claim that Deutsch's theory fails to explain the historical incidence of ethnic states and solidarities outside the context of social and economic modernization (such as the Germanic states and the medieval political community of Western Europe) and instances in which societies emerge from the experience of modernization without an ethnically defined political identity or able to assume a dual identity. This identity, states Janos, is dependent upon the distribution of ethnic and cultural characteristics and a congruity among such components as language, religion, cultural heritage, and physical proximity. Where this congruity exists a particularistic identity and pattern of solidarity is also likely to exist. Conversely, where there are significant incongruities in these components the mobilized individual will opt for an ethnically neutral, universalistic political identity (and it is in this instance that Deutsch's model holds true).[4]

When cultural consciousness precedes political consciousness and presupposes an awareness of other cultures, increased antagonisms are likely to occur. Assimilation is even more of a natural foe to self-determination than the multinational state due to the emotional power of ethnic consciousness.[5]

Social mobilization need not lead to nation building. Deutsch sees several ethnic elements combining through the process of social mobilization to form a nation, but he does not adequately take into account the phenomenon of parallel groups in a society. Deutsch's model of mobilization deals best with vertical groups that have a hierarchical stratification in which ascendancy and social mobilization are restricted by ascriptive criteria. This type of vertical ethnic differentiation is clearly on the decline as has been shown by the demise of the colonial rule. It has been eroded by the spread of egalitarian values, by international contact and communication, and by education.[6] What he did not consider were groups with parallel ethnic structure, each with its own criteria of stratification. These groups are more able to survive as distinct units due to the very fact that there are opportunities for mobilization within the ethnic group and that there exists no ascriptive bar to social mobility.

Communication and the Plural Society

Communication is necessary in the process of mobilization, in the articulation of group preferences, and in the transmission of demands and decisions. Communication in the input portion of the cycle is either information in the form of a demand or in the form of a feedback message sent to alter policies in a more positive direction in relation to the demand group. Communication in the output portion of the cycle is information as a resource for reallocating other resources or as a decision redistributing the resources. The idea of the distribution of communication equally among all ethnic groups in society is of primary importance to achieve the integration of the groups into a viable polity, particularly if specific group autonomy is to be maintained.

The equitable representation of each ethnic community through open channels of communication in all types of social transaction — and particularly in politics — would make possible the integration of autonomous groups into a viable contractual polity. Such a polity is a plural bureaucracy based on a contract relationship between all parts, coordinated by the free flow of information, both laterally and vertically. An example of this contractual integration is Switzerland, a federation of local autonomous groups that can fulfill ethnic demands, while the national government holds a minimum of collective goods. Assimilation is required only to the extent needed to maintain national unity, that is, the maintenance of open communication channels for purposes of coordination; this may or may not necessitate the sharing of the same institutions.

Mobilization is important in the process of integration because it involves an attempt to change perceptions and the salience of perceptions, or awareness. Awareness is a function of salience and perception of alternatives and is a primary factor in the establishment or eradication of ethnic boundaries. The populace is often unaware of the relationships between ethnic and interethnic systems, and the individual often does not perceive his role in these systems.

One can distinguish three phases in the process of mobilization: in the first phase, one achieves self-awareness and "identity"; in the second phase, one is led to an awareness of needs based on the new identity; and in the third phase, demands based on the new needs are expressed or articulated. This process might also be called a process of *demand generation.*

Communication, either intraethnically or interethnically, heightens the awareness of future leaders to inequalities, the possibility of increased power, or some other desired goal. In the first phase of mobilization, the course is set for the direction that the mobilization will take — either in the direction of ethnic integration or of ethnic conflict. The leaders, having reached a new level of awareness, communicate their new perceptions to the ethnic group in question — either stressing the differences from others and reerecting ethnic boundaries or increasing the salience of them; or stressing similitude, expanding boundaries to a national level, and making the ethnic boundary irrelevant.

In the second phase, the salience of the group is raised and group cohesion is heightened; needs based on the new identity are generated. The awareness of self brings an awareness of one's needs. In the third phase, demands, based on the new needs, are made. Political and other types of groups (social or economic) are formed to articulate these demands. Thus, mobilization involves the achievement of interest articulation and interest aggregation.

The demand group of the input function is also the response group of the output function. If there is no feedback (no output) or if the feedback is negative, the demand group will respond, if it is not repressed and if the group is still "mobilized" towards the goal in question. The response of the demand group to this "noncommunication" will be either more intense demands or new demands. Demand generation will continue until a saturation point is reached; at this point, mobilization may follow a different direction, and communication and interaction may involve covert or illegitimate activity.

Competitive politics in the plural society has been characterized by ethnic politics, with ethnicity as the major base for the authoritarian allocation of value. Part of the explanation for the choice of ethnicity as a basis for politics lies in the existence of mobilized resources (including the people themselves) and organizations suited for "political deployment" on ethnic issues. One already has the ingredients of a readily organizable pressure group that can maintain a sustained effort for a relatively long period of time. In ethnic politics, one finds the salience of "primordial sentiments" according to Clifford Geertz; he defines a "primordial attachment" as one that stems from the givens of social existence — congruities of speech, blood, custom, and so forth.[7] He also states that political modernization usually quickens, instead of quieting, primordial sentiments and increased ethnic contact — making these issues salient in the development of structural unity.[8] Emerson refers to the ethnic group as a "terminal community," that is, the largest community that effectively commands men's loyalty.[9]

Value conflicts between communities complicate the political process, with communal institutions of aggregation and articulation rapidly converted into corporate representatives of communal value. An example of this situation was the conversion of a Temne dancing society in Sierre Leone into a political unit that organized the election of one of their members to public office in an attempt to raise Temne prestige in the society and to prevent the desertion of young men to other tribes. In this particular case, the recognition of an opposition of interests by the Temne was more important in integration than in the discovery of similarities.[10]

Often ethnic preferences are intense and not negotiable. One finds two situations common in ethnic politics in terms of individual values: intracommunal consensus and intercommunal conflict. Intracommunal consensus is the identical perception and expression of political alternatives by ethnic members, while intercommunal conflict arises from the disagreement by different ethnic communities on all issues that face the collectivity.[11] One must conceive of consensus and conflict on the basis of degree and not as an all-or-nothing affair.

Another interesting concept is that of perceptual consensus in which alternatives are viewed according to a common perceptual framework. In the plural society the lines of conflict are drawn and hardened in full view of everyone. This is often the work of political entrepreneurs, who succeed in converting natural communities into active and antithetical political communities, often only to further their own interest, i.e., they are "mobilizers for gain."[12] Differences in salience and incompatibilities in preferences contribute to the political stability or instability of a community.

According to the decision theory, individuals make choices on the basis of underlying values. These are possible even if the relationship between alternatives and underlying values is unclear. Preference orderings, and the degree of preferences, have implications for behavior, especially under uncertainty.[13] One is again concerned with awareness. For example, in the preindependence era in many African states, the salient issue was the presence of a foreign power; the existence of alien rule was the impetus to interethnic cooperation and the submergence of ethnic differences. However, to attain ethnic cooperation in the postindependence period when the game changed from the game of extraction (that is, the extraction of gains from the dominant — here, alien — group) to the game of division (that is, gain at the expense of the coalition partners), divisive communal issues have had to be treated with ambiguity.[14]

The change from playing the game of extraction to playing the game of division has been traced by Shepsle and Rabushka in ten steps of ethnic politics:

1. The formation of a broad-based multiethnic coalition during the preindependence period
2. Survival through postindependence
3. Fostered by ambiguous pronouncements on divisive ethnic issues
4. The generation of demand for national issues
5. The emergence of ambitious politicians making appeals to ethnic passions — the political entrepreneurs
6. The resurrection of ethnicity as the salient dimension of political competition
7. The development of the politics of "outbidding"
8. The disappearance of brokerage institutions and the con-

committant ethnicization of public goods

9.   The ineffectuality of moderate elements
10. The decline of democratic competition as a result of electoral manipulation and political violence. (Or are the manipulations an attempt to restore democratic competition to the oppressed group?)

In the proliferation of ethnic communities that results, chaos is rampant in which the momentarily advantaged take steps to secure that advantage.[15] A perfect example is the emergence of Nigeria and the postindependence crises that eventually led to the secession of Biafra and three years of civil war. One notes the three processes mentioned before: disintegration of the old lines of communication and power; the redistribution of power through changes in access to channels of communication and changes in the efficiency of communication; and a reintegration of the people into new aggregates through mobilization.

The outcome of mobilization is ultimately demand generation; and it is the political entrepreneurs who sensitize the electorate to the dimensions and importance of choice. But the success of the demand generation depends both on the choice of issues and the degree to which this choice corresponds to the individual preferences. An ethnic politician can raise the perception and salience of ethnic demands by making his ethnic group aware of discrepancies in the response of the system (for example, the national polity) to their particular group. Ethnic mobilization in this case constitutes a gathering of forces of the subject group to combat, literally or figuratively, or both, the groups maintaining the obstacles to social communication, as described earlier.

Ethnic mobilization occurs when communication is blocked in any aspect or aspects of life – social, economic, political, cultural. Noncommunication, or partial nonresponse (noise, reduced fidelity), is an act of discrimination; to put it more succinctly, discrimination is noncommunication. By discriminating against any one group, one is restricting the redistribution of power, goods, wealth. Scarce resources will continue to be held in the hands of the dominant group that controls access to these scarce resources. By closing the channels of communication the status quo is maintained.

Communication is a means for redistributing scarce resources and information is the resource involved in the redistribution. Communication within the oppressed group about inequalities, stimulated by an ethnic leader or a political entrepreneur, heightens the awareness of the group of their oppressed condition. This heightened awareness makes the group susceptible to appeals to organize for action, to the forces of mobilization directed toward opening new channels of communication, if the old channels remain closed.

This process of opening channels involves a reorganization: disintegration, redistribution, and reintegration. If the old channels are reopened and demands that are generated are met (that is, the system is responsive), there will probably be a move in the direction of greater integration, perhaps even assimilation. But the outcome will be either a more homogeneous society or, if boundaries are more strongly enforced, a more coordinated or "contractually" integrated society. One would expect a greater degree of national unity and a broader perspective from such cooperative efforts.

However, if the old channels remain closed it will be necessary to open new ones. These channels may or may not be legitimate; if not, communication through such channels may be referred to as "covert activities." If the new channels are accepted by the dominant group, one again has a movement toward greater integration. If the new channels are rejected by the dominant group, and there are no channels through which to express and to obtain a response to group needs, there is a strong possibility that the covert activities will generate further competition in the society between the oppressed group and the dominant group (or groups), even to the point of conflict. In such a situation of conflicting forces there is an increased possibility that a leader will arise who finds it to his advantage — and to that of the oppressed group — to develop new covert channels of communication. And he can take advantage of the situation to make appeals against the common enemy, pitting ethnic group against ethnic group.

Continued noncommunication is the communication of expulsion or rejection. By expulsion of the oppressed group the dominant group legitimizes covert activity, and even makes the ground fertile for such activity to germinate. The oppressed group perceives itself "in the right": due to its exclusion from the society, the only types of communication channels the oppressed group can have are ipso facto illegitimate communication channels and, thus, "illegitimate" communications. The state, unwittingly, is the legitimizer of the illegitimate activity, since it has excluded from the system the legitimate activities of the rebellious ethnic group.

When Deutsch speaks of mobilized-assimilated populations and mobilized-differentiated populations, he is speaking of the problem of the degree of coordination between different ethnic systems and the effect of such degrees on the degree of integration in a multiethnic society (or between two separate national polities).

Extremist politics tend to emerge when the channels of communication have been restricted on both sides, so that anything that is communicated is communicated more. There are few counter-communications to balance the effect of the extremist messages and the salience of the extremist communication crescendoes.

Limited or restricted access to channels of communication is one incentive for mobilization against an oppressive group. A proposition to be tested is relevant to the problems of communication, described above, in relation to national unity and legitimacy: the greater the obstacles to communication for a given ethnic community and the greater the awareness that these obstacles exist, the greater the possibility of ethnic conflict. One aspect of this proposition is whether the oppressed are "repressed." If the dominant group forces the oppressed group to keep the channels of communication closed and at the same time forces that group to remain a part of the total society or polity, the oppressed group is also repressed. It is not repressed if, once awareness of the condition is established, the oppressed group is allowed to voice their grievances. If the oppressed are not repressed, there is the possibility of becoming "unoppressed," for communication makes it possible to lift the bonds of oppression. Repression, however, closes the channels of communication and the oppressed remain bound by their condition.

Tribalism vs Nationalism: The Problem of "Subjective Ethnicity"

What are the rewards or punishments that positively or negatively reinforce: (1) discrimination, or noncommunication, of the dominant group against the "oppressed" group? (2) covert communication by the oppressed group in society? And how are these incentives or threats utilized by ethnic leaders and politicians, for exam-

ple, in South Africa or in Nigeria? Will the direction of ethnic mobilization be focused on national unity and a cooperative, integrative
effort of all groups, or will the direction be focused on communal
loyalties and toward greater competition and perhaps conflict?
Will nationalistic symbols and appeals have predominance over
ethnic symbols and appeals? In what way will the group identify
itself?

Pierre van den Berghe has discussed both objective and subjective ethnicity and his comments are of particular importance in the
process of mobilization. He states that subjective ethnicity is more
common than objective ethnicity and that the growth in the scale
of relevant ethnicity or "super-tribalization" is linked with the
rise of nationalism. For example, the Luhya of Kenya and the Ibo
of Nigeria, who have acquired a sense of nationhood, were still
clusters of parochial peasant villages three to four decades ago.
But through the increased flow of communication and the opportunity to make wider comparisons and become acquainted with new
and different alternatives, the parochial villagers found themselves
more similar to each other than they had thought themselves different. Van den Berghe suggests that nationalism was the "transformation of vague, subjective feelings of common ethnicity into a more
articulated form of political consciousness."[16]

Subjective ethnicity is more important than objective ethnicity
in the attainment of an integrated society or national unity. It is
also of more importance in the process of mobilization: does one
perceive oneself more as a member of a locally centered ethnic group
or more as a member of a comprehensive national group (whether
the national community is one ethnic group or a confederation of
diverse ethnic groups)? The perception determines the direction of
the ethnic mobilization, and the perception itself is determined by
intraethnic and interethnic communications that have aroused the
self-awareness of the ethnic group — that is, premobilization communications moving the ethnic group toward awareness arousal
determine the direction of mobilization and the mobilizations
communications. This does not rule out the possibility of a change
in the direction of the mobilization; a similar process would occur
should the direction change, with different issues and different
perceptions becoming the salient ones.

The problem of ethnicity has been called tribalism, parochialism, and communalism. Multiethnic groups in Africa regard ethnic diversity as part of their individuality and desire to retain that identity even as members of the national polity.[17] Ethnic blocs reflect the clash between personal identity and political integrity. How does one provide a solution to this clash? Geertz suggests that primordial sentiments be reconciled with the civil order "by divesting them of their legitimizing force with respect to the governmental authority, by neutralizing the apparatus of the state in relation to them, and by channeling discontent arising out of their dislocation into properly political rather than parapolitical forms of expression."[18] Geertz is demanding specialization of the channels of communication and a reaggregation of interests. He calls this process a "progressive extension of primordial sentiments and differences, generated from the direct, protracted encounter of culturally diverse groups into local contexts to more broadly defined groups in the national context."[19]

The importance of extending the boundaries of identity to achieve national unity is apparent in a historical analysis of many African states. Up to the attainment of power, African nationalism was composed of an anticolonial awareness, Pan-African solidarity uniting all forces against a common enemy on vague and general bases, and being suffused with a strong revolutionary force. Since independence, Pan-African nationalism has been invoked to obtain optimum conditions for complete decolonization, ethnic consolidation,and the liberation of the colonized south.

The counterbalancing force is local nationalism, which is still a cohesive force compared with tribal separatism. Separatist policies practiced by tribal chiefs may be used to salvage the ethnic group and also to retain their privileges in that ethnic group. Similarly, class interests may be hidden by national patriotism.[20] The provocation of regional politics in Nigeria is one of many examples where the political ideology of nationalism was used first as a successful instrument of a united liberal front against a common enemy and later used to obtain new objectives that were diametrically opposed — the division of the people.

Communication and Ethnic Consciousness

Through the examples discussed above, perhaps one will come

to an understanding of the interrelationship between the problems of communication, coordination and control, and of the importance of the direction of mobilization for the persistence of a national polity. The discussion has been based on theories of system interdependence and system persistence; theories of communication; and the concept of self-identification as the determinant of ethnic boundaries.

The proposition made is of contractual integration. A polity that is contractually integrated is one in which the ethnic community maintains its autonomy and has open and free access to the channels of communication; the system is interdependent and the parts are mutually responsive, making adjustments in order that the polity is perpetuated — that is, plural bureaucracies are coordinated by lateral, responsive communication among the separate bureaucracies. There is a "communication democracy" in which there is an equitable distribution of social communication among all groups. Information is a resource for allocating other resources; and communication is the means by which the information is distributed. Therefore, equal access to the channels of communication, equal participation in the communication and mutual sensitivity of all groups allow the possibility of equality of power and the sharing of total resources while still maintaining ethnic autonomy. Coordination, achieved through interaction and mutual adjustment, makes possible (as well as being made possible because of) a free flow of information.

Perhaps this relationship is the reason that ethnic politics is described as a "vicious cycle," a spiralling downward to even greater extremism. But this spiralling effect may also give hope to those countries caught in the grasp of the politics of racial extremism. Once the cycle is broken and the first step is made towards a more equitable distribution of social communication in the polity, the spiral upward could lead to greater national solidarity and political integrity.

Advances in communications and transportation have helped to curtail cultural isolation. These advances in technology also tend to increase the cultural awareness of minorities by making them more aware of the distinctions between themselves and other groups. The individual becomes more aware of alien ethnic groups as well as those who share his identity. An unintegrated state poses no threat to the lifeways of the various ethnic groups but the curtailment of this isolation may lead to a xenophobic reaction. As argued, intraethnic as well as interethnic communications play a major role in the creation of ethnic consciousness.[21] Thus, communications play a pervasive role not only in social mobility and nation building but also in strengthening ethnic consciousness.

Notes

1. Charles R. Wright, "Functional Analysis and Mass Communication," *Public Opinion Quarterly* 24 (Winter 1960): 610–13.

2. Karl W. Deutsch, "Social Mobilization and Political Development," *American Political Science Review* 55 (September 1961): 494. *See also* Karl W. Deutsch, "The Growth of Nations, Some Recurrent Patterns of Political and Social Integration," *World Politics* 5 (January 1953): 169–70.

3. Karl W. Deutsch, *Nationalism and Social Communication* (Cambridge, Mass.: M.I.T. Press, 1966), pp.156–62.

4. Andrew C. Janos, "Ethnicity, Communism, and Political Change in Eastern Europe," *World Politics* 23 (April 1971): 517–18.

5. Walker Connor, "Self-Determination," *World Politics* 20 (October 1967): 49–50.

6. Donald L. Horowitz, "Three Dimensions of Ethnic Politics," *World Politics* 23 (January 1971): 232, 236. For examples of the communication process in ethnically diverse nations in this chapter, we are indebted to the research assistance of Vicki Morey.

7. Clifford Geertz, "The Integrative Revolution," in *Old Societies and New States*, ed. C. Geertz (Glencoe, Ill.: The Free Press, 1963), p.109.

8. Ibid., p.119.

9. Alvine Rabushka and K. A. Shepsle, *Politics in Plural Societies* (Columbus, Ohio: Charles E. Merrill, 1972), p.63.

10. John C. Mitchell, "Tribalism and the Plural Society," in *Black Africa,* ed. J. Middleton (New York: Macmillan, 1970), p.331.

11. Rabushka and Shepsle, pp.65–67.

12. Ibid., pp.2, 67–69.

13. Ibid., p.43.

14. Ibid., pp.73–76.

15. Ibid., pp.91–92.

16. Pierre van den Berghe, "Ethnicity in the African Experience ," *International Social Science Journal* 23 (1971): 511.

17. Geertz, pp.198–99.

18. Ibid., p.128.

19. Ibid., p.153–54.

20. L. Yablotchkov, "L'Evolution du Nationalisme Africain," *Presence Africaine* 74 (1970): 46–53.

21. Walker Connor, "Nation-Building or Nation-Destroying?", *World Politics* 24 (April 1972): 329.

Black Consciousness and American Policy in Africa

J. K. Obatala

One of the most significant developments in international relations in the second half of this century is the rise of racial and ethnic consciousness among Afro-Americans. The actual effect of Afro-Americans on U.S. foreign policy is, as of yet, minimal; however, developments within the Afro-American community over the past three decades, the rise of African nationalism, and the emergence of independent African states along with America's rapidly expanding economic, military, and political role in African countries have created conditions that will result in a more active and aggressive role on the part of Afro-Americans in the shaping of American policy.

The efforts of Afro-Americans to influence U.S. foreign policy in Africa have been mainly concerned with American policies toward southern Africa. A key reason for this is that the issues arising out of the deepening crisis in southern Africa are, in this stage of the conflict, more clearly racial in their implication than those arising out of conflicts elsewhere on the continent. Although the existence of tribalism as an ethnic phenomenon in black-ruled states to the north is acknowledged by most Afro-American activists, scholars, and intellectuals, the racial overtones of the struggle in southern Africa are more in line with the Afro-American's sense of social urgency; because of the racial experience of the Afro-American in the U.S.; he is more likely to address himself to international issues that involve color conflict. He is less likely to become involved with issues that, while ethnic in nature, are not black and white in their dimensions.

The Afro-American's attitude toward U.S. policy in Africa has been conditioned by the national forces that led to his concern for Africa in the first place. These national forces have manifested themselves largely within the context of the struggle for social reform. One of the most significant trends within this struggle over the past two decades has been the rise of racial or ethnic consciousness, a trend that evolved into the black consciousness movement that came to dominate the civil rights effort in the mid-1960s.

There is a definite distinction between color, racial, and ethnic consciousness; the former two are largely biological in their implications while the latter has, for the most part, cultural and historical connotations.[1] Moreover, ethnic consciousness in the strictest sense of the term need not imply racial or color consciousness. However, racial or black consciousness is used interchangeably with ethnic consciousness. The reason for this is that the black consciousness movement of the late 1960s and early 1970s was characterized by a high degree of racial and color consciousness that was, for the most part, accompanied by a cultural yearning, a search for historical roots and the quest for a life-style that would be more compatible with what was termed the black experience.

This sense of cultural deprivation, realized and acknowledged in the 1960s, gave rise to two related trends in the Afro-American community; one was the glorification of the culture of the black masses in this country and the other was the tendency to identify with Africa and its culture abroad. The pull of these two psychological forces, not always working in unison, together with the fact that the black consciousness advocates were among the most Westernized blacks in the world, created the so-called identity crisis about which so much has been written and so little understood. The identity crisis was, in fact, a political crisis: a crisis engendered by the apparent obsolescence of the activist strategies that had been mapped out by nonviolent theoreticians of the 50s and early 60s and the development of serious conflicts between white interests and black aspirations.

By the middle 1960s two significant developments had taken place, both of which would help to influence the extent and nature of the Afro-American's concern with U.S. foreign policy in Africa in the postnationalist era. One was the race-oriented turn taken by the movement in the middle of the decade when activists like Stokely Carmichael and H. Rap Brown began to openly court the masses with their Black Power rhetoric. This strategy became widely employed within the civil rights movement: those not able to overcome the negative implications, rooted deep within the English language, of the slogan Black Power chose the more psychologically acceptable phrase Black Is Beautiful and began what became popularly known as the bourgeois nationalist movement. For example, even though possessing a high degree of militancy, thus appearing violence prone, most of the black student unions actually fell into the classification of bourgeois or cultural nationalist.

A second significant development in the middle 1960s was the increasing level of awareness, economic and political as well as social, of the black urban masses. By the middle of the decade, there had been major social upheavals in New York and Los Angeles, while blacks in the South were beginning to arm themselves.[2] The social agitation of the earlier civil rights activists, together with increasing frustration over their own plight, had resulted in the militant awakening of blacks at all levels. Another factor that facilitated the rise of black consciousness among all levels was the return of white and black activists from the South to the urban slums and the college and universtiy campuses, bringing the movement out of the South, urban and rural, and into the streets and schools of the North.[3]

Those blacks who were the most materially fortunate, those who were in a position to sustain financial, property, and/or job losses of greater magnitude than the average, faced a cruel dilemma: it was virtually impossible for them to openly attack the system that maintained them, while at the same time, if they were to do so, the interests of those attempting to attain the same material status might run countercurrent to their own. Each interest group, however, realized the importance of the other, if only because there is safety (and power) in numbers. While Carmichael could very well have defined the problem of the Afro-American as simply one of power-lessness and left the matter at that, it was necessary for him and other leading advocates of black consciousness to stress blackness in order to camouflage the basic conflict of political and economic interest that existed between the new middle class, on the one hand, and some race-oriented leadership and their largely lower-income shock troops on the other.

There was a third element that was also woven into the pattern of the new race-oriented strategy that was emerging out of the crisis of the 1960s. African consciousness became an intricate part of black consciousness. It involved a greater appreciation and know-ledge of African culture, history, and – to a lesser extent – politics, and was concerned with forging closer links between Africans and Afro-Americans. The roots of modern African consciousness exten-ded past the mid-1960s into the African Nationalist era of the 50s. It was not, however, until after the independence of Ghana and other African countries that African consciousness began to stand its own ground in the arena of Afro-American social thought.[4] One thing that contributed to the new importance of Africa in the black consciousness movement in the sixties was the cold war and the fact that the U.S. was faced with keen competition from the Socialist countries in the struggle to fill the power vacuum left by the retreat of the old colonial powers (except Portugal): Spain (Spanish Morocco, Rio Muñi), France (Djibouti), Britain (Rhodesia, Bechwanaland, and so on). "It needs no underlining," observed Rupert Emerson in 1962, "that the domestic racial difficulties of the United States curtail the possible success of American policies in Africa. Little Rock has entered into the international vocabu-lary."[5] Thus, although African consciousness, like black conscious-ness, served some significant and legitimate psychological functions by helping the Afro-American to deal with his identity crisis, the rise of African consciousness within the Afro-American movement was also sustained, in part, by the political leverage that independent

African states could provide a troubled reform movement in an era of fierce cold war competition. Indeed, internationalist strategy was in no sense a new element in Afro-American politics. Black leadership had learned of the enormous political leverage foreign allies could provide as early as the late eighteenth century when Lord Dunsmore issued his famous declaration giving freedom to any slaves that would join the Loyalist cause, a development that resulted in the relaxation of discriminatory policies barring blacks from the revolutionary armies.[6] In the nineteenth century blacks also demonstrated their grasp of international politics when they exploited British and other foreign antislavery sentiments to raise money and mobilize support for the abolitionist movement here at home;[7] and, in the mid-twentieth century, they themselves had been victimized by cold war pressures when the rise of McCarthyist anticommunism forced most of them to move away from their leftist anticolonial internationalism and take a more traditional rightist stand, concerning themselves mainly with the struggle for civil rights in the U.S.[8]

The rise of African consciousness in the mid-1960s, when large numbers of African states had gained at least token independence, and the splintering of the civil rights movement were hardly coincidental. Neither was it totally a psychological phenomenon. Up to the era of African nationalism, it had been largely Africa itself — apart from the people — that was of great strategic importance as a place to escape white oppression in this country. Now, with the advent of African independence, Africans themselves had become as important in the Afro-American social and psychological strategy as the land had always been. Many black leaders made trips to Africa in the 1960s to drum up support for the Afro-American struggle.[9]

The political relationship between Africans and Afro-Americans in the sixties was not a one-way affair; it was a symbiotic relationship. Africans also considered Afro-Americans to be of great strategic importance. This had been the case ever since the educated African first emerged as a factor in British colonial politics in the last half of the nineteenth century. The African movement reached its peak in the 1890s and in the first two decades of the twentieth century, courting and even recruiting Afro-Americans to come to

Africa to participate in the regeneration of Africa. The increasing involvement of Africans and Afro-Americans with each other was, in effect, a political reflection of America's growth and evolution as a major world power. For Afro-American internationalism would have been meaningless as a political strategy if the United States had not had interest abroad that could have been adversely affected by what happened on the home front. African consciousness would indeed have been nothing more than a placebo if, in the 1960s, the United States had not had interests in Africa that it deemed worth protecting by making concessions to placate an increasingly aggressive black middle class.

Despite this, it is not difficult to understand why close economic, political, and military ties between South Africa, Rhodesia, Portugal, and the United States are likely to continue and may even become stronger. In addition to international pressures, there are some potent social and political forces emerging within the United States that could result in a long-range modification of U.S. foreign policy toward southern Africa. The most significant of these new forces is the black consciousness movement with its direct interest in Africa and concern over developments in southern Africa. Thus, while Tilden J. LeMelle is, for the most part, correct in his assertion that the concern of black Americans for, and their impact on U.S. foreign policy has been rather minimal,[10] the development of the black consciousness movement has had some consequences that could turn out to be of great significance with regard to the future course of American foreign policy in Africa. Seretse Khama, president of Botswana, remarked in 1971 that, "Africa is watching with fascination and sympathy the efforts of black Americans to assert their identity and to win themselves their rightful place in U.S. society." President Khama, whose country shares common borders with both South Africa and Rhodesia, took special note of what he termed the growing influence of Afro-Americans in U.S. politics, especially "developing Black representation in Congress."[11]

This remark underscores the foreign policy implications of the new black American thrust into electoral politics: an outgrowth of first the civil rights and, later, the black consciousness movement. It was the civil rights movement that provided the impetus for the registration of large numbers of black voters, especially in the southeastern United States, while the black consciousness movement succeeded in mobilizing those votes behind black candidates.[12] The results of both phases of the social reform movement that threw the nation into a social and political crisis in the 1950s and 60s can be seen in the fact that, while two decades ago there were no black elected officials in the South, there are more blacks holding elective offices in that region today than anywhere else in the country.[13] Nationally, the success of the black consciousness movement in mobilizing the masses behind black middle-class candidates is evident in the fact that the total number of black elected officials in the United States jumped from 1,185 in 1969 to 2,621 in August of 1973.[14]

The upshot is that there is presently in the U.S. Congress a small, racially conscious cadre of black representatives who are very much concerned about American foreign policy in southern Africa. Organized into a formal structure known as the Black Caucus, they are one of three foreign-policy-oriented movements whose growth and evolution can be linked to the rise of black consciousness and to America's expanding role in African affairs. In addition to this middle-class-dominated legislative movement, there is a widespread but loosely organized propaganda drive that is also largely white collar in composition; however, the membership of groups falling into this category also consists of a large number of blue-collar workers. Their objective is to bring to the attention of the American people what they consider to be the morally repugnant role of U.S. policy toward southern Africa with hopes of creating social sentiment against it. These groups work very closely, and sometimes their membership even overlaps, with a third category of policy-oriented organizations, the social activists. Most of the social-activist groups also engage in public education, but they differ from the propaganda specialists in that they contain a larger number of workers and community organizers than their two more middle-class-oriented counterparts.

The Black Caucus and Congressman Charles Diggs from Detroit have contributed greatly in the struggle to reform U.S. policies toward the white republics and colonial territories of southern Africa. In 1971 and 1972, Diggs led study missions to Africa, one of which went on a People-to-People mission to the Republic of

South Africa. The report of the subcommittee on these study missions is monumental in its importance and has provided a great deal of the intellectual fuel for the flames of black and white protest that are beginning to rage across the American social and political horizon.

The African-American National Conference on Africa was held at Howard University in Washington in May of 1972 and was sponsored by the Black Caucus. The goals of the Conference, as outlined in its *Report*, are a clear indication of the relationship between the black consciousness movement and the black legislative challenge to U.S. foreign policy as it relates to the struggle in southern Africa. "The purpose," notes Diggs, who chaired the conference and wrote the introduction to its *Report*, "was ... to establish a national Black Strategy on Africa; to set priorities on critical African questions; to devise legislative, judicial, political, community, and positive action techniques for achieving these priorities; to institute a nationwide program of support for the liberation struggles; and to establish an ongoing operation for the implementation and the effectuation of these objectives."[15] Significantly, though the conference was sponsored by the Black Caucus, there were representatives and participants from all segments and strata of the black community. The composition of the conference was also an indication that the black legislators were willing to endorse tactics that are much more threatening in their social implications than the mere introduction of bills or even the filing of court suits, such as the one the Black Caucus had filed only a month before the convention was held in a futile attempt to stop the continued importation of Rhodesian chrome into the United States.[16]

Parallel to the development of black legislative action against U.S. policies in southern Africa is a broadening resistance movement in the black community. A key trend in community resistance is the effort on the part of an increasing number of groups to arouse the awareness of students and workers as to the political, moral, social, and economic implications of U.S. policy in southern Africa. These groups have proliferated in great numbers since the rise of the black consciousness movement in the last half of the 1960s.

The Committee of Concerned Blacks is largely a middle-class

organization based in New York whose main objective is to disseminate information about U.S. policy in southern Africa and discourage Afro-American travel to South Africa. They were among the forefront of those groups and individuals that exerted pressure on Muhammed Ali in an apparently successful effort to discourage him from fighting in the Republic of South Africa. Black Concern is a group that carries the endorsement of many prominent Afro-Americans, among them Imamu Amiri Baraka. They have published a widely acclaimed pamphlet entitled, "Black Americans Stay Out of South Africa."[17] Further to the left is the Africa Information Service, another group based in New York. AIS is actually an offshoot of the white-dominated Africa Research Group that turned over all of its files and papers to the former after ARG was dissolved. It has been extremely effective in acquiring and circulating vital information concerning U.S. foreign policy as well as the liberation struggles in Africa. The most important contribution of AIS to the struggle against U.S. foreign policy to date is its filming and circulation of the highly successful *A Luta Continua (The Struggle Continues)*, a documentary on the struggle to free Mozambique from Portuguese domination. The film contains rare shots of South African soldiers guarding the dam site as well as evidences of U.S. participation in the project. The Southern Africa Committee, on the other hand, publishes what is probably the best and most informative journal yet to hit the market of resistance literature. Entitled *Southern Africa: A Monthly Survey of News and Opinion*, it is a well-documented, concisely written chronicle of events having to do with U.S. policy and the struggle in southern Africa. Its main bases of operation are New York and Durham, North Carolina.[18] The Liberation Support movement, predominantly white, has a comprehensive assortment of publications and a film about freedom movements in Africa, and a large black constituency on the West coast. It is probably further to the left than any of the groups mentioned above and, for that reason alone, may not make significant headway among blacks organizationally, aside from the distribution of its film and publications. Afrojournals, such as *Freedomways, Muhammed Speaks, Black Scholar*, and, to a lesser extent, *Black World*, are important information media also concerned with dissemination of facts about U.S. policy in southern Africa. These are by far the most powerful organs of dissent in the black community, all of which have taken stands against U.S. support for Portugal and the white republics of Rhodesia and South Africa.

Legislative pressure for a change in U.S. foreign policy is destined to increase due to the rise in liberal sentiment and the increase in black participation in the political process. One factor, however, that has militated against increased legislative pressure was the relative decline in the power of the Congress in favor of a more authoritarian presidency. Yet whatever the relationship between Congress and the presidency in the years to come, both must either respond to social pressure or join their southern African allies in becoming a racialist dictatorship. For while there may be fundamentally different points of view within the black body politic over issues having to do with U.S. suppression of outright socialism in Africa, such a split is not likely — at least not to any prohibitive degree — over the question of U.S. support for white racism and minority rule. The issue in southern Africa is to most Afro-Americans one of race and not one of class or political ideology; both the middle-class, culture-oriented groups in and out of Congress as well as the more radical community-based groups share a common ground on the question of racial oppression. For they realize, as Tilden J. LeMelle has so aptly observed, that "all classes and all ideological persuasions must be involved in a common effort . . . if Black Americans are going to begin to have an impact on U.S. policy in Africa."[19]

Notes

1. Oliver C. Cox, *Caste, Class and Race: A Study in Social Dynamics* (London: Modern Reader Paperbacks, 1948).

2. Robert L. Allen, *Black Awakening in Capitalist America: An Analytic History* (Garden City, N.Y.: Anchor, 1970), pp.27–28; Robert Conot, *Rivers of Blood, Years of Darkness* (New York: Bantam Books, 1967).

3. Stokely Carmichael, *Stokely Speaks: Black Power, Back to Pan-Africanism* (New York; Vintage Books, 1971), pp.187–90; Allen, pp.21–88.

4. This is indicated by direct and indirect references, as well

as through illustration in numerous publications. *See,* for example, E. U. Essien-Udom, *Black Nationalism: The Rise of the Black Muslims in the U.S.A.* (Middlesex, England: Penguin Books, 1966), p.129; Allen, pp.59–65; Malcolm X, *Malcolm X on Afro-American History* (New York: Pathfinder, 1970), pp.8–11; Joseph S. Roucek, "The Black American and the New Viewpoints in Black American History," in *The Negro Impact on Western Civilization,* ed. Joseph S. Roucek (New York; Philosophical Library, 1970), pp.1–22; John Hendrik Clarke, "The Search for Africa," *Negro Digest* (February 1968); W. E. B. DuBois, "The American Negro and the Darker World," *Freedomways* (Summer 1968).

5. Rupert Emerson, "American Policy in Africa," *Foreign Affairs* (January 1962). *See also* August Meier and Elliot Rudwick, *From Plantation to Ghetto,* rev. ed. (New York; Hill and Wang, 1970), p.253: "Nothing was more helpful to the Negroes' cause than the Cold War, with the Communist powers holding American democratic pretensions up to ridicule before the uncommitted people of the world."

6. Benjamin Quarles, "Lord Dunsmore as Liberator," in *The Making of Black America: Volume I: The Origins of Black Americans,* ed. August Meier and Elliott Rudwick (New York: Atheneum, 1969), pp.125–36.

7. Frederick Douglass, among others, went to England to lecture and raise money. Meier and Rudwick, *Plantation to Ghetto,* p.122; Frederick Douglass, *The Life and Times of Frederick Douglass* (New York: Collier Books, 1962), pp.232–58.

8. James L. Roark, "American Black Leaders: The Response to Colonialism and the Cold War, 1943–1953," *African Historical Studies* 4, no. 2 (1971).

9. Interview with John Lewis, Atlanta, Georgia (17 August 1973).

10. Tilden J. LeMelle, "Black Americans and Foreign Policy," *Africa Today* (October 1971).

11. Sir Seretse Khama, "African-American Relations in the 1970s: Prospects and Problems," *Africa Today* (July 1971). *See also* Representatives Charles Diggs, Jr., J. Irving Whalley, Edward J. Derwinski, J. Herbert Burke, Seymour Halpern, and Guy Vander Jagt, "Faces of Africa: Diversity and Progress — Repression and Struggle," *Report of Special Study Mission to Africa,* 7 February — 7 March 1971, 5 August — 8 September 1971, and 2–25 January 1972,

persuant to House Res. 109, 21 September 1971, Appendix 2 (here-after designated *Report of Special Mission*), pp.293–99.

12. *See* Carmichael, *Stokely Speaks*, pp.31–43. This also seems implicit in Ronald L. Walters, "The New Black Political Culture," *Black World* (October 1972).

13. *Black Enterprise* (September 1973).

14. Ibid. On black politics in the South, *see also Ebony* (August 1971).

15. The Congressional Black Caucus, "Strategy Workshops Report," *African-American National Conference on Africa, 26–27 May 1972* (Washington, D.C.: Howard University Press, 1972); *also see*, for a brief but incisive review of the Conference, Robert Rhodes, "Internationalism and Social Consciousness in the Black Community," *Freedomways* 12, no. 3 (1972).

16. Hyman Lumer, "U.S. Imperialism in Southern Africa," *Political Affairs* (July 1973).

17. *Black Americans Stay Out of South Africa*, prepared and distributed by Black Concern (P.O. Box 523, Bronx, New York 10472).

18. *See* Southern Africa Committee (244 West 27th Street, New York, New York 10001, or 213 North Gregson Street, Durham, North Carolina 27701) for further information.

19. LeMelle.

Ethnic Groups and Developmental Models: The Case of Quebec

Gustav Morf

For the last decade Quebec, the French-speaking region of Canada, experienced considerable unrest and turmoil presaged by the rise of a terrorist movement known as F.L.Q. The national composition of Quebec — eighty percent French, ten percent English, and ten percent immigrants of different nationalities — partially explains why. The Quebecois, as the French-speaking inhabitants refer to themselves, are striving to obtain a new status either within Canada or as an independent country. They feel their survival as an ethnic nation with respect to other Canadian nationalities is at stake, yet political geography is also important in understanding this problem.

The history of French subjugation provides a "usable part" in legitimizing the aspirations of the Quebecois. In the second half of the eighteenth century, the military power of France declined steadi-

76

ly while the might of Britain increased. New England was already a
prosperous English colony with over one and a half million people,
and English settlers, merchants, and adventurers became more and
more active along the Atlantic coast and right up to Newfoundland.
Sharing the land and the commerce in a kind of peaceful coexistence
was an idea foreign to the British. The French fortress Louisbourg,
on the Atlantic coast near Halifax, was attacked in 1745 and had to
capitulate before the superior strength of the English troops. In
1755 the Acadiens, 7,000 peaceful French people engaged in farming in the fertile Anapolis valley on the Bay of Fundy, were deported to Louisiana to make room for English settlers. This was one
of the first examples of a deportation of a whole ethnic group by a
civilized power. Soon afterwards, the English General James Wolfe
set out from England with the express purpose of putting an end to
the French rule in Canada. The war was fought with the usual atrocities (farms burned down, women and children killed). The Canadians fought valiantly, but, receiving very little help from France,
they could not prevail against the superior strength of the invaders.
Wolfe's victory, on the Plains of Abraham near Quebec on 13
September 1859, marked the end of French rule. The surrender was
signed the following year. At that time, the military strength of the
British was 30,000 sailors and 9,000 soldiers, mustered against a
population of 85,000, 5,000 of which died in the war. New France
was then an English colony and would be ruled from Westminster.

These historical facts play a great role in the mind of the French
Canadians. The conquest was a traumatic event that still influences
the thinking of the French minority of North America — especially
the younger generation. Not that the conditions before the conquest
were ideal. But the habitants were governed by people of their own
blood and language. After the conquest they were ruled by foreigners whose mentality and language were incomprehensible. They were
afraid. Would they be deported like the Acadians? Would they be
forced to become Protestants according to the principle *cuius regio,
eius religio?* Would they have to speak English? Everything seemed
possible.

The American revolution in 1774 obliged the British to do
something to keep the allegiance of their French-speaking subjects.
When Benjamin Franklin came to Montreal in 1776 in order to find

support for the American cause, he discovered that not only the
English merchants (numbering about 800) but also the French
leaders did not want to have anything to do with the war of independence. The tolerant attitude of the British Crown had paid
off. The English merchants who came to the new colony found no
hostility. They were soon on good terms with their French-speaking
customers, learned the language, and let their children grow up in
a French atmosphere.

While the English population east and west of Quebec grew
rapidly, French immigration had naturally come to a halt. This
created a problem of survival. It was solved by what has been called
"the revenge of the cradle": an abnormally high birth rate. For two
centuries, and until about 1960, the natural increase (through births)
of the French Canadians more than offset the effect of English
immigration and despite great losses owing to emigration to the
adjacent United States. From 1901–61, the population of Quebec
increased from 1,649,000 inhabitants (of which 327,000 were
non-French) to 5,259,000. Only twenty-seven percent of the increase was due to immigration. The most prolific regions were, of
course, the farming districts where the birth rate reached the
astonishing level of forty-five per thousand (against twenty per
thousand in English-speaking districts) and where the yearly population growth rate was thirty-seven per thousand, when in France this
was only seven per thousand. Since the English colony of Montreal
had the lowest birth rate, the percentage of English-speaking residents of Quebec actually decreased from twenty-four percent in
1851 to 10.8% in 1961. From 1961 to 1971, the English element,
boosted by strong immigration, grew to 13.1%. Since the English
speaking live mostly in Montreal, many counties are actually ninety-
nine percent French. The eastern townships had been settled by the
English, but from 1850 to 1945 the region was literally flooded
with French Canadians.

During the two centuries of British rule, a curious division of
labor took place between the two nationalities. The French Canadians preferred farming, lumbering, and arts and crafts. There were
many intellectuals; priests, lawyers, and physicians. Quebec exported
hundreds of priests to Latin America and Africa. Industry and
commerce became more and more the domain of the English, who

had those business connections in the rest of Canada and overseas which the French Canadians lacked. During the so-called Industrial Revolution, the French Canadians provided the labor, while the businessmen and industrialists were mostly of Anglo-Saxon stock. All business, including banking, was conducted in English, while the lower echelons spoke French. This almost unique state of affairs still exists and has led to ever-stronger protests against this kind of "linguistic imperialism," or "colonialism." The same malaise arose and still exists in the Canadian armed forces. Apart from a few French units, these forces are entirely English oriented, even when half of the soldiers or sailors are French. No officer is expected to know French, while every French Canadian who aspires to become an officer is expected to speak perfect English.

The same applies to civil service and Parliament, where a knowledge of English was a prerequisite to mobility and success. This is why many of the younger generation of French Canadians, especially the intellectuals, found this state of affairs intolerable. They pointed out that at the beginning of the British rule an Englishman who went to court against a Frenchman had to present his case in French. The younger generation is not restorationist. It accepts English as a necessity in most higher occupations. However, they cannot tolerate that an English Canadian who must deal with French Canadians (be it as a business executive or as a civil servant) refuses to learn and speak French.

Apart from the language problem of the Anglo-Saxons refusing to learn French, there are problems in the church, the civil service, and military services. The Catholic church had almost complete freedom but the church leaders and the priests knew that this situation could be altered at any time if Catholicism seemed to threaten the rule of the Protestant king. They did everything to instruct their faithful on the virtues of submission. Under the French regime, the citizens had always had the reputation of being not easy to govern. Under British rule their submission was exemplary. The church leaders, especially the bishop of Montreal, could conciliate his dependence on a Protestant king with his allegiance to the Pope. But the influence of the church also discouraged the French Canadians from going into commerce and banking, which were supposed to be more corrupt than farming, fishing, or wood cutting. (A similar phenomenon took place in the Catholic regions of Europe that remained mainly agricultural, while industry, banking, and commerce flourished in the Protestant countries. It cannot be said, therefore, that the English prevented the French Canadians from going into commerce.) Only during the last ten years have efforts been made to form a sufficient number of French Canadian business administrators and executives. The opening of a new Ecole des Hautes Etudes Commerciales at the University of Montreal in 1970 was a step in this direction.

The question of military service did not arise for some time. Under the French regime, the inhabitants had done compulsory military service without difficulty. Under the new regime, they were exempted from serving under the British flag. But when the English were fighting the native Indians, they thought that these would capitulate more easily if they saw French soldiers fighting side by side with the English. Right or wrong, the English commanders were convinced that the Indians expected help from the French, if not from France itself, and they had to be shown that no such help was forthcoming. But when the British authorities tried to enlist 300 French volunteers, they had the greatest difficulty finding them, despite very good conditions. When, in 1884, a small contingent of French Canadians volunteered to fight for Great Britain in the Sudan, there were protests. The protests were much stronger during the Boer War. In March 1900, there were riots in the streets of Montreal between the prowar English students of McGill University and antiwar French students. Canada was divided: the French Canadians identified themselves with the Boers and the war with the conquest, the English Canadians with the British. After the war, the French member of the Canadian Parliament, Henri Bourassa, demanded that Canada should ask Great Britain to grant the Boers their independence. The proposal was voted down and the rejection celebrated by the singing of "God Save the King."

During World War I, very few French Canadians joined the army voluntarily. The great majority just did not want to fight for the English. In 1916, only 12,000 French Canadian soldiers had been enrolled, 4.5% of the Canadian forces. When Prime Minister Borden, in order to step up the Canadian contribution to the war, announced conscription, violent riots broke out in the streets of

Montreal. Those newspapers which had come out in favor of conscription had their windows smashed. Finally, about 19,000 French Canadians were enrolled while at least 18,000 went into hiding. Most of these dodgers were never apprehended. At the end of the war, 15,000 French Canadians actually fought in Europe.

During World War II, precisely the same situation occurred. Again, the majority of the French Canadian people were against conscription. They were not in favor of Nazi Germany, they just would not serve under the British flag. The situation in Montreal became so volatile that the federal government summoned a division of soldiers from Toronto to reestablish order in the streets of Montreal. Several people were killed in the ensuing street fights.

Understanding the feelings of Quebec, Prime Minister King had first declared that no Canadian soldier would be sent to Europe. He thus averted a new divisive issue. However, when the Americans joined the war in 1942, King was under great pressure. He organized a referendum throughout Canada on conscription and Canadian involvement in Europe. English Canada voted eighty percent in favor of conscription, while Quebec was 71.2% against it. (Since most English in Quebec had voted for conscription, approximately eighty-five percent of the French Canadians of Quebec must have been against intervention.) When the authorities attempted to impose conscription on Quebec, there was massive resistence. Again there were sizable riots and, once more, about half of the soldiers went into hiding with relatives in the backwoods of Quebec. There were so many deserters that it was impossible to bring them before the court and a general amnesty was declared.

Ethnic Bargaining

Several decades after the conquest, England planned to Anglicize Quebec in much the same way as Northern Ireland was being Anglicized: by massive immigration of English Protestants. This attempt failed completely, despite huge propaganda efforts. The vast expanses of land opening up in the Midwest were much more attractive to would-be settlers than the lower shores of the Saint Lawrence. Forty years after the conquest, less than one percent of Quebec's population was English Protestant. It was only after 1812 that the immigration from England picked up somewhat. However, the government and administration (apart from the

church and the courts) were entirely in English hands. This was due
to a very simple trick: every official had to swear an oath of allegiance to the king, "Defender of the Faith," and Roman Catholics
clearly could not accept the wording of this oath.

In 1801, a law was passed concerning the establishment of primary schools. Up to then, there had only been church schools and
junior colleges administered by priests, all of them attended primarily by children of the elite. The new law introduced a plan that
was to have much greater consequences than could be anticipated
at that time: each parish could decide whether to establish English
schools as well. This meant that, wherever such schools existed,
the children of English immigrants would no longer grow up in a
French environment or in intimate contact with French-speaking
schoolmates. They could be brought up separately. The existence
of English schools also attracted more English immigrants and this,
in turn, increased the demand for English schools. This curious
form of voluntary apartheid has remained typical for Quebec,
where thousands of children can still grow up without really becoming familiar with the language, the thinking, and the aspirations of
the French majority. The parents can decide the language of
instruction of their children in the same way as they decide about
their religion. What is known as "linguistic rights" is actually the
right of every inhabitant of the province to choose between French
and English schooling for his children.

The establishment of separate schools in Quebec finally lead to
a quadruple system: French/Catholic, English/Catholic, English/
Protestant, and French/Protestant. The fact that the English schools
effectively shielded the students from any serious contact with
French, language and culture (French in English schools until lately
was taught like a dead language), the further fact that ninety percent
of all immigrants (especially the Germans, Italians, Greeks, and
Jews) were sending their children to English schools is now perceived to be intolerable by many leading French Canadians. The
widespread opinion that science and commerce are best done in
English only has been boosting the prestige of English educational
establishments.

The establishment of separate school systems in Quebec is at
the root of the Quebec "language question." It clearly worked in

favor of the English majority. Once English schools were established, immigrants were attracted to municipalities with English schools, thus boosting the English influence. In 1960, Montreal with sixty percent French population had one French university (Université de Montreal) and three English ones: McGill, Sir George Williams, and Loyola College. Quebec City also had only one French university. Such was the condition at the time when not more than ten percent of the population of Quebec were English born.

The Politicization of Unrest

After 1960, many things changed rapidly in a hitherto rather static Quebec. Three factors created this new situation:

1. *Political changes:* A new provincial government was elected, that is, less paternalistic and less parochial — a change that was called "the quiet revolution."

2. *Religious changes:* The Catholic church within a few years lost its persuasive authority, especially over the young. This meant that the young were no longer as susceptible to the doctrined submissiveness that the church had preached ever since the conquest. The way for contestation and revolutionary actions was open.

3. *Social changes:* The young generation was more impatient, more rationalistic, more demanding, and more obsessed by justice. At the same time, the birthrate of the French Canadians dropped drastically within a decade. From 1971 on, it was barely able to compensate for the deaths. As far as the French ethnic community was concerned, the future looked grim, for the English continued to proliferate at a somewhat greater rate. The immigrants also had a higher birthrate and their children with few exceptions were being Anglicized.

For over two centuries, the great fertility of the French Canadian women maintained faith in the face of Anglo-Saxon pressure. After 1960, the weapon went blunt. Was the dream of the British imperialists of 1760 coming true after all? Would the French Canadians become a minority in French Canada? Many patriotically minded leaders expresses a sense of dismay and impending doom.

The French Canadians were a sturdy race of farmers, lumbermen, builders, and hunters. The children were brought up to help in the fields and in the household, the older ones to look after their smaller siblings. Family spirit was strong. Until well into this century, schooling was neglected. Only the school bus made compulsory school attendance possible. Prior to its introduction there had been no way of getting to school in winter, and in summer the children were needed in the fields and at home. Even now, the number of people unable to write and read is comparatively high. But most children now go to school eight or nine years.

Up to about 1960, the French Canadian was a convinced Roman Catholic who went to mass every Sunday. This is still true of the older generation, but not of the youth. There was once a tradition that at least one child of every family should become a priest or a nun. Since most families had ten, twelve, or more children, the condition was generally easy to fulfill. For over a hundred years, Quebec has thus had a surplus of priests and nuns from Quebec. With the present low birthrate, this supply is bound to dry up, and the Quebec workers are now trying to form indigenous personnel.

The traditional division of labor (French Canadians for manual work; English Canadians for leading jobs in banking, commerce, and industry; French Canadian lawyers and physicians, plus a growing number of engineers; English Canadians as business executives and industrialists) is being challenged. What the defenders of French Canada can no longer accept is the rule that business should be done in English, that factories with 80–90% French Canadian workers should be administered in English only, and that, in order to be acceptable for any higher job, the Quebecois has to master English completely, while his English colleague may get away with his native language alone.

In October 1968, the Federal Commission on Bilingualism and Biculturalism published its findings on this subject, here summarized by Lysiane Gagnon.

51.5% of export goods produced in Quebec are manufactured by American companies, 44% by English Canadian enterprises. In Montreal, 83% of the higher-income brackets in industry and commerce go to the English. Only one in five of these is

expected to know French. In the lower-income brackets
($10,000 per year or less), 60% of the personnel are French,
while the administrators are 80% Anglo-Saxon. Only half
of these are expected to understand French.

Lysiane Gagnon concluded that with the same education and
qualification the French Canadian, even if he spoke fluent English,
had less opportunities to accede to a higher post in industry, banking, or commerce than even a unilingual English colleague. In a perceptive study of this question Rioux concludes: "The young French
Canadian wishing to make a career in industry is faced with the
following dilemma: he feels he must make a choice between his
personal advancement and his cultural identity. In order to succeed,
he must be willing to lose, to a great extent, his linguistic and cultural identity. He is expected to speak, think, and act in English."

For the same reasons, many gifted French Canadians prefer to
work for the provincial government, where such sacrifice is not
necessary because the number of "anglophones" working there is
very small. There should also be opportunities in the federal administration, where less than ten percent of the personnel are bilingual.
But the strongly unilingual English civil servants react with hostility or fear to any attempt of increasing the bilingual personnel in
the higher-income brackets, since such personnel could only come
from Quebec.

The reaction against this process of foreign domination and
linguistic erosion has become increasingly stronger during the sixties. The counterattack has taken different forms, both cultural
and political. The provincial government has painstakingly promoted
French culture. All art forms have experienced a great expansion
during the sixties: theater, ballet, folklore, painting, and music (no
country has such an abundance of popular chansonniers). Quebec
arts and crafts are also flourishing: furniture making, pottery, weav-
ing, wood carving, forged iron, boat building, and so forth.

The cultural life of Quebec, concentrated in Montreal, is overwhelmingly French and has an extraordinary vitality. The Théâtre
du Nouveau Monde, which started as a classical Molière playhouse
some years ago, is now an experimental theater giving the young
French Canadian playwrights and actors a generous opportunity to

show their talents. Another playhouse, the Théâtre du Rideau Vert, has become a real French Canadian family theater and is often sold out weeks in advance. There are two more French playhouses that appeal especially to the young. The ballet Feux Follets draws strongly on French and Indian folklore. All this cultural activity is generously subsidized by the provincial and federal governments.

The expansion of educational facilities, mostly French, has been tremendous since 1960. Two new French universities, thirty junior colleges (all French, except five), a huge engineering school, the School of High Commercial Studies training French Canadian business executives, a French theater school, and a huge expansion of evening courses at the university level are part of the counter-offensive. Behind all these efforts in the artistic and educational fields is the desire to stress the French presence to fortify the French language, to overcome the traditional inferiority feeling of the French Canadian, and to make people proud of their French heritage and identity. These efforts have not been without consequence, and French Canadians seem to demonstrate more vigor and vitality in their cultural and political expressions than ever.

In the political field, too, great efforts are being made to strengthen French influence and to deal with the dangers threatening the French ethnic nation. All of these political movements are characterized by a new militancy. They are led by people who know what they want. They refuse to be absorbed by the Anglo-Saxons of the continent. They reject any melting-pot idea and point to the sad fate of the French in Vermont, Maine, and Detroit. The overwhelming majority of the French people of Quebec want *cultural* independence. The federal government is generously subsidizing the French institutions of learning and the artistic life of Quebec; yet French leaders of Quebec feel this does not eliminate the threat of ethnicide. The drastic fall of the birthrate, the refusal of immigrants of all races to send their children to French schools, the English pressure and domination in the realms of industry, banking, and commerce still favor increasing English penetration. The existence of "two solitudes": the French people, still mainly of the working class, and an English minority which, at least in Montreal, knows all too little about the feelings, aspirations, and needs of the French majority, has become intolerable.

While the independentists (about thirty percent of the French people) maintain that the problems cannot be solved without Quebec becoming independent ("Master in our own house"), other political movements try to achieve the same goal within the Canadian federation. For both groups, however, the language question is crucial. No one has yet suggested the Swiss or the Belgian principle of linguistic territories of schooling. Most will still agree that a parallel English educational system should exist, but only on condition that this system does not shield the students from any real contact with the French Canadian people. In fact, a number of English parents already sent their children to French primary schools with the intention to let them have their secondary education in English. Others, like Michel Chartrand, propose the opposite. In an interview he said: "There is no problem for the anglophone minority at all. We are the nation in the world who has been the most generous for its minorities. We even built Italian schools to permit their kids to learn French the easy way. But we are drowning ourselves voluntarily because eighty-nine percent of the immigrants' children in Quebec are attending English schools. It's insane what we are doing to ourselves. No other country would stand for such a genocide. I believe that English children should go to primary schools in English, but when they reach high school and universities, it should all be in French. Quebec should be a French province, even more than Ontario is an English one. English being the second language, the anglophones could continue to do their business in English. McGill University should become French. ... The next generation will be less patient, more radical, and they will not stand for English (higher) schools anymore. We must be honest enough to tell the anglophones that if we let them keep their linguistic privileges, we shall be contributing to our own destruction."

Despite assurances to the contrary by the leader of the independentist Parti Quebecois (PQ), René Lévesque, it is not likely that an independent Quebec would be able to grant the English minority its present linguistic rights. Union leader Michel Chartrand may seem a firebrand today, but he only expresses what the young French generation actually believes. Compared with countries where the principle of language territories is in force, his suggestions are con-

servative. Very few countries grant their immigrants a choice between two languages of schooling. French Canadians think that non-
English immigrants to Quebec should be barred from sending their
children to English schools. They consider this as one important
measure to forestall a linguistic takeover of Quebec.

The watchword of these militant groups is "prise de con-
science," that is, an attempt to bring people to a greater awareness
of their problems and to prepare political solutions. René Lévesque
puts the problem this way (*La Presse*, June 23, 1973):

> Are we going anywhere? It seems to me we are. It will be
> long, and hard and uncertain till the very end for all of us
> working to bring about the maturity of a society as trauma-
> tized as ours. Is there a people in the world which history
> has repressed so long, keeping it in a dependence that provided
> sufficiently well that one got used to it? Is there another
> people whose elite betrayed it so lightheartedly, almost with-
> out exception? For is it not betrayal to constantly preach
> patience, resignation, and fear of change in order to keep the
> herd well under control? Without doubt, Quebec is a "case,"
> the case of a nation born like others, and capable like others,
> if not better, to flourish and take its affairs in hand, but a
> nation one has tried to smother for ever in the depressing
> cotton wool of a paternalistic social and political climate,
> a nation full of complexes and animated by a "holy" distrust
> of man. . . .Nothing less but independence will correct that
> psychological contraction which they (and ourselves) inflicted
> upon us. With the creation of Israel, so it was said, all the Jews
> in the world suddenly had grown by two inches, standing
> more upright. A national home made all the difference. The
> same thing will happen to us.

The Parti Quebecois, however, was not the first movement of
national militancy and collective self-assertion. In fact, it was the
last, albeit the most mature. Its forerunner was the Rassemblement
pour l'Indéndence nationale (RIN), mainly consisting of young
intellectuals. But to some members, the RIN was not revolutionary
enough. Inspired by the worldwide phenomenon of decolonializa-

tion and by the Cuban and Algerian revolutions, they were mostly young people, idealistic, adventurous, very impatient, who would not wait for any evolution towards a new Quebec. They all had studied Frantz Fanon's *The Wretched of the Earth* and believed in the redeeming, liberating power of violence per se. The first group of extremists was led by the Belgian immigrant Georges Schoeters. Calling itself the Front de Libération Quebecois (FLQ), it began to explode bombs in symbolic places. The members were betrayed, arrested, and incarcerated for a number of years. Two of the group later committed new political crimes (bank robberies), a third became a drug addict, Schoeters wound up in Chile, and others abandoned their objectives.

One year later, another group, led by a Hungarian immigrant, was arrested during a robbery. In 1966, a third group, known as the Vallières-Gagnon group, was arrested after it had caused the death of two persons. The two leaders fled to the U.S.A. where they demonstrated, were arrested, and brought back to Quebec. While incarcerated at the Manhattan House of Detention, Vallières wrote the book *White Niggers of America*, a partisan view of the alienated, "colonized" average French Canadian, justifying indirectly the action of the F.L.Q.

Other F.L.Q. cells formed in 1968, 1969 and 1970. They committed a number of crimes ranging from bank robberies and bomb explosions to hijacking a plane to Cuba, and finally culminating in two kidnappings and a murder (October 1970). After this climax ("the October crisis") and the arrests that followed, the F.L.Q. disintegrated. As one leader said: "You cannot make a revolution with most of the revolutionaries in prison." In May 1971, Vallières officially acknowledged that the F.L.Q. was dissolved.

It is difficult to say whether the dramatic events caused by the F.L.Q. really changed much. Some, such as Mitchell Sharp, minister of foreign affairs in Ottawa, believed the F.L.Q. had only demonstrated the absurdity of independence. (The P.Q. lost half of its membership after the October crisis.) Others contended that the actions of the F.L.Q. had been necessary to wake up the people. Still others considered the F.L.Q. activity as rather puerile, noisy actions of protest without any lasting effect.

The publicity effect of the F.L.Q. was tremendous. Quebec acquired international prominence. English Canadians were shaken, and some began to study French. A number of well-to-do English Canadians (among them forty psychiatrists) left the province. Everybody wanted to know what was wrong with Canada and Quebec, and what Quebec wanted. The fact was that Quebec was and still is profoundly divided. The young generation of intellectuals is predominantly for independence, the older generation and the workers consider independence a journey into the unknown. While everyone agrees that French Quebec must not only survive but also remain strong, there is no agreement as to how this could be achieved. Labor leader Paul Emile Dalpé wrote in June 1973: "Pulled in every direction, the Quebec nation does not know where to go. In the course of its history, many efforts have been made to reveal its soul, but these efforts had only little success. During the past years, very promising attempts were made, but these seem to have foundered on the rock of general indifference." This apathy, Dalpé explains, is due to materialism. Too many would-be reformers were too interested in dialectical (Marxist) exercises that did not impress the masses.

It is doubtful whether Quebec will really become independent in the near future. Unless there is some drastic change, such as an economic or political crisis bordering on a depression, the majority will prefer to work within the present system for the creation of a strong French Quebec.

There are two regions of Quebec with an important English minority where the two races have been living in complete harmony for several decades. One is the suburban town of Verdun, mostly inhabitated by the lower-middle and working class. Here, the shopkeepers, employees, and artisans, both English and French, speak the two languages, as do the city councillors and administrators. The other region is composed of the rural districts south and southwest of Montreal, where almost everyone has grown up bilingual. Both regions prove that harmony and mutual understanding are possible on condition that both linguistic groups are willing to learn and use both languages and to consider each other as equal. In the final analysis, the solution to ethnic conflict in Quebec may lie just beyond the reach of government intervention and ultimately in the reciprocity of respect for different cultures, which only adversary nations can confer upon each other.

Jewish Ethnicity and Latin American Nationalism

The emergence of the state of Israel had significantly mobilized renewing interest in the condition of Jewish communities elsewhere. The three largest such Diaspora communities are in the United States, the Soviet Union, and in Latin America. The condition of American Jewry has sufficient exceptional features to exempt it from the widespread belief, advocated in particular by the Zionists, that Israel alone insures security and long-range satisfaction as well as survival for the Jewish people. It is a widely held (but increasingly debated) belief that the two and one-half to three million Jews within the Soviet Union are fundamentally disenfranchised as Jews and do not possess either the economic or political resources to redress such imbalances. As a result, there is a widespread corollary persuasion that immigration to Israel is the basic solution to the Jewish problem in the Soviet Union.

In each of the preceding situations, minority reports have been filed. Some assert that Jews in the United States may survive as Americans but that long-run assimilationist pressures within this country can only result in the dissemination of that largest of world Jewish communities. Others claim that Israel cannot possibly absorb all of the Jews within the Soviet Union and that the Soviet government must be made to adhere strictly to its own canons on the national question as established during the revolution by Lenin and others, a position that guarantees rights of full autonomy and full citizenship for Soviet Jews.

Because scholars have concentrated their thoughts and research on the question of Jewish survival elsewhere, the situation in Latin America is less well known. While studies of national Jewish communities in Latin America exist, only sociological and demographic research on the status of Jews in Argentina and in Brazil is particularly extensive.[1] Larger issues concerning the future of Latin American Jews have remained shrouded in imaginative conversation rather than firm research. The survival potential of Latin American Jewry remains a major consideration and constraint on a formulation of policymaking in Israel. That is to say, Israeli policy toward Latin American nations is considerably dependent upon their orientations toward the Jewish communities in these nations. The emergence of Socialist regimes in Latin America has further intensified interest in Latin American Jewry since it in turn intensified the relationship between entrepreneurial activities and national priorities.

There are essentially two root sociological persuasions of the Jew in modern history: as a major factor in the development of capitalism and industrialism, and as a major factor in the development of political pluralism and ethnic diversity. The two positions may not be contradictory. Indeed, wisdom increasingly dictates a high degree of similitude and overlap. Yet, insofar as the two positions reveal the Jews as a factor in the development within society, they point out its economic and political sides within a larger sociological framework.

The stark commentaries of Werner Sombart and Simon Dubnow juxtaposed with each other perhaps clarify just what the researcher interested in the relationship between ethnicity and nationality is faced with.

> The importance of the Jews was twofold. On one hand, they
> influenced the outward form of modern capitalism; and on
> the other, they gave expression to its inward spirit. Under the
> first heading the Jews contributed no small share in giving to
> economic relations the international aspect they bear today;
> in helping the modern state, that framework of capitalism, to
> become what it is; and lastly, in giving capitalist organization
> its peculiar features by inventing a good many details of the
> commercial machinery which moves the business of life today
> and by cooperating in the perfecting of others. Under the
> second heading, the importance of the Jews is so enormous
> because they, above all others, endowed economic life with
> its modern spirit. They seized upon the essential idea of
> capitalism and carried it to its fullest development.[2]

In contrast, the searing words of Dubnow indicate far less
concern with the economic support of capitalism than with the drive
toward political sovereignty:

> Our enemies in all generations cry out: "There is a certain
> people scattered abroad and dispersed among the peoples
> and their laws are diverse from those of every other people."
> In modern times they call it "a state within a state." But the
> congregation of Israel goes on in its historical path and says:
> "Indeed, a state within a state," an internal autonomous
> group within an external political group, and the nature of
> things sanctions it.[3]

Jews flourished in the Diaspora in proportion to the degree
that the European medieval contract society was supplanted by the
modern industrial system based on monetary exchange. But, at the
same time, capitalism itself gave birth to a renewed sense of nationalism, and this had its impact on the Jews no less than on other minority peoples.They too were swept by tidal waves of nationalism.
In their case, the nationalism had the full authority of biblical
injunctions concerning Israel as a sacred homeland. As a result,

one can say that both Sombart, in the economic realm, and Dubnow, in the political realm, express the dual realities of Jewish life
in the modern industrial era, a reality given particular poignancy and
urgency by the Nazi holocaust marking the death of six million
Jews. The question then becomes: Can the Jewish people retain an
economic, religious, and national identity in a Socialist or at least
a postcapitalist setting, or is the future of the Jewish community
inextricably linked not so much to socialism but to Zionism or a
return to the notion of a special Jewish sovereignty?

While this question is theoretically fascinating, our task here is
to seek some empirical resolution of the issues since, out of a total
world Jewish population of certainly no more than fifteen million
people, of whom approximately three million reside in Israel, the
majority of Jews, whether voluntarily or otherwise, continue to live
in national boundaries other than their own and yet retain a Jewish
ethnic identity that is as ferociously maintained as that of religious
orthodox groups within the state of Israel itself.

By focusing specifically on the Jewish communities of Latin
America with less than one million people, but nonetheless a significant contributing element to practically every nation in which
they reside, we should derive a keener appreciation of both present
tendencies and future prospects of Jewish community life in the
Diaspora and hence begin to understand the relationship between
ethnic factors and national systems in general.

Where Jewish communities of Latin America are largely middle
class in character and the rest of the society has not been able to
share in the bountiful riches of bourgeois life, these communities
have become inextricably tied to the international capitalist system.
Jews participate in that special brand of postindustrial capitalism,
neocolonialism, that places great store in property and profits but
has all but ignored other shibboleths of capitalism such as free-
market competition and equality of access to personal growth. We
are not talking here about Jewish communities similar to those
begun in Israel, which from the outset were formulated in terms of
agrarian Socialist patterns. My remarks pertain only to the Jews
within the Diaspora as it took Jews to Latin America.

Even in their quasi-radical Communist versions, Jewish
communities always retain their lively sense of bourgeois perspec-

tives. In Argentina, Brazil, and Chile, membership in Communist parties of the traditional variety represents, or represented, a secular expression of Jewish aspirations for a just society. Membership in athletic clubs, private banking societies, and generally well-heeled life-styles was a bourgeois expression of this same aspiration. Thus, when the political crunch comes, Jews — whether as open or closed middle-class members — face a crisis of class membership. The immigrant generation by any standards represented a shallow commitment to Judaism; it was concerned with adaptation to the nations of Latin America as a survival mechanism. The second generation, once removed from the immigrant culture, represented a shallow secularism since once a modicum of integration was achieved economic pursuits became dominant. Thus, for third-generation Jews to become truly radical means an abandonment of Judaism altogether, while to remain overtly and manifestly Jewish implies an identity with the exploiting middle sectors. This then is the untenable truth faced by established Jewish communities in Latin America. It is little wonder that their rage is directed at their special condition as Jews rather than at their condition as members of a middle class in which they are limited participants. The pressure of the political Left in many of these nations further heightens the belief that being Jewish is itself the source of their alienation.

How do Jews fare in a Socialist state such as Cuba, a nation that revolted against capitalist social relationships? And how have Jews fared under neo-Fascist regimes such as those in Argentina, Brazil, and Paraguay, states that have had revolutionary assaults on the classic capitalist model that incorporates the liberal tradition of free criticism and free choice?

These questions avoid the assumption of the new orthodoxy that the Jews are on the verge of catastrophe or the conventional assumption that, as Latin America develops, so too will Jews prosper and profit. The convergence of ethnicity and nationalism was far greater at an earlier period when immigrant labor was a central ingredient to business and labor expansion in Latin America. Now, in the postindustrial era, the need for such labor has given way and confrontation has replaced convergence as the essential dynamic in Jewish-Latin relationships. For example, if one were to ask how the Jewish community of Cuba fared after the Castro revolution, the answer would be not very well. According to the latest and most reliable demographic estimates, there were roughly 10,000 Jews in Cuba at the time of that revolution in 1959. This number has dwindled to roughly 2,000 a decade later.[4] It is argued that the exodus from Cuba was part and parcel of the middle-class exodus and therefore had very little to do with religious sentiment.[5] But that leads us to Sombart's point that Jews and capitalism are so intimately linked that an exodus of the bourgeoisie implicitly means the exodus of large numbers of Jews.

This neat model does not seem quite so applicable to a nation like Chile during its three-year effort at Socialist construction. Immediately after the victory of the Socialist party of Salvador Allende, a Jewish exodus occurred corresponding to a by-now typical postrevolutionary process: a middle-class entrepreneurial exodus. This was heightened by the pro-Arab views of Allende that compelled many Jews to assume would result in a wider anti-Semitism. Yet before this progressed far, a curious reversal took place, the exodus tapered off dramatically. Some Jews quickly stopped being economic entrepreneurs and began functioning as political entrepreneurs. They performed with admirable loyalty to the Socialist regime and exhibited a brilliance that permitted a flowering of a politicized intelligentsia the likes of which has not been seen in South America since nineteenth-century positivism took hold in education. In Chile the Jews had historically participated economically but not politically. Because of a residual anti-Semitism in the new Chile, Jews must travel with light suitcases and heavy hearts whatever the political arrangements. Yet the expected exodus did not take place, nor were Jews physically or spiritually imperiled under Allende. Indeed, in the military *golpe* that followed the overthrow of Allende, many of these highly politicized radical Jews did suffer — as radicals rather than as Jews.

In Argentina under Peron, in Brazil under Vargas, and in Chile under Frei, the Jews fared exceptionally well economically. There were occasional outbursts against Jewish financial interests, but these became increasingly muted after the defeat of nazism in World War II. Jews had not been particularly prominent in political life, and certainly not in the military life, of these countries. There are, of course, rare exceptions, particularly in Brazil, but the overall fact is that Jews have remained in the economic interstices of these nations without exercising any corresponding political role. It would seem that prominent Jews felt this form of accommodation to be quite acceptable if not desirable, given the cycle of Latin American political instability.

To illustrate the volatility of the Jewish condition in the "ABC countries" it is necessary only to review, in brief, the dramatic changes that have already occurred in the 1970s in these crucial nations of South America. This regime instability attests both to the overall worth and complexity in the analysis of Jewish ethnicity within a larger context of Latin American nationalism.

Probably the most dramatic changes took place in Chile where the regime of Salvadore Allende was toppled by a military coup in the autumn of 1973. Given the fact that the Jewish community had polarized (just as everyone else had in Chile) on the purposes and prospects of Chilean socialism, the very character of the investigation must obviously be altered. For instead of being able to examine the impact of socialism on Jewish communal life, the substance of any inquiry must now shift, taking into consideration the impact of the coup d'etat, and whether this latest major event has restored Jewish community life, left it unaffected, or fragmented it even further. It might now be possible to study whether the considerable number of Jews in the Chilean administration of Allende in any way represented the Jewish community or were simply executing their duties on a professional level. Beyond that, it might be possible to stake out the three-year Allende time span and analyze some of the more fundamental issues of the condition of Jews under a Socialist regime. Thus, from an analytic point of view, the abrupt turn of events in Chile enhances both the possibilities and the importance of studying Jewish ethnicity within a larger Latin American nationalism.

Conditions in Argentina likewise were tremendously altered as a result of the return to power, after seventeen years in exile, of Juan Domingo Peron. With his return, and the ambiguous appeals to both the political Right and the political Left, the condition of Argentine Jewry became, if possible, even more problematic. Under the impact of a more sophisticated Arab foreign policy the number of anti-Semitic publications circulating in the *post-interregnum* era increased. At the same time, however, Jewish associations seemed to firm up and extract from the Peronist leadership a ubiquitous but nonetheless explicit promise not to engage in anti-Semitism as a political formula. The basic posture of the Peronist regime toward the Jews, and we have no reason to doubt its continuance under the reign of his wife, is not much different from previous military regimes. This entails an emphasis on national factors; that is, support for_ Argentina as a prime requisite in exchange for a rejection of anti-Semitism as an overt policy. However, the situation in Argentina is extremely fluid, with Left and Right tendencies within Peronism competing vigorously, and even viciously, for power. The Jewish community is in the unfortunate position of having been harrassed and subject to assault by both Right and Left tendencies during twentieth-century Argentine history; and one can hardly doubt that this pattern will continue for some time to come.

The situation in Brazil has remained as stable as any nonparliamentary regime can be. However, here, too, there has been a very recent shift in administration with a more liberalizing tendency in the "election" of the first Protestant president in Brazilian history. Whether such secularization of Brazilian politics will permit greater Jewish participation in the Brazilian national structure is still too early to say. However, it is certain that the Brazilian social structure has come to uniquely favor the middle sectors, those groups in which Jews predominate.[6] Such unique dimensions are not simply part of a Latin American syndrome. The Portuguese background of Brazilian culture created a less harsh climate for Jews. And the Jewish role in the developmental and industrial process has long been acknowledged and even acclaimed by the larger society.

In general, then, Argentina, Brazil, and Chile, for the time being, have moved considerably to the Right, the Chilean shift being the most dramatic and fundamental. Under the circumstances, in order to generate a strong test case of the fate of Jews under Latin American socialism, it is necessary to reconsider our parameters and briefly turn to an analysis of Cuba. The special character of the Cuban revolution of 1959 may not permit any vast generalizations, but at least the stability of its Socialist regime does make possible certain extrapolations about Jewish community life and communal life in general under conditions of Latin American socialism.

One major, international trend that has emerged since the October 1973 round in the Arab-Israeli struggle is the shift toward the Arab position in the foreign policies of many Latin American countries. Brazil has shifted less than Argentina. The Arab League, in one form or another, has been especially vigorous in the last several years in the distribution of anti-Semitic literature. Indeed, with the rise of a uniform Arab foreign policy and the strict separation of anti-Zionism from anti-Semitism in their rhetoric, the support base for Arab national interests in high places of Latin American political regimes has increased. Those countries with a considerable Jewish population,and are therefore susceptible to anti-Semitic literature to begin with, have witnessed a stepping up in such activities. However, it must be added that of all sectors within the Third World, Latin America (including Cuba) has reacted with the least hostility toward Israeli claims and toward the maximum security of its own Jewish citizens in the face of any terrorist potentials.

The condition of the Jewish communities under Cuban communism is perhaps one of the more fascinating issues confronting Jews of Latin America. This fascination derives from the overt development of a Socialist regime in the Western hemisphere, although its level of importance must be measured by the relatively small numbers of people involved. The reduction in population from a thriving, throbbing Jewish community of 10,000 to one of slightly under 2,000 confronts us with the main issue: whether in fact this exodus is a response to the economic superfluity of a middle class in a working-class revolutionary environment or whether the specific inability of the Jew to survive under the new regime led to such large-scale emigration. The librarian of Havana's largest synagogue, Marcos Matterin, answered that the Jewish community remained intact because only the bourgeois community disintegrated. "Actually, nothing happened to the Jewish community. Except that simply with the social change that took place here, since the great majority of the Jews were businessmen and industrialists, they understood that they 'had no future' under a Socialist regime and left the country. But it was not for racial or religious motives — since there was no discrimination here. It was only that they felt themselves affected economically and then left the country."[7]

It should not be thought that the condition of the Jews in pre-Socialist Cuba was especially attractive. Certainly they had no discernible political power and, beyond that, when the crunch came in 1940 and Terman Jewish refugees attempted to land in Havana, they were met by Cuban officials with stony silence and a thoroughly negative attitude. As a result, boatloads of Jews were sent back from this last hope for survival to Nazi Germany where they met their ultimate fate in concentration camps. Not even the intervention of then President of the United States Franklin Delano Roosevelt was able to alter this situation. Thus, one must candidly state that Jewish circumstances in Cuba were at no time in the past especially inviting to the flowering of its ethnic and cultural life. By all reports, the Castro regime has worked hard to meet Jewish religious community needs especially on high holy occasions. No opposition has been forthcoming to the development of a coordinating commission of the Jewish congregations of Cuba, as long as these activities were focused on community performances that had no linkages either to the United States or to Israel, or to domestic counterrevolutionary activities.

The problem in Cuba, as elsewhere, is that the Jews are not just a religious group. Neither are they simply an ethnic group, yet they retain definite feelings of nationhood unto themselves. Whether this was a nationhood of mind or a nation on earth, the fact remains that Zionism is but the Jewish form of nationalism. Jewish national aspirations have long been recognized in Marxian and non-Marxian circles alike.[8] Hence, it would be misleading to assume that the existence of Jews as a community or religious entity resolves the tension of Jews living out of different national frameworks and different economic systems. As a tentative conclusion, on the basis of the fourteen-year experience in Cuba and the three-year experience in Chile, we are confronted with both/and rather than neither/nor situations. Evidence exists that Judaism flourishes under capitalism and tends to atrophy under socialism. Yet, as the positive contributions of Jews to Cuban life make plain (not to mention the continued expression of strength of Soviet Jewry), Jews do not vanish per se behind the walls of socialism.

It is evident that Jewishness as a religion falls in numbers as the general tendency toward secularization spreads throughout the hemisphere. Jews as an ethnic factor continue to liberalize political life and expand economic opportunities. This is especially the case as long as Latin American cultural tendencies remain derivative and dependent. Jews, however, as a national question, are inextricably linked to the fates and fortunes of Jewish communities throughout the world, especially the fate of Israel. At this level, Jewish concerns, whatever their reservations concerning Zionism in general or Israeli foreign policy in particular, remain an essential measuring rod of Jewish consciousness. Even if this sort of horizontal mosaic will not allow simple responses to Jewish life in Latin America, it at least permits an identification of those factors creating religious, ethnic, and political congruence, and this sums up contemporary expressions of Judaism.

Unfortunately a marked tendency to generalize and theorize about Jews either in the Diaspora or Latin America is blind to different possibilities and changed circumstances over time. The role of politics in the Latin American orbit has always been equal, if not greater, to the socioeconomic forces often considered basic. Because societies in Latin America are highly politicized, Jewish power can be measured as effectively in terms of political power as in terms of the conventional measure of economic mobility. With these kinds of variations accounted for and frankly acknowledged, some of the undue concerns for the physical survival of Jewish people can be put in clearer historical perspective, where they somehow seem less ominous, if not necessarily less omnipresent.

In part, the Israeli Jews have escaped the dilemma of surviving outside the framework of capitalism (at least in part) because the national aspirations are isomorphic with Jewish aspirations. Israel is, after all, a Jewish state. Therefore, the Jewish community within Israel links up with problems and processes of the state and the governmental apparatus. The idea of a Jewish state, however, coated with religious values, is at the core of the idea of a state as such, and that signifies the capacity to direct the instruments of control and coercion within the society.

It is the estrangement, the alienation of Jews in the Diaspora from the sources of state power that is responsible for their special connection with the spirit of capitalism. The economic arena alone seems to be hospitable to Jewish talent, or at least it does not subject the Jew to the same level of ire and suspicions of other nationals and other nationalities. Now that Israel has existed for almost a quarter of a century, it is perhaps to be expected that the suspicion of Jewish dual loyalty lurks deep in the rising nationalisms throughout the Third World and not least in Latin America. The very existence of Israel, while providing a support and a shield for the Jews of Latin America, also creates problems for these Jews, since it raises the possibility that Jews might never really be integrated into the national aspirations of each nation in Latin America. Now that such aspirations are increasingly framed by the Left not only as nationalism but also as antiimperialism, the Jewish condition has become ubiquitous. Jews are perceived as marginal economic men (in Marxian terms) and even more marginal neo-imperialists who cannot be absorbed into local nationalism and at the same time refuse to consider nationalism as a salvation.[9]

At this juncture, Jewish organizational fears for survival in Latin America link up with nationalist fears for survival of Latin America apart from dependency relations with the imperial powers. The tragic fate of the Jewish communities of Latin America does not involve a concerted effort of a Torquemada or a Hitler to destroy human life for reasons of religious or political fanaticisms, yet it makes them the victim of the rising tide of national liberation movements throughout the hemisphere, to which Jews are remote and residual rather than central and integral. Jews, classically and historically linked to causes of mass democracy and social equity, and now outside the impulse toward national liberation from imperial domination, that is, outside the very source that would provide for the sort of democratic goals Jews have been linked to historically. There are important exceptions; however, it must be noted that these liberation movements create a causal nexus moving from anti-imperialism to anti-Zionism to pro-Soviet and pro-Arab postures that make it hard for all but the anti-Jewish Jew to participate in.

To pose the problem of Jewish survival as a question of left-wing Latin American nationalism does not absolve the nationalists from anti-Semitism. It does not remove the sting of guerrilla organizations such as the Tupamaros in Uruguay or the Tacuaristas in Argentina, whose singular restrictive badge of honor is that Jews not

be permitted in their respective ranks. In contrast, we can say —
poignantly as well as pointedly — that the historical role of the Jew
as marginal man, while serving the purposes of liberalism and even
radicalism in fully developed and even overripe capitalism, has not
had the same radical thrust in underdeveloped nations with unreal-
ized dreams. If anti-Semitism on the Left led to a condition of what
Bebel termed the socialism of fools, it nonetheless is a fact that the
main threat to Jewish survival is indeed now from the Left. Therefore, the main response of the Jews must be to that Left, and that
response must be affirmative no less than critical; otherwise, the
confrontation will be ominous, with serious consequences for the
Jews of Latin America. Ironically, those Latin American societies
which have been singularly appreciative of their Jewish communities
have been singularly enriched economically and intellectually by
their presence.

This muted fear that the Jews of Latin America, in their very
immersion in middle-sector affairs, may not survive the revolutionary onslaught has given rise to a search for alternatives. In this
search, the leaders of Jewish organizational life have worked dili-
gently to move the Jewish masses away from what is, after all, a
far-from-robust bourgeoisie.

The Jewish leadership in Latin America is plainly worried, not
by the possibility of extermination as in Nazi Germany or even by
the possibility of cultural absorption as in contemporary North
America. Rather, it is concerned by something at once more subtle
and yet evident to anyone who has spent time in Latin America. It
is disturbed by the potential for class absorption, the destruction of
dependent bourgeois societies that have neither the determination of
their North American class counterparts nor the traditions of their
European bourgeois counterparts. The myth of the bourgeoisie
as a bridgehead in Latin America for more rapid development is
being dispelled. Too much poverty exists at the bottom and too
much dependency exists at the top of society for the myth to be
sustained. In the process of inflation, unemployment,and technical
dependency, the fragile status of middle-sector superiority is in fact
subject to severe strains. This is especially so in Argentina and
Peru, less so in Brazil and Mexico. Yet with this general deterioration
of the bourgeois condition, one notes the breakdown of the Jewish

communities.

Jewish organizational leadership in Latin America, often in marked contrast to their own rank-and-file membership, has taken to heart its own marginality and its need to settle accounts with the countries and nations in which it resides. Such leaders demonstrate less a sense of worldwide solidarity among Jews than a sense of remarkable solidarity with the cause of the Third World and of national liberation, in part as Jews and in part as Latins. This is an intriguing development because it means that leaders in the Jewish community are in an antithetical relationship to the capitalist sector and in an ambivalent relationship even to Israel. Such an identification with national goals and movement away from identification with capitalism makes Jewish participation in indigenous and even radical Latin American movements possible, and indeed this is evidently underway. But this also leads to new strains between Jewish bourgeois aspirations and Jewish radical aspirations, not an unusual situation in the history of Judaism.

Spokesmen for the Latin American Jewish community have indicated that anti-Semitism is the product of the unique condition of Jews as representatives of middle-class and upper-class life in Latin America and their essential distance from the cause of the peasantry and proletariat. While this is correct, it is only the most visible part of the problem. For this view expresses the myth of Jewish power without appreciating the degree to which Jews participate in the bourgeois artifact but not in the bourgeois substance. What E. Franklin Frazier once said about the black bourgeoisie of the United States could well be attributed to the Jewish bourgeoisie of Latin America: they represent shadow without substance, good form and good manners without corresponding real power or real wealth. Many other factors contribute to Latin American anti-Semitism other than the Jew's marginal persistence in the middle class, and these have not received the attention they deserve.

Latin American culture is significantly Catholic, and that means it is a monolithic one. Latin America did not have the Protestant leavening of North America. Jews were therefore forced into a much sharper juxtaposition with Catholics than in North America, where just about all religions seem to blend into an American religion of the moral economy. One finds the Jew in Latin American culture confronting Christianity as the Church Triumphant, much as he had to do in medieval European culture, rather than as a fragmented and highly parceled series of churches controlled locally. The absence of Protestantism also represented an absence of pluralistic sensibilities. The pluralisms in North America and their absence in Latin America enabled Jewish marginality to persist far longer in Latin America. This religious dimension helps explain the current tendencies toward anti-Semitism in Latin America. After all, Jews do represent a religious counterforce there, not just a cultural or economic force.

Latin America has seen a more militant form of atheism or positivism than has North America. Secularism has confronted religious belief in a vigorous head-on clash in Argentina, Brazil, and Mexico. Here, too, the Jews have found trouble, for as a religious group they shared with Catholics a set of beliefs that put them beyond the pale of positivism. As a result, they were damned on one hand by the majority religion for being a minority religion, and then damned on the other hand by the antireligious forces for being religious to begin with. Positivism, secularism, and modernism all worked to sustain a low-keyed anti-Semitism in the Latin American environment, though it rarely spilled over into overt manifestations of hostilities to Jewish communities.

These conditions must be dealt with, otherwise we shall become prey to an oversimplified version of the Jewish condition as presented by those who wish us to believe that Jews are culturally dominant and not politically alienated. It would be extremely naive to assume that Jewish power within the intellectual world translates into Jewish power in other sectors of Latin American society.

Jews who perform cultural services in Latin America cannot yet translate these services into political power or into economic power. Nowhere in Latin America do Jews share in significant political power. This is the central fact of the hemisphere. We must therefore go beyond formalistic schemes as to whether politics or economics is of primary importance in the modern world. Rather, we are dealing with a group that is not able to participate in managing the affairs of state in any Latin American nation. Apart from its short-lived "political broker" role in Chile between 1970 and 1973,

Jews lack the strength of other national and ethnic groups that have participated much more fully in the political life of Latin American society. Generally Italians gave up being Italian to become Argentines, and Portuguese gave up being Portuguese to become Brazilian, and Spanish emigrés gave up their loyalty to Spain to become Mexicans, but Jews cannot accept or afford this surrender of traditions and the "nationality of the mind," as Dubnow called it. Therefore, Jews cannot expect to be welcomed with any fervor into the political process.

The Jewish communities in Latin America must also confront not only their Jewishness but also their ideological and national position vis-à-vis Israel. Curiously, Israeli social scientists have simply exhibited the kind of interest in the Jewish communities of Latin America that a devoted elder might show toward a younger wayward relative. But paternal concern avoids the basic fact that what Israel does in relation to Africa or in relation to other parts of the Third World, or how Israel confronts American foreign policy with respect to Vietnam, all have great bearing on the capacity of the Jewish communities of Latin America to develop a significant independent "radical" posture.

The sources of anxiety over the Jews of Latin America extend beyond their heavy concentration in the world of middle-class life and their parallel penetration of the cultural apparatus. At its deepest recesses, the very cosmopolitanism of the Jew, his links not just to the land of Israel but more profoundly his stubborn connection to Jews in the United States, England, France, and even the Soviet Union, appear to be more durable than similar sentiments of other ethnics for the old country. In the latter case, such sentiments pass away rather quickly with the second generation, whereas with Jews such sentiments pass either much more slowly or not at all. Indeed, even among Jews for whom Yiddish is as foreign as Chinese, the revival of Jewish passions has taken place. Of course, there is none of the ruthlessness and hatefulness of the charges leveled by the Soviet Stalinists in the fifties against "rootless cosmopolitanism," but the attitudes are there in the new-found belief by Tacuaristas in Argentina and Tupamaros in Uruguay that Jewish cosmopolitanism compromises Jewish radicalism at the source because of their unwillingness to surrender their links to the imperialisms of America and Europe. Even those Jews attuned to current stylistic forms of New Left sentiment and doctrine find themselves immobilized by anti-Semitism. Hence, the rebellion of third-generation Jews not infrequently involves either intense self-hate taking the form of open repudiation or self-adulation taking the form of a left-winged Zionism — but a Zionism nonetheless. This, of course, in the circular world of anti-Semitic reasoning, only reinforces the belief that Jewish loyalty to Latin America, or really to Argentina or Brazil or Mexico, and so forth, is weak and untrustworthy.

The spirit of antiimperialism and of firm independence from American foreign policy exhibited by Latin American Jewish leadership is mediated by their condition not so much as Jews but as their unique sense of responsibility and commitment to Israel. The norm of reciprocity must finally take effect, and that demands a much greater responsibility on the part of Israel not just for the abstract survival of the Latin American Jewish community, or as an expression of sympathy and concern for their brethren in the Diaspora, but as a concerted effort in the formulation of Israeli foreign and domestic policy. Promoting a more radical posture within Israel would contribute positively to the image of the Jew in the democratic upsurge now taking place throughout Latin America.

There are no easy answers. The problems of nationalism and the Jewish condition cannot be resolved by neat expressions of words and language. Yet we can clarify explicitly the responsibility of each huge cluster, in the United States, Israel, and Latin America, to forge the kinds of political positions that will foster greater pride in being a Jew as well as enforce the Jew's classic expression of concern for the downtrodden and his demand for universal equity, concerns that at least ostensibly are the taproots of Latin American nationalism as well.

Notes

1.   Haim Avni, "Argentine Jewry: Its Sociopolitical Status and Organizational Patterns," *Dispersion and Unity*, no. 12 (1971), pp.128–62. Heinrich Rattner, "Tradicao E. Mudanca: A Comunidade Judaica em Sao Paulo. Sao Paulo: Federacao Israelita do

Estado de Sao Paulo e pelo Instituto de Relacoes Humanas do Comite Judaico Americano" (mimeograph, 1970).

2.   Werner Sombart, *The Jews and Modern Capitalism,* trans. M. Epstein (Glencoe, Ill.: The Free Press, 1951).

3.   Simon Dubnow in *Nationalism and History: Essays on Old and New Judaism,* ed. Koppel S. Pinson (Cleveland, Ohio and New York: The World Publishing Co., Meridian Books, 1961).

4.   Institute of Jewish Affairs, *The Jewish Communities of the World: Demography, Political and Organization Status, Religious Institutions, Education, and the Press* (London: Andre Deutsch, 1971).

5.   Donna Katzin, "The Jews of Cuba," *The Nation* (25 May 1974), pp.658–60.

6.   Heinrich Rattner, "Occupational Structure of Jews in Brazil: Trends and Perspectives" (Sao Paulo, Brazil: University of Sao Paulo, mimeograph, 1973).

7.   Katzin.

8.   *See* Irving Louis Horowitz, *Israeli Ecstasies/Jewish Agonies* (New York and London: Oxford University Press, 1974).

9.   Anthony Leeds, "Economic-Social Changes and the Future of the Middle Class," in *Proceedings of the Experts Confererence on Latin America and the Future of Its Jewish Communities* (London: Institute of Jewish Affairs, 1973).

The Political Significance of Ethnonationalism Within Western Europe

Walker Connor

This chapter's concentration upon the political role of ethnonationalism should not be construed as a conviction that ethnicity constitutes the key to Western European politics. Political developments are the product of the interplay of a multitude of personal and impersonal forces, and single-factor analyses are therefore intrinsically deficient. However, the exclusive focus upon ethnonationalism within Western Europe is an attempt to draw attention to an important political force that has been largely ignored in political analyses of the region. Frictions between Fleming and Walloon, between Tyrolean Germans and Italians, between Basques and Castilians, and between the French- and German-speaking elements of Bern canton have been well publicized, as has the revitalization of nationalism by the Scottish and Welsh peoples. But many other intrastate situations involving ethnic differences are less well known.

No study has addressed itself to the impact of ethnicity upon interstate relations within the Western European region. The purpose of
concentrating upon the ethnonational factor is, therefore, not to
claim for it a determinative role but to illustrate some of the ways
it continues to influence the internal and external affairs of the
Western European countries. In some instances its presence is conspicuous, in others more subtle. In some intra- and interstate situations its role is primary, in others incidental.

Another justification for concentrating upon the role of ethnonationalism concerns the general study of nationalism, which has
tended to regard European experiences as the principal source of
precedents and analogies. As the cradle of the modern state system,
Western Europe is often portrayed by scholars as the most promising
respository of answers to problems currently being faced by the
newer states of Africa, the Americas, and Asia. It is widely assumed
that the lengthy experiences of the region's states should prove
instructive for states of later vintage at comparable historical stages
of development. Problems arising from ethnic diversity have been
no exception. The countries of Western Europe have been quite
consistently depicted by prominent authorities on nationalism as
having long ago achieved the assimilation of their respective populations.[1] The manner in which disparate ethnic elements were
transformed, for example, into Britons, into Frenchmen, or into
Spaniards is often applied today to the fate of multiethnic states
located outside of Europe. The European experience is therefore
held to justify optimism that the divisiveness of ethnonationalism in
the new states will prove of short duration and that these states
will ultimately emerge as victors over their ethnic groups in the
competition for loyalty and identity.

There are several reasons why this analogy is invalid. One
reason involves the time element: examples of successful assimilation that occurred in Europe prior to the advent of the age of
nationalism are not pertinent to contemporary affairs. For a generation schooled to accept as an article of faith that all nations have
the right to self-determination, it is psychologically difficult to
remember that popular perception of this "self-evident" association between ethnicity and political legitimacy has only developed
over the last two-hundred years. The self-determination principle

holds that any people, simply because it considers itself to be a separate national group, is uniquely and exclusively qualified to determine its own political status, including, should it so desire, the right to its own state. The concept, therefore, makes ethnicity the ultimate standard of political legitimacy.

As noted, this linkage of ethnicity and political legitimacy is a recent development, necessarily postdating the spread of the doctrine of popular sovereignty. Prior to the nineteenth century, political legitimacy was dependent upon such diverse and often overlapping attributes as divine right, title to land, conquest, inheritance, or marriage. All of these justifications stemmed from the view that the right to rule emanated not from below but from above, that is, the basis for political legitimacy was not to be sought among the governed. The notion of popular sovereignty therefore represented a truly revolutionary philosophical about-face by maintaining that the source of political legitimacy resides somehow in the people as a whole. From this doctrine it was but a short step to the idea that any group who deems itself a separate people also has the right to determine its own political allegiance. The beginning of the gestation period of this doctrine coincides roughly with the Napoleonic era, so analogies based upon the experiences of multiethnic states prior to 1800 are at best suspect.

To the degree that post-1800 European experiences are germane elsewhere, the destabilizing effect that ethnicity has had upon political borders within post-Napoleonic Europe hardly merits optimism concerning prospects for global stability. The Greek national war of independence from the Ottoman Empire in the 1820s, the secession of the Flemish and Walloons from Dutch control in 1830, the abortive Polish uprisings against Russian domination between 1830–32 and again in 1863, the similarly unsuccessful revolts throughout Europe in 1848 (particularly those involving the Italians, Hungarians, and Germans), the militarily achieved consolidation of Italy (1859–70) and of Germany (1864–71), the successful movement for the autonomy of Hungary in 1867 and the achievement of independence by Romania and Serbia in 1878, by Norway in 1905, by Bulgaria in 1908, by Albania in 1912, by Finland in 1917, and by Estonia, Latvia, Lithuania, and Poland in 1918 all revolved around ethnopolitical demands.[2] Although the statesmen representing the victorious powers in World War I endorsed the principle of self-determination of nations, they intended to restrict it to the territories and possessions of the defeated states. In Europe, this restriction meant its application (or, with an eye to such polyethnic creations as Czechoslovakia and Yugoslavia, its misapplication) to Eastern Europe only. But nationalism proved more unruly than the victors had anticipated. Continuing agitation in the centuries-old battle for Irish independence led to the creation of Ireland in 1921. The interwar years also witnessed autonomy movements among the Basques, Catalans, and Galicians of Spain and the Bretons of France; and *anschluss* or pan-German movements found supporters among German-speaking people of Austria, France (Alsace), Italy (South Tyrol), and Switzerland, as well as in countries to the east of Germany. During the war years Iceland achieved full independence (1944).

The impact of ethnonationalism upon Europe has therefore been enormous. In the period from 1815 to the end of World War II Portugal, Spain, and Switzerland were the only European states not to have been either created or to have undergone territorial alterations as the result of ethnic aspirations. Portugal, as one of the world's most ethnically homogeneous states (a true nation-state), is immune to such considerations. Spain and Switzerland were not totally free of ethnic tensions prior to the end of World War II and, more significant, are among those countries of Western Europe that have experienced in the postwar period an upsurge of ethnonationalist sentiment in segments of their populations.

Ethnic tensions within postwar Western Europe point out still another element overlooked by those who regard the area as a model of effective nation-building. Many of the region's older states whose origins antedate the Napoleonic Era still contain significant elements that successfully resisted losing their distinctive group identity in the larger melting pot. While the governments of these states had indeed made substantial gains toward the creation of a group identity among all segments of their populations prior to the age of nationalism, the process was far from complete and little subsequent headway is discernible.

Identifying these residual groups is often not a simple matter. Considering that we are dealing with modern states, characterized in part by a need and a capability for compiling statistics on their respective populations, it is often very difficult to uncover adequate information on their ethnic minorities. Either as a result of laxity or as a matter of policy, official data on ethnic groups within Western Europe are usually fragmentary or nonexistent. The general inadequacy of such information was highlighted in a U.N. global survey that based its data on the censuses conducted by states between 1945 and 1955: not a single Western European state reported statistics on ethnicity and Denmark, France, Iceland, Ireland, Italy, Luxembourg, the Netherlands, Portugal, Spain, Sweden, and the United Kingdom furnished either extremely inadequate or no information on linguistic groups.[3] Difficulties arising from the inadequacy of data are particularly pronounced in the case of France.[4] The United Kingdom was substantially better but far from ideal. For example, statistics indicating the number of people living within Wales are readily available, but it is considerably more difficult to ascertain the proportion of Wales's population that is of Welsh background as contrasted to English or some other ancestry. A similar uncertainty surrounds the number of Basques or Catalans within Spain.

To the problem of governmental recognition of ethnic diversity is added the general ambiguity surrounding the determination of who or what constitutes an ethnonational group. Cultural and psychological assimilation are vitally different concepts. A national group may surrender any or all of its overt cultural characteristics, including language (the majority of Irish, Scottish, or Welsh, for example), without its members losing their intuitive sense of a separate national identity. Conversely, people who share a myth of common blood can afford sharp intragroup distinctions in cultural characteristics, including language (mono-English versus mono-Celtic speakers within Ireland, Scotland, or Wales, for example), while retaining a profound sense of sameness or oneness. Since the ultimate test of the existence of an ethnonation is abstract — a matter of attitude, it is often a matter of conjecture whether or not a group harbors the necessary intuition of a fundamental uniqueness that sets it apart as a national group. If not, the group constitutes a subnational grouping because, in a test of loyalties, the sense of identity as a member of the predominant group within the state will prove stronger than the sense of uniqueness that sets the subgroup apart from the dominant element. In the words of Rupert Emerson, "the nation is today the largest community which, when the chips are down, effectively commands men's loyalty, overriding the claims both of the lesser communities within it and those which cut across or potentially enfold it within a still greater society. . . ."[5]

Until a group furnishes evidence of a separate national consciousness, the question of the existence of its fundamental sense of identity may quite expectedly occasion conflicting assertions.[6] By and large, however, observers have erred in denying any sense of separate nationhood to minorities. This propensity is often the result of mistaking the absence of current ethnic discord as proof that the assimilation process has been completed. Over the decades, the literature has been filled with assertions that Scottish and Welsh identities had been replaced by a sense of being British, that Flemish and Walloon identities had become lost in a sense of being Belgian, that a Swiss identity had vanquished those of the country's French-, German-, Italian-, and Romanch-speaking components and that France and Spain had similarly each achieved a single uninational self-image.[7] Events in the immediate post-World War II era produced little to challenge this portrait of ethnic homogeneity within states. But the 1960s witnessed an upsurge of nationalism among several peoples whose ethnic names were by this time supposed to be merely quaint and politically contentless holdovers from an earlier epoch.

The United Kingdom

The United Kingdom offers a striking case in point. Authorities on the area conventionally emphasized the remarkable homogeneity of the state, specifically noting the absence of ethnic diversity. As late as 1964 Richard Rose, a recognized scholar of the British political system, noted that "today politics in the United Kingdom is greatly simplified by the absence of major cleavages along the lines of ethnic groups, language, or religion. . . . The unimportance of these differences is demonstrated by the failure of Scottish and Welsh nationalist parties to maintain representation in Parliament. . . . The solidarity of the United Kingdom today may be due to fortuitous historical circumstances; it is nonetheless real and important."[8] The rapidity with which circumstances altered is reflected in the title of two subsequent studies by Rose, *The United Kingdom as a Multi-National State* and *Governing Without Consensus* (the latter being an assessment of political loyalties on the part of the Irish and Ulstermen of Northern Ireland). Among the elements that had destroyed the conventional portrait of the United Kingdom were unanticipated improvements in the fortunes of the Scottish and Welsh nationalist parties; some militant activities on the part of non-English, secessionist elements (particularly among the Welsh); the outbreak and rapid acceleration of violence within Northern Ireland;[9] and the publication of polls indicating that a substantial percentage of the people living within Scotland and Wales felt that their present government did not adequately reflect their national (that is, ethnic) interest. Thus, a Gallup poll conducted in 1968 indicated that a surprising number of people in both Scotland and Wales favored actual separation from the United Kingdom while many others favored a major structural revision:[10]

		Scotland(%)	Wales(%)
1.	Support a separate Scottish/Welsh Parliament with control over all affairs. No representation in the British Parliament	11	6
2.	Support a separate Scottish/Welsh Parliament handling all Scottish/ Welsh affairs including financial affairs, but with joint Scottish-English (Welsh-English) defense and foreign policies. No representation in the British Parliament	18	5
3.	Support a separate Scottish/Welsh Parliament handling Scottish/Welsh affairs in much the same way as the Northern Ireland Government operates within overall British constitution. Representation in the British Parliament	10	8
4.	Support a separate Scottish/Welsh Parliament, but Scotland/Wales and		

	England to continue as one government	14	10
5.	Against separate Parliament	35	50
6.	Do not know; no opinion	12	21

The poll therefore indicated that between one-fourth and one-third of all people in Scotland desired political separation from the United Kingdom and a majority favored a substantial increase in political autonomy. The lower figures for Wales (11% and 29% respectively) were challenged by the results of a separate and almost concurrent poll conducted in Wales by the Opinion Research Centre.[11] In the latter, 18% of the interviewees favored complete independence and 59% favored the creation of a Welsh parliament. Moreover, it appears safe to assume that the results would have reflected an even greater level of ethnonationalistic attitudes if an attempt had been made to exclude the large percentage of people of non-Welsh ancestry from the sample. Among speakers of the Welsh tongue, 25% favored complete separation and nearly two-thirds (64%) favored the creation of a Welsh parliament.

Events in Scotland, Wales, and Northern Ireland appear to have exerted a catalytic affect upon the ethnonational awareness of still other non-English groups within the United Kingdom such as the Celtic Cornish and Manx, the Norse-descendant Orcadians, and the French-speaking residents of the Channel Islands. This sudden outbreak of nationalism on the part of Britishers occasioned broadscale astonishment. As late as 1967, for example, the leader of the Conservative party, Edward Heath, showed his disdain for the influence of the Scottish nationalists by referring to them disparagingly as "flower people." But the following year, the British Broadcasting Corporation presented a program "The Disunited Kingdom," which emphasized the growth of self-determination sentiment among the Scottish and Welsh peoples. The seriousness and potential long-range consequences of these attitudinal changes were given formal governmental recognition in the fall of 1968 when the queen announced the formation of a commission on the Constitution to determine the wisdom of introducing structural changes in the official relations among "the several countries, nations and regions of the United Kingdom." Even a reference to countries and nations within the *United* Kingdom would have been unthinkable a few years earlier. Westminster had been forced to recognize that the assumption that the political loyalties of the Scottish, Welsh, and other non-English peoples were practically indissociable from those of Englishmen was no longer viable, if indeed it ever had been.[12]

Spain

Meanwhile, Spain and France were undergoing somewhat similar experiences. Prior to World War II, Spain had been troubled by growing nationalist sentiments among many of its non-Castilianized people; the Basques, Catalans, and Galicians had even voted themselves what proved to be very abbreviated periods of autonomy under the short-lived Spanish republic of the 1930s. Franco's government reinstituted the centuries-old policy of programmed Castilianization, purging the proponents of autonomy and permitting only Spanish to be used in the schools and in the communications media. For more than two decades this policy appeared to be working. However, just as in the United Kingdom, the 1960s witnessed an upsurge of ethnonationalism among all groups, prompting Franco to lift some of the restrictions, including the linguistic ones. Despite these concessions, agitation continued, particularly in Basque country where assassinations, kidnappings, and other terrorist activities drew world attention.[13] Although Madrid was intent at this time on creating a more democratic image in order to decrease its isolation from the regional trend toward Western European economic integration, it nevertheless viewed the situation as sufficiently serious to compel it to declare martial law and to hold a number of widely publicized trials in which Basques (including a disproportionately large number of priests) were found guilty of such charges as "promoting direct and violent action against the unity of the Fatherland by encouraging separatism and the dismemberment of the nation."[14] Such activities on the part of the state, and particularly the trial of sixteen Basques held at Burgos in late 1970, appeared to generate only greater national consciousness and resentment on the part of Basques, Catalans, and, to a lesser degree, Galicians. While nationalistically inspired activities on the part of the other non-Castilianized peoples have not as yet reached the level of the Basque activists, demonstrations of support for the Basque movement in themselves constitute an important

means of signifying their own national aspirations. As a scholar of
Catalan nationalism has noted:

> The ethnic factor may not always be readily evident, in fact
> it may be subsumed or hidden rather than manifest for the
> very good reason that direct expressions of ethnicity carry
> the danger of repression. But having stripped away such
> protective coloration, the message is clear... [and it] is a
> phenomenon of displacement or identification that leads
> Catalans to champion the cause of minority groups other than
> their own.[15]

France

The problems associated with identifying the ethnic factor are
even more troublesome in France, a fact that appears to be in-
consistent with that country's markedly more open society. As
noted earlier, the government has been reluctant to even acknowledge the existence of non-French elements. This reticence is probably more the result of misperception than of calculation. Members of
the dominant ethnic group within a state are seldom able to compre-
hend, much less to sympathize with, antistate sentiments on the part
of minorities.[16] Subject to no inner conflict between their French
ethnicity and their French citizenship, most Frenchmen are unaware that there are groups long resident within France who feel
a disinclination to identify themselves totally as Frenchmen. An
excellent example of this ethnocentric phenomenon has been unwittingly offered by a French citizen who is a specialist on French
minority problems. In an article "The Popular Press and Ethnic
Pluralism: The Situation in France," Collette Guillaumin restricted
ethnic minorities within France to peoples from overseas departments, Jews, and Gypsies. She was seemingly unaware of the Al-
satian, Basque, Breton, Catalan, Corsican, Flemish, and Occitanian
communities within her own country.[17] Similarly, an otherwise
extremely detailed study of the French population, although men-
tioning foreign migrants, contains no references to ethnic minorities.[18]

Evaluating the political significance of ethnicity within France
is, therefore, a difficult task. Policies are seldom acknowledged to

have their roots in ethnic discord. It is apparent, however, that evidence of growing ethnic unrest within the country was an element in de Gaulle's decision to campaign for a radical decentralization of political power during the late 1960s. This is not to contend that ethnicity was the major element. The multifaceted, acephalous rebellion that paralyzed the central government in the spring of 1968 had made it clear that many segments of the society felt the government was too remote and unresponsive to their particular problems and needs. Many of the groups who participated in the rebellion reflected economic interests, and de Gaulle's support for regionalization was viewed primarily as a response to economic problems. Yet ethnicity was not an unimportant consideration. Several of the new regional units were designed to correspond closely with ethnic distributions, and the regional governments, when and if created, were to be charged with social and cultural, as well as economic, funtions.

Growing dissension on the part of the Bretons played a particularly important role in de Gaulle's deliberations. Nationalistic activities have a long history among this Celtic people. The immediate post-World War II period was one of remarkable quiescence, but just as in the case of the United Kingdom and Spain the 1960s witnessed a sudden upsurge in nationalistic activity, including recourse to terrorism. In supporting the consolidation of five departments into a single unit with the emotion-evoking title of Bretagne, the government was all too aware that it was flirting with an ethnonationalism that had only recently caused much civil discord; de Gaulle openly acknowledged this awareness during a highly publicized visit to Brittany made in response to the area's spreading disorders. After coupling the observation that Brittany would always have its "own character" with the hardly veiled warning to separatists that Brittany has nonetheless "always been an integral part of the body and soul of France," de Gaulle turned to the forthcoming referendum on regionalization, remarking that "if the changes within Brittany — within the changes which our times demand from the whole of France — carry a Breton stamp, this is simply the application of what must henceforward be a principle of our development."[19]

Consonant with this plan, other regions were also to reflect ethnic distributions. The Alsatians were to have their own province, bearing the ethnohistoric title of Alsace. Occitania was to be composed of several units, but names such as Languedoc and Provence also trigger historic associations of an ethnic coloration.[20] At the opposite end of France, the Flemish-speaking residents would also have their own province termed Nord. Perhaps most suggestive of de Gaulle's recognition of the growing importance of the ethnic factor was his decision to designate Corsica as a separate unit, in contrast to earlier plans that had considered it a subpart of one of the units on the continent. Thus, it was only the Basques and Catalans whose ethnicity was not recognized under the plan. The fact that de Gaulle's prime minister felt compelled to assure the parliament that the plan "would in no sense threaten national unity" further suggests that others also saw the program as catering to ethnic sentiments.

Some measure of the level of national sentiment among the various groups may be gleaned from the vote on the subsequent referendum on regionalization, whose overall defeat resulted in de Gaulle's retirement. Unfortunately, the issue is clouded because of de Gaulle's insistence that the same referendum contain a generally unpopular proposal to weaken the strength of the French senate. Nonetheless, it is noteworthy that more than half of the relatively few metropolitan departments that did vote in favor of the referendum represented zones principally populated by Alsatians, Basques, Bretons, Flems, or Occitanians.[21] A majority of Corsicans voted affirmatively. The lack of support demonstrated by the Catalans is partially explained by the lack of recognition that would be accorded them under the proposal.

Interest in regionalization has continued to be manifested by the government in the post-de Gaulle era, but how much of this is attributable to a desire to placate ethnic sentiment is unknown. Breton unrest has continued, and Basque nationalism within France has shown signs of revival.

The French Basques have traditionally been much more tractable than their counterparts in Spain. But in 1963 a nationalist organization (Embata) originated in France, demanding as a short-run goal the creation of a single department coterminous with the distribution of Basques within France, and as a long-run goal, the creation of a single independent state for the Basques of both France and Spain. Nationalistically inspired incidents among the Basques of France showed a marked increase in the early 1970s, and the French government responded by arrests, by forcing Basque exiles from Spain to settle outside of the French Basque region, and by increasingly cooperating with Spain to apprehend Basque activists. In turn these activities elicited an acceleration of violent responses from Embata and its sympathizers.

Ethnic unrest has been far less evident in the case of Alsace. Between the wars, various forms of separatist sentiment were rife, and the three political parties who favored autonomy garnered more than forty percent of the vote in 1928.[22] Some possible reasons for the apparently low level of ethnonationalism during the Nazi and postwar eras will be discussed at a later point, but that such sentiment is not totally absent is indicated by the creation in late 1970 of a Mouvement Regionaliste d'Alsace-Lorraine, whose proclaimed minimal goal was autonomy within a federal structure.[23] In addition to the Breton flag, those of Corsica, Occitania,and "other minorities" (not further described) were also reported to have been prominently displayed during the rebellion of 1968.[24]

Switzerland

France's next-door neighbor, Switzerland, has also experienced growing ethnic unrest. Switzerland's ethnic policies have historically been quite different than those of the United Kingdom, Spain, and France. Rather than promoting cultural assimilation, the Swiss system has tolerated the perpetuation of cultural distinctions, as evidenced by the fact that French, German, and Italian are all officially recognized languages.[25] At least until quite recently scholars were almost unanimous in their insistence that Switzerland was proof that ethnonationalism was conquerable. All felt that a single Swiss consciousness had obliterated any cleavages predicated upon an awareness of being French, German, or Italian. In part, this consensus among scholars was due to a misreading of Swiss history, in which the absence of ethnic strife was taken to be evidence of the absence of strong feelings of ethnic differentiation. But in reality the allegiance of Switzerland's population has never been severely tested during the age of nationalism because of the country's strict adherence to a foreign policy of neutrality. While the reasons for its neutrality are multirooted, there is substantial reason to question whether the government could have relied upon a united populace had it elected to take sides in any of the struggles in which Germany, France, or Italy were pitted against one another. During the Franco-Prussian War, World War I, and the early stages of World War II, for example, even the official policy of nonpartiality was threatened by considerable sympathy for France or Germany, particular preference following ethnolinguistic lines. Although the government, for quite obvious reasons, has not publicly laid stress upon this reason for its neutrality, a member of the Federal Council as recently as 1962 noted that neutrality "constitutes a guarantee of internal cohesion in a country which stands at the crossroads of three civilizations, comprises four language areas, and practices two main religions."[26]

A second element that causes scholars to assume that Switzerland had successfully conquered its ethnic problems has been confusion concerning the confederal nature of the state. There has been a tendency to assume that Switzerland resembles a modern, highly centralized state, when in fact the primary responsibility for legislating in the areas that are most apt to trigger ethnic sensibilities (such as language policies, education, and so forth) rests with the individual cantons. Even the seemingly statewide political parties are but loosely organized, cantonally based units. The primacy of the canton in social matters tends to compartmentalize ethnic issues, preventing them from becoming statewide struggles. In turn, the generally clear-cut distribution pattern of ethnic groups within Switzerland (Germans predominate to the east, Frenchmen to the northwest, and Italians to the south) causes very few of the cantons to be potentially susceptible to ethnic conflict. Most of them are remarkably homogeneous (in fourteen of the twenty-two cantons, the German-speaking element accounts for more than ninety-three percent of the population), and the distinct ethnic patterns within many of the remainder have limited interethnic contacts and tensions.[27] However, recent events in a canton that is potentially susceptible to ethnic conflict illustrate that the population of Switzerland enjoys no special immunity from ethnonationalism. In Bern the French minority has militantly demanded to be separated from that German-dominated canton. Separatist movements among the Bernese French date to the late nineteenth century, but broad-scale popular support is a post-World War II development. As in the case of the Basques and Bretons, the 1960s witnessed a rash of terrorist activities in the name of ethnonationalism. Indeed, in its tactics and demands, this movement appears to differ from those of the Basques and Bretons only in that its target has been a subunit of the state (a canton) rather than the state itself. However, it is significant that the movement's goal has only been secession from its own canton and not total independence or union with France.

It could be said, then, that Switzerland has remained viable by compartmentalizing its ethnic problems within a system that politically decentralizes combustible social issues and that it has been aided in this endeavor by a number of unique topographic, locational, and historical phenomena.

But can this problem be avoided much longer? If increased modernization and industrialization link Switzerland's parts and peoples more closely through improved communication and transportation networks and if the greater centralization of the decision-making process that traditionally accompanies modernization occurs also in Switzerland, will the level of ethnic cacophony not also rise? We have noted that Switzerland's avoidance of strife in the past is at least in part attributable (1) to the lack of contacts between groups and (2) to the decentralization of decision-making in matters involving ethnically relevant issues. We have further noted that the major exception has involved the field of foreign policy, but that potential ethnic conflicts remain manageable through the country's traditional policy of neutrality. However, the probability that the state government may increasingly find it difficult to sidestep issues with statewide consequences of an ethnic nature was illustrated by the grassroots effort during the late 1960s to cut back the number of foreign immigrant workers. Immigration policy is the responsibility of the federal government. Aware of rising resentment against foreigners, the government attempted to head off a statewide referendum that might demonstrate a polarization of attitudes corresponding to ethnic categories. In this attempt it failed, and the referendum indicated that the greatest hostility to the immigrants, most of whom were from Italy and the Iberian Peninsula, was located in rural, German-speaking areas where actual contact with immigrants was slight. By contrast, the French- and Italian-speaking areas did not perceive a threat of the same magnitude in this Latin immigration. Ethnic attitudes were thus given a state-wide airing, and the unity of Switzerland was the poorer for it.

Belgium

The cases of the United Kingdom, Spain, France, and Switzerland demonstrate that these governments have failed to eradicate the wellsprings of ethnonationalism among groups whose political subservience to their governments long antedates the advent of the age of nationalism. The Belgian experience is distinguishable from these other cases because it has existed as an independent state only since 1831. However, the fact that Flemish-speaking and French-speaking people (Walloons) achieved their independence in a common struggle against the Dutch, that they subsequently decided to create a single state, and that the state appeared free of ethnically delineated strife had until quite recently convinced most observers that being Belgian was more important to them than being Flemish or Walloon. The Belgian case therefore does not differ in its essentials from our earlier illustrations. Closer observers of the Belgian scene could have detected the growth of Flemish resentment against the politically and culturally dominant Walloons prior to World War I and noticed its escalation (including the appearance of Flemish nationalist parties) during the interwar period. Only since the early 1960s has the ethnic issue become *the* major issue within the state. It would be difficult to exaggerate the animosities that this struggle has subsequently engendered. Politics became quickly polarized: Walloon parties appeared in response to the Flemish parties, and older statewide parties developed discernible ethnic wings. Attempts of the more moderate elements to preserve a unitary political structure failed to appease either extreme element. In 1963, the state was divided into two major ethnic zones; in one the Flemish language and culture would dominate, in another the Walloon language and culture would dominate. A third zone was set aside for the small number of German-speakers. The capital district of Brussels was to be a fourth and officially bilingual district, but subsequent debates over the delineation of the Brussels district, the nature of the powers to be accorded to the new zones, and the question of whether a father had the right to "denationalize" his offspring by opting for his heir's education in the "other" language resulted in riots and a number of governmental crises.

The intractable, uncompromising fervor with which the conflict has been waged is illustrated by the impact that the struggle has had upon the country's oldest and largest university. The University of Louvain is located within the Flemish zone, and in the early 1960s Flemish elements demanded that the campus be purged of all French-speaking faculty and students. The bishops responsible for university policy adamantly rejected such a suggestion as inimical to the best interests of the school and contrary in spirit to all that the university symbolized. But following three more years of campus unrest the bishops felt compelled to relent, acquiescing in the creation of a new campus within the Walloon sector to house the expellees.

In other arenas as well, Belgium, since 1960, has evidenced a rapidly accelerating trend toward ethnic polarization. This state, whose creation was due to the voluntary cooperation between two ethnic groups, finds its survival seriously threatened by the conflicting ethnonationalisms of the same two groups slightly more than a century later.

Italy

Unlike all of the previously mentioned countries, Italy was ostensibly created to fulfill ethnopolitical aspirations. Italy has therefore traditionally been viewed from its inception in 1970 as a true nation-state and as one of the very earliest illustrations of the principle of self-determination in practice. True, the original borders included a small French-speaking area (Val D'Aosta) in the northwest, and the government of Italy violated the self-determination principle following World War I when it annexed from Austria a German-speaking area in the north (South Tyrol) and a Slovene-speaking area in the northeast. But these exceptions aside, Italy has been depicted as essentially coterminous with a people who are sensitively aware of shared Italian kinship. Contrary to this view, there is substantial reason to question the degree to which the concept of Italianness had formed prior to the creation of the Italian state and even the degree to which such a national consciousness has subsequently permeated popular sentiments. During the 1840s, the Austrian statesman Metternich contemptuously dismissed the notion of an Italian nation with the comment that Italy was only a "geographical expression." That his charge was not totally baseless was later acknowledged by a leader of the successful movement to unify Italy when he stated that "having made Italy, we must [now] make Italians." More recent developments strongly suggest that the process of making Italians is far from completed.

The experience of Mussolini's Fascist movement is a case in point. The movement preceded Hitler's by a decade, and Hitler and his cohorts copied many of the techniques and symbols Mussolini employed to evoke nationalist fervor. One constant in Mussolini's internal propaganda was the appeal to Italianness as captured in el Duce's 1935 announcement of the invasion of Ethiopia:

> Blackshirts of the Revolution, men and women of all Italy, Italians scattered throughout the world, across the mountains and across the oceans, listen! A solemn hour is about to strike in the history of the fatherland. Twenty million men are at this moment gathered in the piazzas throughout the whole of Italy. Never in the history of mankind has there been seen a more gigantic demonstration. Twenty million men: a single heart, a single will, a single decision. This demonstration is meant to show and it does show to the world that the identity between Italy and Fascism is perfect, absolute, and unchangeable. .... Not only is an army marching toward its objectives, but 44,000,000 Italians are marching in unison with this army. ... Never more than in this historic epoch has the Italian people revealed the force of its spirit and the power of its character.[28]

Despite such exhortations, however, in its first real test — the landing of Allied forces on Italian soil — the movement's roots proved astonishingly shallow in comparison to the fanatical devotion and monumental sacrifices that Hitler was able to demand in the name of the *Volksdeutsche,* even though he had a decade less in which to prepare the soil.[29] Under the rule that enough of a quantitative difference makes a qualitative difference, Italianness proved to be a completely different species than Germanness.

A postwar opinion survey of Italy under the direction of two

well-known American political scientists also found broad-scale
rejection of all centralized institutions among Italians and further
noted that "the Italians are particularly low in national pride."[30]
Unfortunately, the study did not elucidate the reasons for the
weakness of a statewide identity. One possibly profitable avenue
for investigation would be the relative importance ascribed to being
Italian as contrasted to being, for example, Abruzzese, Calabrian,
Neapolitan, Sicilian, or Venetian. Regional differences may well be
considered by many to be more significant than common Italianness. During World War II, for example, separatist movements were
active in both Sicily and Sardinia.

One obvious barrier to the development of a feeling of solidarity
is a popularly perceived racial division along Nordic and Mediterranean components. This belief may account for the disinterest
and often disdain that northerners (Nordics) commonly display
toward the people and problems of the south. The myth of common
kinship, which forms the psychological backbone of ethnonationalism, can hardly be expected to operate throughout a population
popularly convinced of its own diversity. A desire to obliterate this
strongly divisive issue would help to explain the prominence that the
Fascist regime accorded the "Manifesto of the Racist Scientists"
which it had publicized throughout all of Italy on 14 July 1938.
More an article of faith than a scientific treatise, part of its credo
read: "The root of differences among peoples and nations is to be
found in differences of race. If Italians differ from Frenchmen,
Germans, Turks, Greeks, etc., this is not just because they possess a
different language and different history, but because their racial development is different. . . . A pure 'Italian race' is already in existence. This pronouncement [rests] on the very pure blood tie that
unites present-day Italians. . . This ancient purity of blood is the
Italian nation's greatest title of nobility." [31]

While the racial barrier remains Italy's most salient barrier to
the formation of a sense of Italianness, it is certainly not the sole
problem. Within either segment of this division group designations,
such as Neapolitan or Calabrian in the south or Florentine or
Venetian in the north, suggest not only the geographic area of one's
ancestral home but also stereotyped human characteristics attributed
to the group as a genetically distinct people.[32] If a feeling of

common Italian ancestry could pervade the subconscious convictions of the population, the self-perceived differentiations between Calabrian, Sicilians, and so forth could be accurately described as regionalism and could be expected to dwindle as transportation and communication networks link the country more intimately. However, that many prominent politicians are convinced that Italianness has not yet achieved this stature is illustrated by Italy's postwar experience with plans for political decentralization. As insurance against the resuscitation of Fascism, the constitution of 1948 called for the creation of nineteen regions, described as "autonomous bodies." Five of these were singled out for special status that would carry greater "self-autonomy." The inclusion of Sicily and Sardinia among the special regions reflected concern with the previously mentioned wartime separatist movements; Val D'Aosta's inclusion was also, in part, a response to a secessionist movement active among the French-speaking populace both during and after the war; Trentino-Alto Adige contained the South Tyrol where the treatment accorded to the separatist-minded, German-speaking people had represented a serious irritant in the relations between Austria and Italy for many years (an irritant that was to continue for decades after World War II); finally, Fruili-Venezia Guilia was included because it housed the Slovene minority and because it was involved in the larger dispute with Yugoslavia concerning sovereignty over the Trieste area.[33] Pressured then by the need to counter separatist tendencies, four of the regions were quickly established; problems delayed the creation of Fruili-Venezia Guilia, but these were overcome by 1963. In contrast, strong opposition to the creation of the "regular" regions prevented implementation of the constitutional provisions throughout the length of peninsular, "Italian" Italy until 1972, a quarter of a century after their constitutional authorization. Among the reasons for the opposition was the often-expressed fear that state unity would be strained by creating units with strongly emotional historical associations. Subsequent events have done little to eradicate such fears. When Calabrians in 1971 engaged in prolonged and bloody rioting over the selection of their regional capital, a newspaper located at the extreme other end of the country (Milan's *Corrier della Serra*) described the strife as "an expression of Calabrian separatism." As one student of the

Italian scene has noted, many of those who are closest to the political pulse of Italy are convinced that "even after close to a century of legal unity and two decades of virulent nationalistic propaganda by the Fascists, large sections of the people of the country still lacked a sense of national identification."[34]

The experience of the United Kingdom, Spain, France, Switzerland, Belgium, and Italy therefore make it abundantly evident that the influence of ethnonationalism throughout Western Europe has continued into the post-World War II era. This runs counter to an image of Western Europeans as politically sophisticated cosmopolites who have come to recognize that nationalism is a dangerous anachronism in the modern age.

Notes

1. *See*, for example, Joseph Strayer, "The Historical Experience of Nation-Building in Europe," in *Nation-Building*, ed. Karl Deutsch and William Foltz (New York: Atherton Press, 1966), pp.17–26.

2. In addition to Finland, Estonia, Latvia, and Lithuania, at least nine other groups seceded from Russia during 1917 and 1918 and created separate states. With the exception of the people of Finland, Estonia, Latvia, Lithuania, Bessarabia, and what had been Russian Poland, the Soviet government succeeded in reabsorbing all of the groups within the next few years and, as a result of World War II, reabsorbed all of the remaining groups except the Finns.

3. "Special Topic: Ethnic and Economic Characteristics" in *United Nations Demographic Yearbook, 1956* (New York: Statistical Office of the U.N., 1956). According to information on linguistic diversity offered in Table I of Dankwart Rustow's *A World of Nations* (Washington, D.C.: Brookings Institute, 1967), only Portugal could justify such an omission on the ground that the state contained no linguistic minority.

4. *See* section on France below.

5. Rupert Emerson, *From Empire to Nation* (Boston: Beacon Press, 1960), pp.95–96.

6. Contrast, for example, Guy Heraud's assertion [*Peuples et Langues d'Europe* (Paris: Editions Denoël, 1967), p.203] that the Corsicans are "profondément intégrée à la nation française" and that

"l'attraction italienne y est faible," with the letter to the New York *Times* of 10 December 1967, asserting that justice requires that the Corsicans be politically reunited with their brethren in Italy.

7. For several illustrations of authorities confusing the absence of ethnic strife with the achievement of psychological assimilation in these and other cases *see* Walker Connor, "Self-Determination: The New Phase," *World Politics* 20 (October 1967): 30–53; and "Nation-Building or Nation-Destroying?", *World Politics* 24 (April 1972): 348–50. Some of the more notable authorities include John Stuart Mill (in 1861), Lord Acton (in 1862), Sir Ernest Barker (in 1927), Alfred Cobban (in 1944), and Karl Deutsch (in 1966).

8. Richard Rose, *Politics in England* (Boston: Little, Brown and Co., 1964), pp.10–11.

9. Due to the heavy coverage of the Irish issue by the United States news media, details concerning it have been omitted here. However, it is important to stress that the issue is ethnic and not religious, as it has been popularly depicted. The struggle is between those of Irish lineage contrasted with those of English and Scottish ancestry. (*See* Connor, "Nation-Building or Nation-Destroying?" pp.339–41).

10. *The* [London] *Daily Telegraph*, 21 September 1968, p.21.

11. *Western Mail* (Cardiffe), 25 September 1968, p.6.

12. There had been at least one partial exception to the tendency to dismiss Scottish and Welsh nationalisms as extinct. Though not flatly predicting their revitalization, the study of the Royal Institute of International Affairs, *Nationalism* (New York: Augustus Kelley, 1966), which was first published in 1939 under the chairpersonship of E. H. Carr, did warn of the vestigal influence of the Scottish and Welsh identities (*see* page 139).

13. For an informative study covering all minorities within Spain, *see* Juan Linz, "Early State-Building and Late Peripheral Nationalisms Against the State: The Case of Spain," paper presented at the UNESCO Conference on Nation-Building, Normandie, France, August 1970. For an exhaustive study of Basque national-ism, *see* Milton da Silva, *The Basque Movement* (Ph.D. dissertation, University of Massachusetts, 1972). *See also,* da Silva's "Moderniza-tion and Ethnic Conflict," published in *Comparative Politics* 7, no.2 (January 1975): 227–51. The latter employs the Basque ex-perience to test several current theories on ethnic integration.

14. *Keesing's Contemporary Archives,* p.24405.

15. Oriol Pi-Sunyer, "The Maintenance of Ethnic Identity in Catalonia," in *The Limits of Integration: Ethnicity and Nationalism in Modern Europe,* ed. Oriol Pi-Sunyer (Amherst, Mass.: Department of Anthropology, University of Massachusetts, 1971), pp.132–33.

16. For a fuller discussion of this phenomenon and a number of examples, *see* Walker Connor, "The Politics of Ethnonationalism," *Journal of International Affairs* 27, no. 1 (1973): 15–16. With specific regard to the manifestations within Europe during the late nineteenth century, *see* the insightful treatment of Carlton Hayes, *A Generation of Materialism, 1871–1900* (New York: Harper and Row, 1941), pp.267–72. In the case of the English, for example, Hayes notes that "Englishmen who profusely sympathized with 'oppressed' peoples on the Continent and warmly upheld their right of national self-determination could perceive slight justification for the exercise of any such right in Ireland." Supporting his assertion with several illustrations from the experience of European states (including France), Hayes concludes that "though of varying intensity in different countries, the phenomenon was ubiquitous."

17. The article appears in translated form in *International Social Science Journal* 22 (1971): 576–93. The author's oversights are the more instructive because she is a research officer at the National Center of Scientific Research at Paris and because she otherwise offers some excellent and objective insights into ethnopsychology, particularly on the part of the dominant group.

18. J. Beaujeu-Garnier, *La Population Francaise* (Paris: Armand Colin, 1969).

19. *Keesing's Contemporary Archives,* p.23391.

20. In 1892, some members of the Félibrige Society formally demanded "Provençal autonomy" within a French federation for a region that would incorporate Provence, Languedoc, and Acquitaine. Carlton Hayes (p.279) has noted that Basque, Breton, and Corsican spokesmen immediately announced their support for the Occitanian cause, but nothing much came of the movement.

21. Out of a total of 95 metropolitan departments, only 24 cast a majority of votes in the affirmative. Of this number, 13 were populated predominantly by minorities.

22. Susan Koch, *Integration in Alsace: A Study in Pluriregionalism* (Ph.D. dissertation, Harvard University, 1972).

23. *Le Figaro,* 5 July 1971.

24. David Fortier, "Breton Nationalism and Modern France,"

in *The Limits of Integration: Ethnicity and Nationalism in Modern Europe,* ed. Oriol Pi-Sunyer (Amherst, Mass.: Dept. of Anthropology, University of Massachusetts, 1971), p.99.

25. A fourth language, Rhaeto-Romanche, is spoken by less than one percent of the population.

26. Cited by Jácques Freymond, "European Neutrals and Atlantic Community," in *The Atlantic Community,* ed. Francis Wilcox and H. Field Haviland, Jr. (New York: Frederick Praeger, 1963), p.86.

27. The topography of Switzerland has also played a role, tending to isolate villages and regions from one another. Thus, French- and German-speaking villages, though in the same canton, are not apt to have extensive contacts.

28. Reprinted in Charles Delzell, ed., *Mediterranean Fascism* (New York: Harper and Row, 1970), pp.193–94.

29. In 1931, Carleton Hayes remarked on Fascism's deep roots among Italians, and their shallowness among Germans. Carleton Hayes, *The Historical Evolution of Modern Nationalism* (New York: Macmillan, 1931), p.308.

30. Gabriel Almond and Sidney Verba, *The Civic Culture: Political Attitudes and Democracy in Five Nations* (Boston: Little, Brown and Co., 1965), p.308.

31. Delzell, pp.174–77.

32. *See,* for example, John Adams and Paopo Barile, *The Government of Republican Italy* (Boston: Houghton Mifflin, 1961), pp.11–31; and Joseph La Palombara, "Italy: Fragmentation, Isolation, Alienation," in *Political Culture and Political Development,* ed. Lucien Pye and Sydney Verba (Princeton, N. J.: Princeton University Press, 1965).

33. At least in the last two cases, the borders of the region were drawn so that the cession of greater cultural autonomy conferred upon the minorities was offset by grouping them with larger Italian-speaking areas.

34. Norman Kogan, *The Government of Italy* (New York: Thomas Crowell, 1962), p.162.

Ethnicity in Yugoslavia: Roots and Impact

Nikolaos A. Stavrou

Speaking before the Slovene Academy of Sciences in 1948, Marshal Tito declared the national question of Yugoslavia "settled." However, his optimism proved to be premature in light of later events. In fact, one of the major problems that confronted the post-World War II leadership was the periodic emergence of intense ethnic conflicts. These contradictions, at odds with Lenin's teachings to be sure, are attributed by Yugoslav theoreticians to the presence of two types of "harmful nationalism": *separatism,* which is normally but not exclusively attributed to Croat "bourgeois elements": and *unitarianism,* which assertedly emanates from remnants of "Serbian hegemonism." These two *isms* inevitably complicated the internal development of the country and adversely affected its international image. During the 1970–72 period, ethnic conflicts intensified to the point that they overshadowed all other concerns of the Titoist

leadership. Thus, in sharp contrast to Tito's earlier views and contrary to theoretical predictions of fusions of nations, the army was
alerted to deal with widespread ethnic animosities and "restore"
Socialist unity.[1] The contrast between 1948 and 1972 was all too
apparent when Tito visited Zagreb and was greeted "as if he were
some foreign chief of state."[2]

The recent reenforcement of an identity below the level of
Yugoslavism defies the Socialist interpretation of the nation and
contradicts theories of political integration that are anchored on the
hypothesis that economic progress reduces political conflicts and
makes possible the identification of adverse ethnic groups with a
supraethnic ideology. Apparently, the assumptions of develop-
mentalists are at variance with postwar Yugoslav experiments.
The economic advances achieved in that country did not eliminate
or appreciably lower the barriers erected by narrow ethnic identity.
On the contrary, ethnic animosities reached a high level of open
conflict at a time when Yugoslavia enjoyed relative economic
prosperity and substantially expanded freedom.

The Marxist analogy of scientific socialism also fails to explain
the presence of narrow ethnicity in a supposedly classless society.
Lenin's theory of nationalism, often invoked by Edward Kardjel,
failed the test of its implementation. These two sets of theories —
developmentalist and Marxist — therefore, do not provide a valid
explanation of Yugoslav neoethnicity. A better understanding of
ethnic conflicts in that country must be sought in the historical
context of Balkanization of the area as a whole. The evolution of the
identity of the southern Slavic subgroups and particularly the
fragmentation of their political culture have retarded efforts of well-
meaning leaders to fuse them into a community and to create a
state based on monoethnicity.[3]

Yugoslavia is a relatively new country. Its present borders were
established by the Versailles Treaty and include half a dozen major
ethnic groups (Serbs, Croats, Slovenes, Muslims, Macedonians,
and Montenegrins) and a dozen minor ones, but few people identify
themselves as Yugoslavs.[4]   The members of these groups have
retained a distinct but local ethnic identity and culture. This makes
Yugoslavia a state and a government, yet not one nation. The oft-
repeated joke that Yugoslavia has several nations, six languages,

three religions, and one Yugoslav (Tito) is expressive of its ethnic makeup and underscores the absence of a supraethnic nationalist ideology.

The concept of the nation-state, which during the last fifty years has been viewed as the terminal political association, is both irrelevant and misleading in the Yugoslav context. This concept presupposes the presence of a shared identity. Yugoslavism – an ideology viewed as the common denominator of all ethnic categories – still remains a concept underscoring aspirations, which are taken more seriously by political elites rather than by the people as a whole. Yugoslavia has not reached the status of the terminal community, that is, a state based on the affinity of a people conscious of a corporate will to form one nation. Yet, the concept of Yugoslavism has been present for more than one century.

In Croatia and Montenegro, Yugoslavism was promoted by Bishop Strossmayer, a Croat, who became an early advocate of unity of the Catholic and Orthodox churches as well as unity of all Slavs "from the Adriatic to the Black Sea."[5] It appears that church unity, not ethnic consolidation, was the primary goal of the bishop. A strong supporter of unity of Slavic groups was the Russian empire, which in the course of its dealings with the then major powers superimposed Panslavism over Yugoslavism.[6] Panslavism made no concrete headway in the area, either. By 1880 the Serbian kingdom and the Slavs outside it adopted the slogan, "Balkans for the Balkans."It was aimed at keeping the great powers out of their affairs, and that included the Russian Empire.

Initially the Serbs, the largest of all the South Slavic groups, regarded the inclusion of the Croats, the Slovenes, and the Macedonians within the borders of an expanded state as the fulfillment of their destiny: to liberate all South Slavs and, in the process, help eliminate the two empires.

The Yugoslav state that emerged as a result of World War I started off haphazardly. Mistaken in their assessment of the feelings of other liberated groups, the Serbs sought to create a unitary state made up of "one nation known by several names." The first postwar constitution (the Vidovan Constitution of 1921) formalized the state, which was to be ruled by a constitutional monarchy. The central government was to be the fountainhead of nationalism, which meant in practice that nationalism was to be legislated in Belgrade.[7] Objections to the hegemonistic practices of the Serbs were soon raised by the other ethnic groups. Before the new state could formalize its existence and adopt its new name — Yugoslavia — the non-Serb political elites turned their attention toward their own kinsmen, giving rise to ethnically based political parties. In the interwar period, only the Communist party was explicitly nationwide in structure.

The post-World War I state benefited from the ideology of Yugoslavism, but it did not adopt the name of Yugoslavia until 1929. Fearing reaction among its various ethnic groups, it was officially known as the *Kingdom of Serbs, Croats, and Slovenes.* Despite the change in name and intensified efforts to produce unity, the ethnic groups that were brought together at the end of World War I went in the opposite direction. As a rule, they were suspect of the central government, strongly opposing the Serbian interpretation of nationalism.

Non-Serbian groups viewed the content of post-World War I nationalism as an externally imposed value system that aimed at domination in the name of unity. Despite the lapse of fifty years and a Socialist revolution, "unity" still retains the negativism of the interwar period. For many, it is a Serbian slogan expressing hegemonistic objectives.[8] Those who objected to unitarianism as an evil form of nationalism are themselves criticized for separatism. Generally speaking, these are the two forms of contemporary Yugoslav nationalism and both are traceable to the policies of the pre-1940 Yugoslav state. Behind these two labels lie cultural, linguistic, religious, and ideological contradictions that test the basic assumptions of the Marxist-Leninist theories concerning the nation-state.

Yugoslavia emerged in 1945 as an orthodox Communist system. Tito's regime claimed immediately that it had solved the nationality question in accordance with the general lines of Lenin's teachings. These general lines should be examined briefly prior to an evaluation of the current ethnic relations in Yugoslavia.

Marx and Lenin considered the nation to be a by-product of economic relations and class antagonisms. As such, it would follow the fate of the state; it would disappear as a concept when society reached the Socialist stage of development. In his pamphlet, "The Right of Nations to Self-Determination," (an answer to Woodrow Wilson's Fourteen Points), Lenin argued that national isolation and parochial identification would end with the emergence of a Socialist culture. He stated: "The aim of socialism is not only to abolish the present division of mankind into small states and all national isolation; not only to bring the nations closer to each other, but also to merge them."[9]

On the basis of the Leninist principles, to which Tito still expresses adherence, the ethnic groups of Yugoslavia should have merged into one, united by class interest and consciousness. "Class interest" was to unify, while cultural-separatist tendencies were expected to diminish. A true merger of nations, according to Lenin, will occur when their freedom is maximized. And maximization of freedom is best exemplified by the freedom of a nation to secede from a federation or any other form of union. If a nation can exercise such a right, Lenin argued, it means that it has absolute freedom and secession becomes superfluous. True freedom, according to Marxism-Leninism, exists only in a democratic-Socialist society, consequently there is no valid reason for nations to seek separation from Socialist federations. If nations seek to abandon a Socialist federation, it is for one of two reasons: either they are still exploited or the system is not socialistic. Yugoslavia claims to be a Socialist and nonexploitative state, and this claim makes recent outbursts of nationalism unique.

When the Yugoslav Peoples Republic was established, the only model of a multiethnic Socialist system in existence was the Soviet Union. Borrowing heavily from that model, Tito established a Federal Peoples Republic by administratively dividing the country along linguistic or ethnic lines and by giving recognition to the existence of more nationalities than had previously been the case. Macedonians, Montenegrins, and Bosnians were recognized as non-Serbian ethnic groups and constitutionally guaranteed their cultural identity. The unifying force of these groups was to be the Communist party of Yugoslavia, whose membership was crossethnic.

Between 1945 and 1953 there were no obvious nationalistic conflicts in Yugoslavia. In retrospect, one can say that this period of quiescence was more the result of a harsh regime than the appearance of instant peace among nationalities. Unity, brotherhood, and equality among ethnic groups emerged as a vague policy of the early years. Mindful of the interwar experience, the non-Serbian nationalities viewed the Titoist slogan of unity and brotherhood as another form of Serbian domination. Following the 1948 break with Stalin, a new nationalities policy was fashioned in order to prevent foreign sponsorship of national conflicts in Yugoslavia. This policy had to be compatible with Tito's brand of communism, it had to develop an ethnic policy uniquely suited for the Yugoslav experience and acceptable to all groups with a minimum of coercion.[10]

The task of working out the basic doctrines of national communism fell upon Edward Kardjel, who as a first step rejected the Stalinist doctrine of nation. Stalin, like Lenin, viewed the nation as the by-product of the bourgeoise and consequently as a contradiction in a Socialist setting. Kardjel's views were similar but not identical. He saw a nation as "a community of peoples arising on the basis of the social division of labor in the epoch of capitalism," and it was not necessarily a negative concept.[11] But in the federal republic of Yugoslavia Kardjel saw only the existence of regional ethnic identity, an identity that in his view was primitive. Because this primitive identity had to be superseded by a higher form of nationalism that all ethnic groups could aspire to, this higher form could be nothing else but Yugoslavism.

Kardjel's theses aimed at two objectives: to unite the various nationalities under the federal republic and to create a nation based on the emasculated principles of economic determinism in order to free the Belgrade leadership to attack "proletarian internationalism" emanating from Moscow. Kardjel based the success of his theory on two acts of faith: first, he hoped that Yugoslavism would be accepted by all ethnic groups this time and, second, he expected the concpet to grow along with economic development. Kardjel and others perceived that such a goal could not be achieved by Stalinist methods. Thus, economic and political reforms were initiated as soon as the threat of Soviet attack subsided.

The first substantial reforms of 1951 decentralized economic production and transferred more responsibility to republican authorities.[12] Agriculture was decollectivized and the party cadres were given tacit authority to see the reforms carried out in the six republics and the two autonomous regions. It was hoped then that, along with the new reforms and the expected economic gains, Yugoslavism as a new national consciousness would take hold. But it did not. Despite the relative economic progress as a result of economic decentralization, the problem of nationalities persisted. In direct contradiction to theories that cultural barriers become less rigid as a result of economic integration, Yugoslav neoethnicity intensified proportionately with industrial progress. It was apparent to the Titoist regime by the mid-fifties that a more comprehensive examination of ethnic matters was necessary.

The first postliberation attempt to sort out cultural conflicts was made in December 1954 when the Conference of Cultural Societies convened in the city of Novi Sad with the task of resolving linguistic and other cultural conflicts. The participants to the conference agreed that the Serbian, Croatian, and Montenegrin languages were variations of one and the same language and that a common dictionary was to be produced. In accordance with the resolutions of the Novi Sad gathering, efforts were made to merge cultural societies and to encourage non-Slavic groups to learn Serbo-Croatian. Such efforts were not enthusiastically received by the non-Slavic people (for example, the Albanians, Muslims, and Hungarians). Thus, while the large ethnic groups were aiming at cultural interdependence in accordance with the Novi Sad agreement, the smaller ones were not because they feared cultural absorption. In the Albanian region the situation deteriorated so much that when the opportunity arose a violent outburst occurred.[13]

Despite setbacks and criticism from various quarters, Tito continued his policy of decentralization-liberalization as the best way to fulfill the aspirations of the various ethnic groups. The federal constitution was repeatedly amended, gradually shedding its Stalinist image and borrowing heavily from the federal provisions of the U.S. Constitution. For a time, the party retained its structural unity and strong grip on the country. However, this too had to change.

In the Fourth Plenum of the Central Committee of the L.Y.C., meeting on the island of Brioni in July 1966, the de facto federalization of the party was introduced. Dominated by the Croat leadership, the participants of the Plenum sought and achieved further liberalization and freedom for the local-party organizations, similar to that already achieved at the governmental and economic levels. The symbol of unitarianism and chief of the secret police, Aleksander Rankovic, was removed from all party and government posts ostensibly because of his opposition to the new economic policy of market socialism and self-management and for using "statist, strong-arm tactics" in dealing with the nationalities question. The removal of Rankovic facilitated many new reforms. The party's Central Committee decided that the implementation of any new policies in the economic sphere required local initiative and decentralization of decision-making. The republics were to take over a key role in implementing such policies, while the federal government's role declined substantially. The success of new policies, however, required domestic harmony among ethnic groups. The party and the government were expected to go beyond symbolisms (that is, removal of Rankovic) in addressing themselves to ethnic grievances.

The Fourth Plenum rejected "unitary nationalism" as harmful to the development of the republics, it reaffirmed the decisions of the Eighth Party Congress and measures were taken to redress grievances.[14] The constitution was once again amended (1968) and in the new order the Chamber of Nationalities was elevated in power, while the Federal Chamber was reduced to a debating sociopolitical assembly. Despite the liberalization measures, which were facilitated by the downfall of Rankovic and economic gains, the ethnic groups of Yugoslavia intensified their demands for greater autonomy in all spheres of political and social life.

In Croatia, nationalist demands reached new extremes: separation from the union, self-determination, and membership in the United Nations.[15] In the Socialist context the Croatian developments constitute a paradox but, compared with similar occurrences on a global scale, they follow the recognizable pattern of a reawakening of the ethnics and prove the failure of Communist ideology to create a new consciousness among the many ethnic groups or to sell Yugoslavism as a higher form of national identity. The Yugoslav developments also suggest that economic progress does not reduce national tensions and contributes very little to the detribalization of society. Indicative of this is the fact that the first Croatian grievances centered on noneconomic issues. Cultural associations and groups of Croat intellectuals repeatedly attacked "Great Serbian chauvinism," which, according to them, appeared under the Titoist slogan of unity and brotherhood. No sooner had Rankovic disappeared than the 1954 Novi Sad agreement on Serbo-Croat linguistics came under attack by Zagreb intellectual circles because the Serbs had misconstrued its meaning.

On 17 March 1967, nineteen Croat cultural organizations published a resolution demanding that the Croatian language be recognized as equal to the Serbian, that the two languages be separated, and that, a new Croatian dictionary be produced. To stress the linguistic differences, those who drafted the resolution brought into use long-forgotten but politically significant words. The reaction of Serbian culture circles was also political. Two days after the Croat resolution, forty-five Serb intellectuals drafted a reply (never published) in which they demanded that Serbs living in Croatia be taught the Cyrillic rather than the Latin alphabet.[16]

The Croatian resolution, which touched off similar demands in other areas, was published in a journal *(Telegraph)* whose editor was a member of the Central Committee of the Croatian League of Communists. Thus, it appears that even the Communist party was affected by ethnic feelings. The editor was subsequently removed from all of his posts, but the practice of party involvement in local politics has not been reversed to this date.

The emergence of the party as an articulator of national interests in the narrow sense of the term is, according to Yugoslav observers, the result of conflicting ideological pronouncements. For example, between 1966 and 1971, Communists who criticized ethnic manifestations were denounced as Rankovicites, cominformists, centralists, and chauvinists. As a result critics of diversity were forced into passivity while the republic rights spokesmen emerged as the dominant group.[17] The latter group had the support of the party hierarchy and Tito himself, who also denounced the evils of Serbian unitary nationalism and sought to redress the complaints of other republics and autonomous regions by shifting more power in their direction. Following the Brioni Plenum, decentralization became a dogma and a party goal.

In order to provide the legal foundations of decentralization and self-management in the economy, the government amended the constitution for the seventh time since the establishment of the federation. In addressing itself to ethnic demands, the new constitution provided for expanded local autonomy and proportional representation in federal bodies. Eventually, proportional representation was interpreted as meaning a quota system of participation in all federal agencies and institutions. Thus, a war of statistics ensued with the Croats pointing to their inadequate representation in the civil service, army, and diplomatic corps. Tito responded by concessions and "good example." As a first step, he expanded the presidency to twenty-three members, but later reduced it to nine with himself president for life. But even such measures did not dampen Croatian nationalist feelings. Nationalism there moved in the direction of separatism. Between 1968 and 1971, Croatian leaders, intellectuals, and, especially, students behaved as a nation within a nation. Croatian flags, coats of arms, and ecclesiastical symbols of the Catholic church replaced the federal symbols. Croat nationals recounted their oppression under the centralist system in existence until the Fourth Plenum. A president of a commune in the city of Split gave the following account of the ethnic oppression:

> Before the war, the village of Bravnice, here in the vicinity of Split, received a Croatian flag from the emigrant organization in America. In the period of Centralism the police took away that flag so that no one might hang it. The flag was valuable also because it was woven in gold. The flag is a national emblem and people are very sensitive about that. See, such things surely did not happen in other regions of Yugoslavia and now it is difficult to comprehend this national awakening, which at this moment is absent in other regions of Yugoslavia.[18]

Historical factors make Croatia sensitive to Serbian domination. The republic entered the federation during the Serbian domination in the twenties and never felt comfortable within it. During World War II, it became a Hitler puppet-state and the Serbs, who bore the brunt of Nazi atrocities, did not forget the behavior of Croatian Ushtashis. Thus, whenever the Croats raised the issue of Serbian chauvinism, Serbian elitist groups would retort by widely publicizing a World War II Ushtashi atrocity.[19] In the conduct of such polemics, the party did not remain neutral.

Having become a "6 + 2 federation" (that is, six republican parties and two for the autonomous regions), it eventually paid more attention to local interests than to nationwide goals. Yugoslav scholars saw this role of the party as a negative but unavoidable development because the success of economic self-management made centralization obsolete, even for the party. Branko Horvat, a Yugoslav economist, considers the emergence of nationalism as an indication of an identity crisis for the Yugoslav individual but one that could not have developed to this extent without the support of the political bureaucracy. Horvat states: "The basic question of Yugoslav society, when it is a matter of relations among our nationalities, is precisely which social forces are the bearers of demands for national emancipation and sovereignty in the new social conditions. . . . National interests among all nationalities are today formed by the political bureaucracy, the national intelligentsia as a whole, the so-called middle class."[20] The federalization of the party and its contradictory policies are also to blame, according to Horvat.

In the Croatian case, party leadership placed itself at the forefront of the nationalist awakening. Party leaders were linked with the *Matica Hrvatska* journal and other communications media that progressively promoted only Croat national interests. Initially, the journal published articles with "safe" subjects, such as economic policies that originated in Belgrade and adversely affected Croatia. For some time statistical polemics, which aimed at proving ("numbers never lie") "exploitation" by "outsiders" (the Serbs), were exchanged. The arguments were documented and ran something like this: only nine percent of the civil servants are Croats, as against sixty percent Serbs; the Yugoslav Bank, controlled by Serbs, takes away all but ten percent of the foreign exchange, while Croatia brings in sixty percent of the national total; the Army High Command is eighty percent Serbian and Montenegrin, and so is the diplomatic service.[21] University students adopted these slogans and converted them into demands for greater national independence. Croat party members joined in support of a generalized quota system. Retired general and Central Committee member Janko Bobetko proposed republican control of the national guard and the armed forces; young people and workers demanded an end to the draft for service outside Croatia; factory managers drew up lists of the ethnic composition of their working force in response to demands for reducing the number of Serbs working in Croatian enterprises.[22]

By November 1971, the cries for greater economic and political independence of Croatia reached confrontation levels. At that time, a few months after Tito had visited the state and was greeted as "the chief of some foreign state," the Croat University Student Association called a strike to protest the practice of siphoning foreign exchange earned in Croatia to Belgrade banks. The strike ended by direct federal intervention and the removal of the entire Croatian party leadership, which at the height of events had adopted some of the student slogans. Tito called the whole affair a counterrevolution and treated it accordingly: he sent troops to Croatia to impose law and order, an action the Croats called "Czechoslovak-type invasion."[23] In his postmortem, he identified the "enemy," which in his opinion proved beyond doubt that ethnic interests have brought together strange ideological bedfellows. A "committee of fifty" was managing events, Tito stated, and *Matica Hrvatska* articulated them publicly. Behind the committee was an assorted group of "various members of the lumpen proletariat, counterrevolutionaries, various nationalists, chauvinists, and the devil knows who else."[24]

The Croatian events, as it turned out, had significant domestic and foreign repercussions. The issues raised by separatism were echoed in various other Yugoslav republics. Slovenia, a rich republic in the north, protested the use of its funds for the development of backward southern regions and the use of the Serbian language in military training. In the Albanian autonomous region of Kosovo-Metohia, students staged a violent strike in the summer of 1971 demanding a lower quota for the non-Albanian students admitted to Prishtina University. At the same time, the Albanians demanded republic status, a piece of Macedonian territory, and better relations with Albania proper. Macedonia, on its part, demanded more investment funds and better relations with the Macedonians in Bulgaria.[25] The predominantly Muslim republic of Bosnia-Hercegovina sought greater autonomy and closer religious ties with the Arab Muslims in the Middle East. And practically all political units blamed the federal authorities either for the lack of economic progress or for the misuse of their wealth outside their borders.

However, the impact of Yugoslav neoethnicity was more acutely felt in external affairs. Tito had based the foreign relations of his country on a policy that came to be known as *nonalignment and active coexistence*. An implicit expectation of this policy was that ethnic groups would serve as links with their kin across the borders and thus help to improve relations with bordering states. The intensification of ethnic demands, however, caused him to have second thoughts. Tito found "meddling" by foreign powers in domestic-ethnic affairs. In support of these accusations, he pointed to the "invasion" of Croatia in the summer of 1972 by a band of World War II Ushtashis, who boldly announced the "commencement of guerrilla warfare" to liberate the republic and to the noises created in Tirana and Sofia in support of ethnic factions in Yugoslavia.[26] Following the "miniinvasion," Tito announced a new crackdown on the two forms of nationalism: Serbian unitarianism and Croatian separatism. Trials of Zagreb students commenced, as did attacks by Serbian "chauvinistic" circles.[27]

To a large extent, the handling of conflicts among nationalities in postwar Yugoslavia is determined by foreign-policy considerations. It is a basic assumption among Yugoslav leaders that domestic conflicts invite "someone else to defend socialism" — an obvious reference to the Brezhnev doctrine.[28] In order for them to retain order and independence, they claim it is necessary to control all forms of "harmful nationalism," but specifically separatism and unitarianism.[29] Either type could develop and intensify with external support originating in the East as well as in the West.[30] To minimize the impact of foreign meddling, Tito and the party leadership are in the process of reexamining the policy of active coexistence. Such an examination in the past resulted in a temporary improvement of relations with the Soviet Union and a cooling of relations with the West.[31] Domestically, it resulted in regression. It is perhaps this experience that suggests further changes in the domestic and foreign relations of Yugoslavia. Tito and his colleagues seek to recreate an avant-garde party loyal to the federation rather than to the republics. The very necessity of such efforts indicates a need on his part to formulate a nationalities policy that could result in harmonious relations among the nineteen ethnic groups.

Several conclusions can be drawn from this analysis. First, the identification of the individual with his ethnic group has not been eroded by almost thirty years of socialist development. Despite early efforts to make the class a concept of individual identification, it appears that the various ethnic groups insist on retaining their narrow culture rather than accepting a new value system. The merging of nations, as predicted by Lenin and initially supported by Kardjel, has failed to materialize.

Second, there is no Yugoslav model of ethnic relations that could be used in resolving similar conflicts elsewhere. Like other matters, the Communist party of Yugoslavia fashioned policies simply to meet crises, not to develop models. Tito started off with the dubious slogan of unity and brotherhood, but this policy was perceived by non-Serbian ethnic groups as a continuation of Serbian domination. And the efforts of ideologues to portray local national-ism as primitive and Yugoslavism as a higher form of national iden-tity were viewed with skepticism. Yugoslavism, the official policy until 1964, can hardly be called a success. Increasingly the concept was viewed as harmful and incompatible with a decentralized econ-omy, market socialism, and cultural independence of ethnic groups. So far, no comprehensive nationalities policy has emerged to replace the deemphasized Yugoslavism. Only persistent criticism of the two negative forms of national behavior — separatism and unitarianism — remains, and criticism can hardly be a viable substitute for policy.

Yugoslavia is witnessing the same problems that multiethnic nation-states are experiencing elsewhere. A unified party and de-pendable instruments of coercion remain the two pillars of their nationalities policy. But their very presence confirms the vitality of the ethnics in modern Yugoslavia and the inadequacy of Yugoslav-ism as a concept for supraethnic identification.

Notes

1. Jure Bilic, "Basic Characteristics of Yugoslavia's New Constitution," *Review of International Affairs,* no. 572 (5 February 1974), p.4.

2. Anatol Shub, "After Tito...," The New York *Times*

Magazine (16 January 1972), p.44.

3. For the recent goals of the leadership *see* Secretariat for Information, *Speeches by Tito, Kardjel, and Dolance: Ideological Offensive of the League of Communists of Yugoslavia* (Belgrade: Secretariat for Information, 1973), pp.12–15.

4. Nineteen groups are listed in official Yugoslav publications. *See Yugoslav Statistical Yearbook* (Belgrade: Statistical Service, 1972).

5. *See* Bogdan Raditsa, "The Disunity of the South Slavs," *Orbis* (Winter 1967), p.1,088.

6. *See* Ivo J. Lederer, ed., *Russian Foreign Policy: Essays in Historical Perspective* (New Haven, Conn.: Yale University Press, 1962), pp.417–52.

7. Ivo J. Lederer, "Nationalism and the Yugoslavs," in *Nationalism in Eastern Europe,* ed. Peter F. Sugar and Ivo J. Lederer (Seattle, Wash.: University of Washington Press, 1971), p.398.

8. George J. Prpic, "Fifty Years of Yugoslavia," *America* 120 (26 April 1969): 499–502.

9. V. I. Lenin, *The Right of Nations to Self-Determination* (New York: International Publishers, 1951), p.76.

10. *See* Charles P. McVicker, *Titoism: Pattern for International Communism* (New York: St. Martin's Press, 1957).

11. *See* Paul Shoup, *Communism and the Yugoslav National Question* (New York: Columbia University Press, 1968), p.203.

12. *See* Benjamin Ward, "Political Power and Economic Changes in Yugoslavia," *The American Economic Review* 58 (1968): 568–79.

13. Jonathan Randal, "Yugoslav Worried by Albanian Minority," New York *Times* (6 December 1968).

14. *See* R. V. Burks, *The National Problem and the Future of Yugoslavia* (Rand Corporation Study no. 476, October 1971), p.20.

15. Veljko Rus, "Current Relations Among the Yugoslav Nationalities: Questions for Discussion," *International Journal of Politics* (Belgrade) 2 (Spring 1972): 6.

16. Alvin Rubinstein, "Reforms, Nonalignment, and Pluralism," *Problems of Communism* 17 (April–March 1968): 39.

17. Rus, pp.6, 10.

18. Quoted by Branko Horvat in "Nationalism and Nationality," *International Journal of Politics* (Belgrade) 2 (Spring 1972): 25.

19. The massacres of Jasenovac, where as many as 800,000 people (mainly Serbs) died, is a favorite reminder of Croation cities.

20. Horvat, p.63.

21. *See* F. Singleton, "The Roots of Discord in Yugoslavia," *World Today* 25 (April 1972): 172. *Also*, Zdenko Antic, "National Structure of the Top Yugoslav Administrative Bodies," *Radio Free Europe Research Report*, no. 1485 (19 July 1972).

22. Paul Lendvai, "National Tensions in Yugoslavia," *Conflict Studies*, no. 25 (August 1972): 9.

23. Slobocan Stankovic, "Yugoslav Paper Protests Czechoslovak Identification of Zagreb and Prague Trials," *Radio Free Europe Research Report*, no. 1517 (21 August 1972).

24. *Borba* (Battle, 1 December 1971) quoted in Singleton, p.178.

25. *See* Dennison I. Rusinow, "The Macedonian Question Never Dies: The San Stefano Trauma Again – or When Is a Macedonian Bulgarian?", *The American Universities Field Staff* 15, no.3 (March 1968). For a more comprehensive analysis of the issue, *see* Evangelos Kofos, *Nationalism and Communism in Macedonia* (Thessaloniki: Institute for Balkan Studies, 1964).

26. The writer was in Yugoslavia on a research trip when the last of the "invaders" was killed in an ambush. Most of those involved were traced to Western countries.

27. Four Serb members of the Central Committee and Executive Buro were removed, including Koca Popovic, who was considered the number two man.

28. *See* Lendvai, p.16.

29. *Politika* (3 December 1971). Also all Yugoslav radio stations (10 September 1972), 1130 hours.

30. *See* speech by General Franjo Herljevic in *Vecernje Novosti* (Belgrade), 2 September 1972. In it the general blamed both sides for meddling in domestic affairs in general and the Croat events in particular.

31. A long-range economic program was negotiated with the Soviet Union in 1972 involving $1.3 million. *Suddeutsche Zeitung* (in translation), (Munich, 5 September 1972). Concerning relations with the West, *see* Dan Morgan, "Tito Seen Trying to Halt Westward Tilt," The Washington *Post* (8 February 1972).

Ethnic Autonomy
in the Soviet Union

Teresa Rakowska-Harmstone

As one of the superpowers and a leading actor in the international arena, the Soviet Union has for years projected an image of total national identity to foreign partners. Internally the same image also prevails. At the twenty-fourth Congress of the Communist Party of the Soviet Union (C.P.S.U.) General Secretary Brezhnev stated, "In the years of Socialist construction, a new historical community of people – the Soviet people – arose in our country."[1]

Even though the very name, the Union of Soviet Socialist Republics, indicates a de jure federal structure, customary foreign references to the country's activities are couched in terms of "the Russians," with little thought and understanding of the fact that Russians constitute only half of the Soviet population and that the other half consists of a multitude of other ethnic groups, too important and too numerous to be dismissed as merely minorities.

When in 1944 the Soviet Union attempted to enlarge its representation in the United Nations (then in the planning stage) by requesting separate seats for all of its constituent republics, this was a surprise to the international community. Their national sovereignty questionable, only two of the republics, Ukraine and Belorussia, were admitted to the U.N., a result of a compromise.[2] They and the U.S.S.R. have since spoken in one voice in the international arena, and thus have done little to undermine the Soviet Union's image as a homogenous state.

The image notwithstanding, the Party has been engaged from the outset in a vigorous effort at nation building, attempting to forge a Soviet state within the largely unchanged boundaries of the old Russian Empire. Early discussions and disagreements among Bolshevik leaders — as they searched for a formula that would reconcile the Party's proclaimed principle of the right to national self-determination with the need to preserve a national power base required for survival — were resolved by the adoption of the so-called Leninist nationality policy. This provided that the new society would be "national in form and Socialist in content." Politically, it has been reflected in federal constitutional forms, the leadership of which is provided by the Party. Culturally, it promotes formal aspects of national minority cultures' media, with the message tailored to the requirements of the current Party line. In practice the policy imposes basic limitations on the exercise of either political or cultural autonomy.

Although the concept of the Soviet nation was formulated within the ideological class matrix of Marxism-Leninism, it became almost totally infused with ethnic Russian political and cultural heritage. The nation-building process concentrated on a three-pronged effort: to build an industrial base, to transform the society to conform to Marx's classless vision, and to create a "New Soviet Man" imbued with Socialist ethics and norms. The first part of the effort proved to be by far the easiest. In the half century since the Revolution, the Soviet Union made great strides in economic development. The society was transformed, but class differentiation remains, and the Party's intensive political socialization did not fully succeed in creating a "New Man" and a common Soviet national consciousness. The great Russians equate their national heritage with

Soviet patriotism, but other ethnic groups not only stubbornly re-fuse to abandon their separate national identity but also promote it through various means at their disposal. Ethnic antagonism be-tween the dominant Russians and all other groups is gaining in in-tensity and is assuming an increasingly divisive character.

Salient Variables

Problems of ethnicity, as they interact within the Soviet politi-cal system, require examination of the nature and characteristics of the key variables: the demographic and political base, character-istics and role of the Great Russians, other ethnic groups, and demographic and economic trends and requirements.

Demographic and Political Base.

The last Soviet population census of 15 January 1970, listed 90 separate nations and nationalities (plus an "other" category of over 100,000) in the total population of 242 million. Of these, 129 million (53 percent of the total) were Russians, and the three Slavic groups – Russians, Ukrainians (the second largest with almost 41 million), and Belorussians (the fourth largest with nine million) – together accounted for three-fourths of the total Soviet population. The Uzbeks (with 9.2 million) replaced Belorussians as the third largest population group since 1959, and they were followed by the Tatars (5.9 million), the Kazakhs (5.3 million), the Azerbaijani (4.4 million), the Armenians (3.6 million), and the Georgians (3.2 million) as the fifth through ninth largest groups, respectively. Four other national groups numbered between two and three million people – Moldavians, Lithuanians, Jews, and Tadzhiks – and ten between one and two million – German, Chuvash, Turkmen, Kirgiz, Latvians, the peoples of Daghestan, Mordvinians, Bashkirs, Poles, and Estonians.[3]

Under the Soviet federal structure, numbers alone do not guarantee an ethnic group a union republic or even an autonomous republic status, for other conditions have to be met, such as com-pactness of settlement, geographic location (border location is necessary for a union republic), economic unity, and a common psychological makeup. While not listed among formal requirements, political considerations are also of major importance. Thus the Volga Tatars have an autonomous republic, but Crimean Tatars, deported during the war, are dispersed throughout Central Asia. Most Jews refused to settle in an autonomous province assigned to them in Eastern Siberia and are scattered throughout the Soviet Union,[4] and the Germans (deported from their Volga region) and the Poles (war deportees and nonrepatriated inhabitants of western Ukraine and Belorussia) do not have an autonomous unit at all. Large ethnic groups have either a union or an autonomous republic, smaller groups have either an autonomous province or a national region. In the early seventies there were in the Soviet Union fifteen union republics, twenty autonomous republics, eight autonomous provinces, and ten national regions.[5]

The C.P.S.U. enjoys the monopoly of power and directs all activities in the Soviet political system. Unlike the state structure, the organization of the Party does not recognize the federal principle. The unitary principle of a single, centralized Communist party with a single, directive Central Committee was adopted by the Eighth Party Congress in 1919 and remains in force.[6] Even federal constitutional provisions leave little autonomy to the union republics, because under the 1936 Constitution, the all-embracing enumerated powers are reserved to the All-Union government. The centralized character of the C.P.S.U. and the government is, in addition, safeguarded by the application of democratic centralism as the ruling operational principle, the main feature of which is that decisions of higher bodies are unconditionally binding on the lower bodies, and that once made, the decisions cannot be questioned.[7]

Russian Role

The vast numerical preponderance of Great Russians tells only a part of the story. Traditionally the ruling group in the Russian Empire, their hegemony survived intact in the succeeding Soviet state. The continuity of the Russians' leading role was based on several factors. They constituted an overwhelming majority of the revolutionary (later bureaucratic) elite, represented the most dynamic and advanced elements in the country, and controlled its key economic base. The Russians interpreted Marxism through their own national prism and, in the process, the revolutionary goals and the goals of the new Communist society became one with national Russian goals and needs. It was in the period of postrevolutionary consolidation that Russian character was indelibly stamped on the new regime.

The identification of Great Russian national interests with the interests of the Soviet state and society continued and became stronger in the period of Stalin's rise to leadership (ethnically Georgian, Stalin acquired all the characteristics of a Great Russian nationalist),[8] in the struggles for collectivization and industrialization, and particularly in the Great Patriotic War (World War II). The influx of non-Russian members modified the excessive predominance of Great Russians in the C.P.S.U., but their weight in the leading bodies of the Party and the government and especially in public administration remained disproportionately small.[9]

Ethnic Minorities

By the early twentieth century, the non-Russian groups represented a conglomerate of peoples of widely varying levels of historical, cultural, and economic development. Peoples of the western borderlands, as well as Georgians and Armenians in the Caucasus, were Christians, had a unique and in some cases ancient political and cultural heritage (including independent statehood), and either equaled or excelled Great Russians in the degree of social and economic development. All had a strong sense of separate national identity and possessed well-developed nationalist movements. The peoples of the southeastern borderlands, mostly Turkic, shared the Muslim religion and a strong sense of Muslim unity. Generally economically backward and bound by traditional social institutions, as in the case of the sedentary Uzbeks of Turkestan and the Khanates, some — like Volga Tatars, Crimean Tatars, and Azerbaijani Turks — had a middle class and developed regional nationalist movements. Nomads of Central Asia and the Siberian and Far Eastern peoples had, in general, little national consciousness and primitive social and economic organization. The ethnic settlement area of many of these groups extended beyond Imperial boundaries, with contacts maintained across them.

Brought into the expanding Empire by conquest or incorporation, all had historical grievances against the Russians and a recent memory of harsh Russification policies. Inevitably, with the breakup of the Empire, the major groups opted for separation. Regular Red Army campaigns were needed to bring the Ukraine, the Caucasus, and the Muslim borderlands back into the fold. Poland, Finland, and the Baltic provinces succeeded in gaining independence;

the Baltic states invaded and reincorporated again in 1941. Since the consolidation, national movements among the non-Russian peoples have been suppressed and traditional, middle-class, and even Communist nationalist elites destroyed.

In the subsequent periods, however, as a new economic base and a new labor market appeared, as social relationships were transformed and a mass-education system established, new minority elites came into being. Soviet educated, and encouraged to enter economic and professional jobs and administrative and political hierarchies of their national areas, their meaningful participation has nevertheless met with continuous frustrations under the limits imposed by the system with its characteristic Russian hegemony. At the same time, ethnic-cultural revivals fostered under the cultural aspects of the nationality policy have provided a focus and a means of identification for the new ethnic elites' sense of national consciousness, despite the Party's efforts to expurgate ethnic cultures of genuine national content. The old ethnic antagonism has been reinforced by another powerful conflict of interests — that which is generated between the central and local authorities under excessive centralization of the Soviet political system. Governmental structure, based on territorial units identical with the ethnic divisions, makes the ethnic and the administrative antagonisms coterminal. Political frustration adds to the attraction of the old heritage, seen both as means of cultural expression and as the source of legitimacy and the base for political assertion in relation to All-Union authorities. Thus, and increasingly, it is the new ethnic elites and not the surviving traditional elements as alleged by the authorities, who are the bearers of new ethnic nationalisms among the non-Russian peoples of the Soviet Union.[10]

Demographic and Economic Trends

Demographic and economic variables bear significantly on the problems of ethnicity. It was the Great Russian area that provided the jump-off base for Soviet economic development and, despite substantial economic growth of Siberia and the southeastern regions, the European part of the country still provides the base for what economic geographers call the *effective national Territory*. As the Soviet Union entered the seventies, its economic core area was still contained within the broadly settled triangle based on the line extending from the southwestern Ukraine to the Volga, with its apex tapering off north of Moscow.

The Ukraine and the Central Asian and Transcaucasian regions have begun to assume greater economic importance because of past development policies, and, currently, the new trends in demographic structure. Population statistics indicate a significant decline in birthrate for the U.S.S.R. as a whole; the decline, however, affecting only the population groups of European Russia. Consequently, their weight in the total population has begun to decrease, while that of the Asian and Caucasian groups increases. In the last two population censuses the relative weight of the Great Russian group fell from 54 to 53 percent between 1959 and 1970, and that of the Ukrainian group from 18 to 17 percent.[11] In comparison, and with a much smaller population base, the combined weight of the five major population groups of Central Asia (Uzbek, Kazakh, Kirgiz, Turkmen, and Tadzhik) and the three major groups of the Caucasus (Georgian, Armenian, and Azerbaijani) has increased from 10 percent of the total population in 1959 to 12.8 percent in 1970.[12]

This kind of change in population patterns invites either a dispersal of capital outlays to labor surplus areas or else a reversal in migration trends, bringing non-Russian workers into the economic core area. Ethnic intermixture of Soviet peoples is one of the avowed goals of the Party, but Asian labor is mostly unskilled and traditionally unwilling to leave home areas. Further buildup of the economic base of the border republics, on the other hand, might serve to strengthen the cause of local nationalisms. One political consequence of demographic change can be seen already in an increase in the weight of titular nationalities and a corresponding decrease in the weight of the Russian group in all of the Central Asian and Caucasian republics in the 1959–70 decade, a reversal in the trend of the preceding thirty years. Western minorities, on the other hand, share in the decline of the natural rate of growth of the Slavic groups. For Latvians and Estonians, in particular, this rate is catastrophically low from the point of view of their national survival, as Russian migration into the two republics continues at a fast rate.

The future course of Soviet economic development has to take into account demographic and ethnic as well as economic factors. Economic rationality increasingly emphasizes obsolescence of an administrative structure based on ethnic rather than on regional economic considerations,[13] and current distribution of resources indicates that the European core is still an optimal area for economic development. Both these considerations seem to indicate a need for a change in the constitutional structure. Yet, a step in this direction taken in 1957 (Krushchev's creation of regional economic councils) was resisted by the republics that found themselves bypassed, and Party leadership backed down, at least in part, in 1964. Also, there is evidence that vested interests of the republics are increasingly difficult to ignore in central planning, and that there is vigorous infighting between them for a largest possible share of resource allocation and distribution.[14]

Party Policy

The relative relaxation of the early Khrushchev period and the uneasy factional balance inherent in the system of collective leadership have provided an opening for the forces of ethnicity that, contrary to expectations, grew rather than diminished with the application of the nationality policy and in conditions of the building of socialism. By the late sixties and early seventies the Party leadership had recognized the national problem to be "one of the critical sectors in the struggle between socialism and capitalism, [in the struggle] of Marxism-Leninism with bourgeois and revisionist ideology."[15] Writing in the *Kommunist,* Mikhail Suslov, a Central Committee secretary and long an ideological spokesman for the Politbureau, singled out ethnic antagonism as one of the three major antagonisms that stand in the way of Communist growth in the Soviet Union.[16] Carefully restating the key ideological premise that the disappearance of class antagonisms removed the basis for ethnic antagonisms, he nevertheless pointed out that a major effort was needed to eradicate national survivals that were not about to disappear by themselves. In response to the growth of ethnic pressures, the Party leadership decided not only to intensify the application of the old long-range assimilationist policies in the political, economic, demographic, and cultural spheres, but also to augment them with a political education campaign of major depth and intensity directed primarily at the Party and state cadres, and professional and creative intelligentsia.

The new hard-line approach is mirrored in practice. Old

personnel policies continue. A recent demotion of two Politbureau members from their posts as Party secretaries of two major republics appears to be connected with their inability to deal with resurgent nationalism in their republics.[17] Their removal has been followed by changes in positions in the Central Committees and in city/province first secretaryships in the Ukraine and Georgia.[18] The discussion of the need for constitutional change has been revived. It is said again that in the ongoing process of internationalization, ethnic-based territorial entities lose their validity; the area of joint All-Union — republican — jurisdiction is mentioned most frequently as ripe for reexamination.[19] This time also, economic reasons for regional-based rather than republic-based development are brought to the fore. Gradual change is favored — such as a merger of smaller republics into broader entities, reminiscent of Khruschev's consolidated regional economic councils. Economic considerations here support political needs, since regional mergers would remove the institutional territorial base as a focus for national identity for at least some ethnic groups.

Foreign-policy implications are less clear-cut. The existence of national republics, and particularly the Asian republics, have proved to be an asset in Soviet foreign policy in dealing with the Afro-Asian world and the Arab Middle East. Also, in the case of border-straddling ethnic groups, Soviet republics provide a convenient focus for the extension of influence outside.[20] Economic development, social change, and modernization that took place in the Soviet Asian areas have provided attractive examples of a Socialist solution to the problems that preoccupy Third World countries. On the other hand, the 1944 constitutional amendments give union republics a clear legal base (in the Soviet as well as in international law) for claiming sovereignty and the right to separate, which, given favorable circumstances, may prove dangerous to Soviet unity. China figures prominently in foreign-policy considerations. The Chinese have repeatedly criticized Soviet assimilationist policies and pose as champions of the rights of Soviet Asians, in addition to claiming portions of Soviet territory.

In the light of the force of nationalism in the world at large, it is important for Party leaders to weigh the advantages of projecting an image of a harmonious multinational state in their pur-

suit of world influence, against the internal danger of potential
Balkanization. Because of recent policy trends, domestic considerations may well outweigh foreign-policy benefits.[21]

Pressure Points

The growth in the sense of ethnic identity and the articulation
of ethnic demands by Soviet minorities depend on the whole range
of factors — not all of which apply equally — in each case. The
highest point of nationalist agitation (and repression) in the early
seventies has been reached in three areas: the Ukraine (particularly
western Ukraine), Georgia, and the Baltic republics, although other
Caucasian republics[22] and Central Asia are also affected. In general,
ethnic dissatisfaction and anti-Russian antagonism coalesce around
three major grievance areas: a desire for broader political autonomy;
recognition of republican needs in resource allocation; and the
demand for complete cultural autonomy.

Pressures for broader political autonomy are reflected in particular in an effort by local elites to obtain control of the power
structure and decision-making process in their republics, and to
achieve fair representation for themselves and their local needs
at the All-Union level. However, political autonomy is incompatible with the two key principles of the Soviet political system: the
leading Party role and democratic centralism.

Because of the ethnic base of Soviet administrative structure,
pressures for local autonomy, common to all centralized systems,
have become identified with the ethnic issue. With all the agitation,
however, these have not reached separatist overtones, with a possible exception of the Ukraine. The problem, nevertheless, affects
all the ethnic elites even in the republics that have traditionally
enjoyed a relatively high degree of local elite participation, such
as the Ukraine, Belorussia, and the Caucasian republics, and in the
most highly internationalized republics, such as Kazakhstan and
Kirgizia, where the titular nationality is a minority of their population.

Pressures for the largest possible share of the All-Union pie,
directed primarily toward building a firm power base for one's own
republic, have surfaced only recently as benefits of economic
development and population change began to be felt in an environment of relative post-1956 relaxation. The reverse side of grasping

for resources is the reluctance to service other parts of the country before satisfying the republic's own needs. The extent of the problems these kinds of practices cause for the Soviet economy indicates not only that they are widespread, but also that there must be a broad complicity on the part of the republics' Party and state leaders to make them possible. Each republic's behavior is shaped by its individual needs. Anxious to develop further, Central Asian republics appear to be pushing hard; Latvia and Estonia, on the other hand, which are highly developed and where new growth inevitably brings more Russians, are satisfied with less.

Cultural grievances and the desire to develop national cultures on traditional lines free from the infusion of Russian elements and of the Party's ideological censorship, constitute the most abrasive and also the most explosive aspect of national relations. The most important grievance areas include freedom of religion, distortion of national histories, use of national languages, and freedom of artistic and literary expression.

For most ethnic minorities, religion forms an integral part of their national identity, and freedom of religious worship and education assumes political as much as cultural importance. The Party recognizes the significance of religion in the growth of ethnic nationalism, as seen, for example, in a 1972 *Pravda* editorial that stated: "In today's conditions, it is very important to reveal the connection between religion and nationalist survivals. It is known that in a number of cases churches and sects lay claim to the role of custodians of national values."[23]

Roman Catholic religion has been an integral factor of the growth of Lithuanian nationalism, as has been the Uniate Church in western Ukraine, and the ancient orthodoxy of Georgia and Armenia. For peoples of Central Asia, for the Tatars, the Azerbaijani Turks, and others, Islam provides the unifying bond against the Russians and an integral part of their cultural distinctiveness and separate way of life. The Protestant religion of Latvia and Estonia forms a part of their Western heritage that makes them distinct from the Russians.

Soviet historiography requires that national histories of each ethnic group be evaluated from the point of view of Leninist class criteria, that is, that distinction be made between the progressive and the reactionary stream in their national heritage. In practice this has meant distortion of historical truth and condemnation of any past event that championed national self-assertion vis-à-vis Russian encroachments, both before and after 1917. The battle of historiography has been going on since the thirties. Here also, the post-1956 relaxation has generated an unprecedented number of incorrect interpretations. Currently (late 1972) two Georgian historians, two Kirgiz historians, an Armenian writer, and a journalist were all under fire for nationalist deviations in recently published works.[24] Prior to 1956, the sins in national historiographies consisted by and large of minor misinterpretations in otherwise correctly class-conscious monographs. By the late sixties, however, the number of books actually published in local languages (publication implies prior approval by local cultural, academic, and Party authorities, and availability of printing facilities, and so forth) that clearly espoused a nationalist rather than a class point of view reached serious proportions.

The key to the language problem is the resistance of ethnic minorities to the officially sponsored replacement of their language by Russian, as the language of politics, public administration, and culture, and as the language of higher and technical education. Though a common language is necessary in a multilingual community, its widespread use in administration and culture is a function of the unwillingness of the Russian elite to learn minority languages. On the other hand, a non-Russian's advance up professional or administrative ladders is predicated on his facility in Russian. The 1970 census indicates that only three percent of the Great Russian group knew any minority language compared to 17.3 percent of members of minority groups who were fluent in Russian. While the numbers of members of more advanced minorities who speak Russian fluently are well in excess of the All-Union average, members of major Asian groups fall below average in this category, notably the Uzbeks, Azerbaijani, Turkmen, and Tadzhiks.[25] Preservation and development of national languages as a means of cultural national identity has been especially important in the advanced republics where the Russian group is particularly large.

Great Russians versus Ethnic Groups

Ethnic nationalisms constitute a major obstacle on the road to national integration and the building of the Soviet nation and are so recognized by the leadership. The relative success of economic and social integration has not counterbalanced the failure of political socialization in the task of building a uniform Soviet political culture. The hoped-for "national in form, Socialist in content" new society has, in fact, evolved into one that is Socialist in form and national in content, with the content part an arena of conflict between the Great Russians and all other nationalisms.

Rooted in the pre-Revolutionary past and inadvertently promoted by the Party's national policy, ethnic antagonisms have grown rather than disappeared as Lenin had expected, and may, in an event of external conflict, contribute to the disintegration of the Soviet state. Of policy alternatives available to the leadership for the solution of the problem, none seem to promise the type of leadership wanted: to have the systemic status quo and to have also the successful assimilation of the minorities. A change toward genuine federalism might satisfy ethnic demands but is not viable in the current systemic context. A constitutional change leading to abolition of federal forms and enforced integration (possibly with a token cultural autonomy continued for a time) seems to be currently a favored alternative, at least by the dominant factions in the leadership. It may not be viable either, however, because of the strong vested interests of the major republics within the Party itself, and because nationalism suppressed is bound to reemerge with increased intensity. The continuation of the present system and policies, the easiest alternative, would not diminish the problem. A most likely policy seems a combination of the third alternative with some aspects of the second, such as a merger possibility for the smaller republics and intensified integrationist policies.

Notes

1. Report to the 24th Congress of the C.P.S.U., in *The Current Digest of the Soviet Press (C.D.S.P.)* 23, no.14: 3.

2. Legal justification for the request was provided by an amendment to the U.S.S.R. constitution adopted in 1944 whereby union republics were given the right "to enter into direct relations with foreign states and to conclude agreements and exchange dip-

lomatic and consular representatives with them" (Article 18a) and
to have their own "republican military formations" (Article 18b).
Except for the two republics' membership in the U.N., the two
clauses remain inoperative.

3. Tsentral 'noe Statisticheskoe Upravlenie pri Sovete Minis-
trov S.S.S.R., *Narodnoe Khoziaistvo S.S.S.R. v 1970 g. Statistiche-
skii Ezhegodnik* (Moscow: "Statistika," 1971), pp.18–21.

4. Despite the Party's attempt to treat Soviet Jews like any
other ethnic group, they are unique in many ways and thus outside
the scope of this discussion. The Jewish Autonomous Province,
Birobidzhan, has only about 200,000 inhabitants and is of little
importance to the Russian Jewish community. Scattered throughout
the Soviet Union the Jews contribute disproportionately to the
scientific and cultural elites of the country as a whole. In 1970
they constituted eight percent of the Soviet scientific elite *(nau-
chnye rabotniki)* while their weight in the population was only 0.8
percent of the total (comparable statistics for Great Russians are 66
and 53 percent, respectively), ibid., pp.15, 658. The Jewish community as a whole has no territorial-administrative base and no
pertinent cultural facilities to serve as a focus for their national
aspirations. Their national focus is abroad, in Israel, which the
Soviet authorities regard as an unfriendly state. The existence of
Israel, the Soviet Middle East policy, and the strength of the Jewish
community in the West have made their status in the Soviet Union
a foreign-policy issue. Historically, also, they have a unique position
because of the pre-1917 discrimination and the prominent role
Jewish Communists played in the Revolution.

5. Ibid. The union republics were: R.S.F.S.R. (Russian Soviet
Federative Socialist Republic), the largest and the most important,
which extends from the western borders to the Soviet Far East;
Ukraine S.S.R., Belorussian S.S.R., Uzbek S.S.R., Kazakh S.S.R.,
Georgian S.S.R., Azerbaijan S.S.R., Lithuanian S.S.R., Moldavian
S.S.R., Latvian S.S.R., Kirgiz S.S.R., Tadzhik S.S.R., Armenian
S.S.R., Turkmen S.S.R., Estonian S.S.R.

6. Reporting to the 22nd Congress of the C.P.S.U. on the
draft Party Statutes, Frol Kozlov (then Khrushchev's heir apparent)
restated the principle in no uncertain terms: "It must . . .be made
clear that the C.P.S.U. is not a federation of parties or Party
committees. It is a centralized organization." In *Current Soviet
Policies 4; The Documentary Record of the 22nd Congress of the
Communist Party of the Soviet Union,* ed. Charlotte Saikowski and

Leo Gruliow (New York and London: Columbia University Press, 1962), p.205.

7. For the most comprehensive explanation of the principle of democratic centralism, *see* Merle Fainsod, *How Russia is Ruled,* rev. ed. (Cambridge, Mass.: Harvard University Press, 1964), ch. 7.

8. Incensed by Stalin's brutality in dealing with the Georgian party in late 1922, Lenin sharply criticized Stalin's Great Russian chauvinism and warned of the dangers of national injustice: "That Georgian who . . . accuses others of 'social-nationalism' (while himself being not only a genuine and veritable 'social-nationalist' but also a crude Great Russian Derzhimorda) [brutal police agent in Gogol] — that Georgian in reality violates the interests of the proletarian class solidarity, because nothing delays so much the development and consolidation of the proletarian class solidarity as does national injustice, and offended members of minority groups are of all things most sensitive to the emotion of equality and to the violation of that equality by their proletarian comrades. . . ." Quoted in ibid., p.285.

9. *See*, for example, Abdurakhman Avtorkhanov, "Denationalization of the Soviet Ethnic Minorities" in *Studies on the Soviet Union,* n.s. 4, no. 1 (1964): 74–79; and Seweryn Bialer, "How Russians Rule Russia," *Problems of Communism,* no. 5 (September–October 1964), pp.45–52.

10. For a case study of the formation and characteristics of the new Tadzhik elite, *see* Teresa Rakowska-Harmstone, *Russia and Nationalism in Central Asia: The Case of Tadzhikistan,* (Baltimore, Md., and London: The Johns Hopkins Press, 1970), ch. 5, 8.

11. Concern over the low birthrate has already been voiced in the Soviet press. *See C.D.S.P.* 24, no. 37: 1.

12. Calculated on the basis of data in *Narodnoe Khoziaistvo S.S.S.R. v 1970 g.,* pp.15–16.

13. A Western observer comments: "The republic and 'economic region' of Kazakhstan disrupts the natural unity of the wheat and metal region of the West Siberian plains on the one hand and the irrigated oases of Middle Asia on the other, and its center is an empty desert. This geographical violence is done on ethnic grounds that are now quite invalid, since the Kazakhs are only a small minority in the northern half of the republic," and, "it is maintained throughout, that regional analysis will be bedeviled from the outset if it is locked into units that are meaningless, vague, or actual-

ly distorting." David Hooson, "The Outlook for Regional Development in the Soviet Union," *Slavic Review,* no. 3 (September 1972), p.552.

14. *See,* for example, Leslie Dienes, "Issues in Soviet Energy Policy and Conflicts over Fuel Costs in Regional Development," *Soviet Studies,* no. 1 (July 1971), pp.26–58; and Violet Connolly, *Beyond the Urals* (London, New York, and Toronto: Oxford University Press, 1967).

15. Resolution of the C.C. C.P.S.U., " O podgotovke k 50– letiiu obrazovaniia Soiuza Sovetskikh Sotsialisticheskikh Respublik," *Partiinaia Zhizn,* no. 5 (March 1972), pp.3–13.

16. M. Suslov, "Obshchestvennye nauki – boevoe oruzhie partii v stroitel'stve kommunizma," *Kommunist,* no. 1 (January 1972), pp.18–30.

17. The underground *Chronicle of Current Events* reported (in an article by a known dissenter, V. Chornovil), that in 1965 the Central Committee of the Ukrainian Party (headed then by Shelest), transmitted to Moscow (with apparent approval), a ten-point memorandum by a Ukrainian minister of professional higher and secondary education, Dadenkov, proposing changes in the Ukrainian educational system in favor of its Ukrainization, which was rejected by the C.C. C.P.S.U. As reported in "Kronika Ukrainska," *Kultura* (in Polish), no. 11 (1972), p.98. In 1972 Georgia was rocked by a scandal involving two prominent historians' new interpretation of the history of the establishment of Soviet power in Georgia (*see* footnote 24).

18. *See Pravda Ukrainy* (6, 7, 11 October 1972), and *Zaria Vostoka* (2 November 1972).

19. *See* "K piatidesiatiletiu obrazovaniia Soiuza S.S.R.," *Sovetskoe Gosudarstvo i Pravo,* no. 1 (1972), pp.3–10; and S. L. Ronin, "Sotsialisticheskii internatsionalizm Sovetskogo prava i edinstvo zakonnosti v Soiuze S.S.R.," ibid., no.9 (1972), pp.63–70.

20. The promotion of the Tadzhik A.S.S.R. to the status of a union republic was clearly generated by a desire to extend Soviet influence into Afghanistan, Iran, and the then British India (*see* Rakowska-Harmstone); Ukraine's "sovereign" status was emphasized in the transfer, from Czechoslovakia of Carpathian Ruthenia; the formation and subsequent abolition of the Karelo-Finnish Union republic was clearly motivated by the role it played in the Soviet policy toward Finland (*see* Vernon Aspaturian, "The Union Re-

publics and Soviet Diplomacy; Concepts, Institutions, and Practices," *American Political Science Review* (June 1959), pp. 383–411. Soviet Kazakhstan and Kirgizia are inhabited by the same ethnic groups, which live in Chinese Sinkiang.

21. For a discussion of the role of the union republics in Soviet foreign policy, *see* Aspaturian, and Vernon Aspaturian, *Process and Power in Soviet Foreign Policy* (Boston: Little, Brown and Co., 1971), chs. 13, 14.

22. *See* Avtorkhanov.

23. *Pravda* (15 September 1972), cited *C.D.S.P.* 24, no. 27:8.

24. In Georgia: U. I. Sidamonidze for a book on the role of the Georgian Mensheviks in the period of revolutionary consolidation, and A.I. Menabde, for an attempt to rehabilitate "nationalist deviationists by condoning their struggle against the Transcaucasian Federation." Ibid., no. 11, pp.8–9. In Armenia: A. N. Mnatsakanyan for an article on Lenin and the national question in a historical journal (ibid., no. 44, p.15); and a novelist, Zertaganyan, for a thirteenth-century setting novel *(The House of Cilicia)*, which "distorts class essence of historical process." In Kirgizia: two historians for national deviations *(Christian Science Monitor* [29 December 1972]).

25. *Narodnoe Khoziaistvo S.S.S.R. v 1970 g.*, pp.15–17.

Ethnic Conflict in
a Strategic Area:
The Case of Cyprus

Paschalis M. Kitromilides and Theodore A. Couloumbis

In the following pages we present a general survey of the politics of ethnic conflict in Cyprus, and we outline and evaluate a number of initiatives, attempted at a variety of levels, aimed at a resolution of the problem.[1] Although our focus remains political, we appreciate the need for a comparative study of the historical roots and the structural and attitudinal dynamics of the conflict between the two Cypriot communities.[2] Finally, we offer some relevant ideas suggesting the direction that future research should follow.

The Politics of Ethnic Conflict: From Coexistence to Segregation

The contemporary problem of Cyprus originates with the Ottoman conquest of the island, which had been occupied by the Venetians, in 1570–71. The most momentous effect of the Turkish conquest was the creation of a Muslim minority in Cyprus. According to Ottoman practice, part of the invading forces settled in Cyprus as *sipahis,* or military landholders, taking over as their *timars* or *chifliks* the feudal estates of the former Frankish nobility. These were the original forefathers of the Turkish minority. Its numbers were soon swelled by the Islamization of Greek inhabitants who were induced to escape the lot of subject *rayas* by adopting the religion, thus enjoying the privileges of the ruling *millet.*[3] These Islamizations can be systematically documented from tax registers that have survived from the period of Turkish occupation. There is convincing evidence that there were conversions of Greek Cypriot villagers to Islam as late as 1825—28. The best testimony however is afforded by the names of Christian saints borne by several Turkish villages in Cyprus, for example, Saint John, Saint Nicholas, and Saint George, and the fact that, until recently, many of the Turkish Cypriots, especially in the Paphos area, were Greek-speaking Muslims.[4]

These Muslims lived in peace with the Greek Cypriots who formed the overwhelming majority of the population throughout the centuries of the Turkish occupation of Cyprus. This extended to Cyprus the pattern of peaceful symbiosis of Orthodox Christian and Muslim peasants that obtained in Anatolia, especially in such areas as Cappadocia and Pontos until the Greeks were expelled from Asia Minor in 1922—24. Peaceful coexistence manifested itself in a shared folk piety and a common life-style that survived intact in those areas of Asia Minor that remained away from the battlegrounds of the Greek-Turkish war that raged during 1919—22 in western Anatolia. The memories of this peaceful past are still invoked by the moving receptions of those Greeks who in recent years have been returning to visit their erstwhile villages. The same is largely true of those parts of rural Cyprus where Greeks and Turks lived in mixed or neighboring villages. In this context, an undeniable tradition of mutual help and cordiality in the personal sphere survived the vicissitudes of political history.[5]

This was the social legacy of intercommunal relations inherited by the British when they took over the administration of Cyprus in 1878 in the context of a rearrangment of power relations in the Near East sanctioned by the Treaty of Berlin.[6] In the span of eighty years of British rule between 1878 and the late 1950s, only one minor incident of intercommunal violence is reported.[7] It is true that in the intricate politics of the Legislative Council that functioned from 1881 to 1931 the colonial rulers managed repeatedly to play the representatives of the two communities against each other.[8] Political representation in the Legislative Council reflected the traditional Ottoman system of social organization based on religious communities *(millets),* which was retained by the British and which formed the fundamental principle of their handling of the politics of Cyprus. In the context of this policy, the *millet* system was gradually politicized and provided the organizational foundation for the national differentiation of the Cypriots.[9] Despite this process, which was encouraged by British policy, the Turkish members of the Council sided occasionally with their Greek compatriots to promote the common interests of the island, especially regarding taxation and finance. The two communities did not come to blows, even over the issue of *Enosis,* the demand for union with Greece for which the Greek Cypriots had been clamoring for generations. True, the Turkish Cypriot leaders consistently registered their opposition to *Enosis,* but this disagreement was never strained so far as to be expressed in violence.

The *Enosis* movement emerged in the nineteenth century. It essentially represented an extension to Cyprus of the wider historical phenomenon of European nationalism. In its social character and political aspirations, the *Enosis* movement was similar to the Italian *Risorgimento,* the movement for German unification, and the irredentist movements of the Balkan nations. Similar *Enosis* movements aspiring to unification with the kingdom of Greece had developed in Crete, Macedonia, and the seven Ionian islands in the nineteenth century. While it was timid under the Ottomans in the nineteenth century, the *Enosis* movement was intensified under the British and reached a peak in the nationalist rebellion of October 1931.[10] Meanwhile, in 1925 Cyprus had become a British crown colony after Turkey had renounced all rights of sovereignty over the island by the Treaty of Lausanne of 1923.[11] The 1931 uprising, aspiring to *Enosis* with Greece, was forcefully put down by the British, and the civil liberties of the Cypriots were suppressed. The repression of political life and national expression that followed this uprising was largely responsible for the intransigence that the *Enotist* leaders manifested in dealing with the constitutional proposals of the British government after World War II.

In the wake of World War II, the national demands of the Cypriots were formulated as a claim of self-determination in the context of the movement of decolonization.[12] A plebiscite organized by the Ethnarchy of Cyprus in 1950 — after the British rulers refused to conduct one — showed an overwhelming majority of the Greek Cypriots favoring union with Greece.[13] The British refused to discuss the future of Cyprus even in the face of increasing political agitation on the island.[14] The subsequent intransigence growing on all sides in the years 1950—55 culminated in an anticolonial guerrilla rebellion lasting between 1955 and 1959, and spearheaded by E.O.K.A., the underground National Organization of Cypriot Fighters.[15]

Until then the conflict had been primarily between the Greek Cypriots and the British, while the Turkish Cypriots remained relatively uninvolved. It was not until 1957—58 that the tensions prevailing in Cyprus generated intercommunal violence on a considerable scale for the first time. The eruption of ethnic violence in the late 1950s came as the result of a process of increasing differentiation between the two Cypriot communities that had until then coexisted in a traditional society. Socioeconomic modernization, slow but steady under the British, and the spread of literacy transformed the traditional religious and linguistic differences into the bases of the development of a distinct Greek and a distinct Turkish national consciousness. In the political sphere, as nationalism grew among Greek Cypriots and as demands for broader political participation rose against British colonial rule, the Turkish Cypriots as well became increasingly conscious of their ethnic identity and their rights of participation in Cypriot affairs. Further, since the educational systems of the two communities were modeled on those of Greece and Turkey, respectively, the symbolism of nationalist antagonism that grew out of the long historical confrontation of the two nations was transposed to Cyprus. As a result, a commonly shared system of social communication that could conceivably form the basis of an integrated society was precluded from developing.[16]

Against this background, contention emerged over the spoils of independence that was felt to be imminent once the British indicated their willingness to hand over the government of the island to the Cypriots themselves.[17] Fortified in their antagonism by the support of their respective motherlands and by British colonial policy, which as a rule discouraged ethnic integration in the territories of the Empire,[18] the two Cypriot ethnic communities found it increasingly difficult to compromise. Discord developed over both the form and the method of independence. The Greek Cypriots fought for union with Greece through the exercise of the right of self-determination. The Turkish Cypriots expressed interest in continuing British rule or in securing a partition of Cyprus between Greece and Turkey to be decided by those outside powers and Britain. The irreconcilability of these positions led to heightened tensions that exploded in violence. The workings of social mobilization and the political choices of the years 1945–55 resulted in the translation of the traditional religious and linguistic differences into ethnic conflict.

Accommodation or drastic surgical solutions were extremely difficult in view of the communal demography and ethnic geography of Cyprus. The Turkish Cypriot community never exceeded twenty-five percent of the population. Indeed, since the 1920s its numbers had dropped below twenty percent.[19] Being an overwhelming majority of the population, the Greek Cypriots remained firm in their claim for self-determination by majority rule. Conversely, the extreme dispersion of Turkish Cypriot settlements over the island made it impossible to find a geographic basis for partition – a solution suggested first by the British and espoused by Turkey since the mid-1950s.[20]

The continuing anti-British guerrilla struggle of the Greek Cypriots, the endemic diplomatic confrontation among Britain, Greece, and Turkey and mounting pressures from NATO and the world community built up to such a point of tension that the parties to the conflict finally settled for a compromise; on 16 August 1960, following the Zurich and London agreements of the previous year and protracted negotiations in Cyprus, the island emerged as an independent state.[21]

The Zurich and London agreements concluded in February 1959 reflected the ethnic duality of Cyprus as well as the power balance of the contracting parties. The British acquiesced to the loss of a colony but secured rights to sizable sovereign bases on

Cyprus. In the confrontation between Greek and Turkish Cypriots the mainland Greeks felt so pressed to reach a settlement that they gave up more than their fair share of bargaining chips to the Turkish side. The United States, being intimately involved with both Greece and Turkey, applied continuous pressure on both junior allies as well as on the Cypriots to settle amicably and to heal the "festering sore" in the southeastern flank of NATO.[22]

The Zurich and London agreements and the constitution that was based on them set up the Republic of Cyprus, which was granted sovereignty and independence and soon attained U.N. membership. However, on independence day Cyprus was bound by three treaties. The Treaty of Guarantee among Cyprus, Britain, Greece, and Turkey (the three guarantors) was designed to safeguard the territorial integrity and independence of Cyprus, while it simultaneously permitted the guarantors to interfere in concert or independently in Cyprus to uphold the state of affairs created by the 1960 treaties and to prevent either *Enosis,* the Greek maximalist position, or *Taksim* (partition of the island between Greece and Turkey), the Turkish answer to *Enosis.* The Treaty of Alliance committed Greece and Turkey to come to the aid of Cyprus in case of external aggression and allowed them to station one military contingent each on Cyprus on a 60:40 ratio. By the Treaty of Establishment, Great Britain secured two sovereign base areas at Dhekelia and Akrotiri-Episkope in southern Cyprus.[23]

The basic principles of the constitutional organization of the Republic of Cyprus were agreed at Zurich between the prime ministers of Greece and Turkey. During a subsequent London conference, they were presented to the Cypriots to guide the work of the commission, which was to draft the constitution of Cyprus. The constitution took more than a year to draft and its major provisions were as follows: Cyprus would have a presidential regime with a Greek Cypriot president and a Turkish Cypriot vice-president, each elected by his respective community and each possessing final veto power on matters dealing with foreign affairs, defense, and internal security; the Council of Ministers would include three Turkish Cypriots out of ten members; at least one of three important ministries (Defense, Foreign Affairs, and Finance) would go to a Turkish Cypriot citizen. The Turkish Cypriots also secured quotas of forty percent in the army and security forces and thirty percent in the civil service — well in excess of their eighteen percent share in the population. The fifty-member legislature would be composed of Greek and Turkish Cypriot deputies on a 70:30 ratio. Each ethnic community would elect its deputies separately. Separate majorities in each ethnic caucus would be required to pass legislation on such matters as taxation, electoral procedures, and municipalities. Exclusively communal affairs would be administered by the Greek and Turkish Communal Chambers. Further there were provisions for separate Turkish and Greek municipalities, separate taxation, and separate administration of justice. The Treaties of Guarantee and Alliance were annexed to the constitution. Article 182 of the constitution declared that the provisions of final veto, separate majorities, and fixed ethnic ratios as well as the two incorporated treaties would be basic and unalterable.[24]

The constitutional framework of the Republic of Cyprus was designed to contain the ethnic conflict by satisfying some of the most basic requirements of the two Cypriot communities by ruling out both union and partition. Beyond this however the Cypriot constitution, premised on ethnic dualism, did not contribute anything toward a substantive resolution of past or potential inter-communal conflict. Its intricate formulas and cumbersome structures were precisely designed to freeze and perpetuate the ethnic division. Instead of encouraging cooperation it institutionalized separatist tendencies in its provisions for ethnic voting in Parliament and split municipalities. The public life of Cyprus was oriented by the very spirit of the constitution toward ethnic antagonism instead of toward democratic development of socially based party politics. Constitutional experts everywhere concurred that the Cyprus constitution despite its ingenuity was practically unworkable.[25] In real life, efficient government proved impossible and controversies quickly arose. The danger points centered on the question of the army's composition (that is, at what level should the units be ethnically integrated), the passage of tax legislation, the establishment of separate municipalities, and the implementation of the 70:30 ratio in the composition of the civil service.[26]

Predictably the psychological dynamics of the postindependence situation in Cyprus intensified these disagreements. The Greek

Cypriots resented what they felt to be an unfair share of the bargain; although they had set aside their cherished aspiration for *Enosis*, the final settlement gave them less than what the hard facts of their proportion in the population and their contribution to the economy would warrant. At the same time, the Turkish Cypriots were quite zealous in pressing for full enjoyment of their prerogatives under the constitution, arguing that this was the only way to cope with the overwhelming numbers of Greeks. The Turkish Cypriots remained extremely suspicious of any suggestions to change the status quo. The outcome was tension and escalating discord, to the point that by 1963 the government could not collect taxes because the Turkish members of the legislature would not vote for the income-tax bill, not out of any reservations regarding its fairness to their community, but as a tactical move to force the establishment of separate municipalities and the immediate implementation of the ethnic ratios provided by the civil service clauses of the constitution.[27]

In November 1963, with this stalemate in the background, President Makarios offered for consideration thirteen amendments designed to make the 1960 constitution workable.[28] These amendments sought primarily to abolish the requirement for separate ethnic majorities in the legislature, to merge the separate judicial systems for the two communities, and to eliminate the veto powers of the president and the vice-president. While the Turkish Cypriot community was studying these proposals, Turkey immediately and flatly rejected them and admonished the president to respect the provisions of the externally guaranteed Cypriot constitution.

In the ensuing climate of heightened tensions, a small incident escalated into all-out violence between the two fired up communities during the last week of December 1963. Turkey threatened to intervene militarily as the new year was dawning. Active American pressure on all sides averted the escalation of the conflict into a Greek-Turkish war.[29]

The communal violence that erupted in 1963 and punctuated the following year was a later and more intense phase of the ethnic conflict that emerged in the late 1950s. It not only underlined the fact that ethnic conflicts tend to be of long duration and to persist over time despite intervals of (usually) uneasy peace, but it also showed that the bicommunal experiment conceived at Zurich and London primarily to meet NATO objectives was ill-founded and failed to contribute toward conflict resolution. The constitution ignored the real issues and further distorted the relations of the two Cypriot communities by institutionalizing external interference in the politics of Cyprus.

Following the crisis of Christmas 1963, the British intervened using troops stationed at their bases to reestablish order, separate the combatants, and achieve a cessation of hostilites. It was at that time that the "Green Line" was drawn along a narrow street in the old city of Nicosia by the British military authorites. This line has since separated the Turkish quarter of Nicosia from the remainder of the city and has remained a symbol of ethnic division.

In the critical days following the British intervention, the initiative shifted to the old British metropolis. London, with strong U.S. backing, attempted to set up a multinational NATO emergency force whose task would be to police the tenuously established truce lines. Greece and Turkey reluctantly agreed to this proposal, but Archbishop Makarios — fearing partition — staunchly opposed a NATO-generated solution for Cyprus. After a conference in London among the three guarantor powers and representatives of the two Cypriot communities failed in February 1964, the government of Cyprus brought the problem to the U.N. Security Council.

With its resolution of 4 March 1964 the Security Council called on all member states to refrain from actions that might endanger the territorial integrity and independence of Cyprus; the Council urged restraint on all parties and recommended the establishment of an international peacekeeping force to be dispatched to Cyprus. The U.N. Cyprus Peacekeeping Force (U.N.F.I.CYP.) had as its primary purpose to interpose itself between the combatants after the ceasefire and to act as an objective observer and facilitator of peaceful bargaining. The size of U.N.F.I.CYP. has fluctuated from 6,400 at its peak to about 2,400 at the time of this writing.

U.N.F.I.CYP. was staffed primarily with contingents from Britain, Finland, Canada, Denmark, Ireland, and Sweden. It was divided into brigades, companies, squadrons, and other units commanded by their national commanders who, in turn, received their orders from U.N.F.I.CYP.'s commanding officer. The force was dis-

persed throughout the island to patrol city streets and the countryside in order to discourage the accidental outbreak of local incidents.
The U.N. Secretary-General has been represented by a special en-
voy in Cyprus.

U.N.F.I.CYP. has been responsible to the U.N. Security Council,
which authorizes and renews the force's life twice a year. However,
most day-to-day authority over this force has been delegated to
the Secretary-General. Its activities have included the following:

1. Pacification Efforts (negotiation, mediation, good offices),
2. Civic Action (aid in the reestablishment of normal services
   and institutions),
3. Information Gathering (aid in establishing a detached and
   accurate empirical base of facts that could facilitate negotiations).

In short, U.N.F.I.CYP. has been acting both as a buffer and a link
between the two ethnic communities. U.N.F.I.CYP.'s mandate,
however, has clearly excluded the "forceful imposition of peace"
in Cyprus. Whenever armed hostilities break out, the role of
U.N.F.I.CYP. becomes more political-diplomatic and less military.

In the ten years of its operation between 1964–74,
U.N.F.I.CYP. performed quite admirably and was welcomed by all
sides. The only criticism made of the U.N.F.I.CYP. was that it
unwittingly contributed to the freezing of the status quo (that is,
the de facto separation of the communities), and that its presence
became addictive for all the islanders who have grown psychologically dependent on this externally administered painkilling operation.
It could be said that U.N.F.I.CYP. managed to control but not to
eliminate ethnic conflict, especially when the latter was exacerbated
by externally planned interventions in the political affairs of Cyprus.[31]

Since the period of 1963–64, a stalemate had developed
between the two communities involving a de facto separation of
Greek from Turkish Cypriots. The Turkish Cypriot community had
been in enclaves scattered throughout the island. These enclaves
were based primarily in the Turkish quarters of the six major cities
and in a number of clusters of Turkish villages in the countryside.

In the climate of tension and fear that prevailed during the ethnic confrontation in 1964, the inhabitants of a number of small and isolated Turkish villages and the Turkish quarters of some mixed Greek and Turkish villages were abandoned by their population, which moved to the areas that later were consolidated into the enclaves.

Originally this movement appeared as the result of a quest for safety and refuge during the charged up atmosphere of hostilities. As time went by, however, and life returned to its normal pace, especially after 1968, it became evident that the creation and sealing off of the enclaves was a measure designed to modify the ethnic demography of Cyprus and to create at least a partial geographical basis for a political federation of the island to replace the unitary state of the Republic of Cyprus.[32] Documentary evidence that has become available subsequently tends to corroborate this view.[33] The Turkish Cypriot enclaves remained inaccessible to the government of Cyprus and have been forbidden areas for Greek Cypriots. The Turks gradually developed separate administrative structures (military, police, tax, and judicial) within the enclaves and withdrew from participation in the Cypriot government, which remained as the only internationally recognized authority on the island.[34]

The intensification of ethnic differentiation precipitated by the growth of Greek and Turkish nationalism in Cyprus and the ethnic violence of the 1950s prevented, once Cyprus had attained independence, an "integrative revolution" from occurring on the island.[35] In the case of Cyprus, the preconditions for some form of social, though probably not ethnic, integration were present in the substratum of traditional coexistence still surviving in the countryside. The institutionalization of ethnic dualism in the Cypriot constitution and the consequent political climate of communal divisiveness effectively blocked any policy initiatives that might have exploited the potential for social change in the direction of some form of integrative evolution.

In addition, a number of powerful exogenous factors also arrested the possible development of a pattern of coexistence. At the origins of the ethnically based political disintegration of the Republic of Cyprus lay the legacy of British colonial policy, which, as noted earlier, tended to solidify ethnic divisions by means of the separate organization of communal groups in the colonial territories. Even more powerful factors have been the close linkages between the two Cypriot communities with Greece and Turkey, respectively.

Since independence and especially since the constitutional breakdown of 1963–64, the interethnic intransigence of both Cypriot communities has been considerably fortified by the policies of Greece and Turkey. Both countries, Turkey more effectively than Greece, have been dealing with their respective ethnic communities on Cyprus with scant regard to Cypriot sovereignty. Clearly, support and directives emanating from Ankara to the Turkish Cypriot leadership had been a major factor in the creation of the enclaves and the promotion of the separation of the two Cypriot communities throughout the 1960s.[36] Support from Ankara also made possible the neutralization of all moderate elements in the leadership of the Turkish Cypriots and the solidification of the separatist course advocated by the extremists. The escalation of extremism among Turkish Cypriot political elites in turn enabled Turkey to exercise total control and to maintain a firm grip over the enclaves that remained dependent on economic aid and military protection from the mainland.[37]

Conversely, the vitality of the Cypriot economy and the effective political leadership of President Makarios combined to allow a considerable degree of independent initiative in the effort of the Cyprus government to secure the continuing independence of the island. The military dictatorship that came to power in Greece after the coup of 21 April 1967 attempted to quell the independent line of Archbishop Makarios by undermining his authority. The intraethnic conflict that developed among the Greek Cypriots as a consequence complicated all attempts at ethnic conflict management in Cyprus.

From Legal Arguments to Attempts at Conflict Resolution: 1964–74

During the ten years of ethnic crisis (1964–74), both communities advanced sets of well-developed legal arguments designed to bolster their respective positions, while they worked substantively on the political level in order to crystalize a status quo consonant with their interests.[38] Archbishop Makarios, the unchallenged spokesman of the Greek Cypriot point of view, sought a solution through direct negotiations among the communities, while making maximum use of the good offices of the U.N. General Assembly and minimizing, to the extent possible, influences from Greece, Turkey, Britain, the United States, and NATO in general. President Makarios consistently argued that the 1960 constitution and the treaties had been forced upon the Cypriot people and that these treaties were blatantly inequitable.[39] Makarios's position is that the provisions of the Treaty of Guarantee that permit the intervention of third states (the guarantor powers', as well as the fact that no amendments were permitted to the Cypriot constitution — on which the Cypriot people never had the opportunity to vote — are clearly incompatible with internationally recognized principles of sovereignty and independence.[40]

On the political side, the Greek case rests heavily on General Assembly Resolution 2077 (20) of 18 December 1965, which takes "cognizance of the fact that the Republic of Cyprus, as an equal member of the United Nations is, in accordance with the Charter of the United Nations, entitled to enjoy and should enjoy, full sovereignty and complete independence without any foreign intervention or interference." The Assembly has further called upon all nations "in conformity with their obligations under the Charter, and in particular Article 2, paragraphs 1 and 4, to respect the sovereignty, unity, independence, and territorial integrity of the Republic of Cyprus and to refrain from any intervention directed against it."[41]

Resting its case on the international recognition of Cyprus's sovereignty and evoking the generally acknowledged principle of majority rule and minority rights, the Cypriot government has consistently offered the following concessions in an attempt to compromise the most thorny interethnic issues:

1. The adoption of a code of fundamental rights to protect the minority;
2. The requirement that the Turkish Cypriot participation in Parliament should be on the basis of proportional representation to the population of the Cypriot Turks;
3. The authorization for the minority of Turks to direct

the "education, culture, religion, and personal status of
its members";

4. The acceptance of a U.N. commission that would oversee
the protection of minority rights for a specified period of
time.[42]

The Turkish Cypriot position has also adopted a mixture of
legal and political arguments in order to protect its interests. The
Turkish Cypriots have accused President Makarios of failing to
implement faithfully and equitably the 1960 constitution from
the very beginning. His Thirteen Amendments (November 1963)
fly in the face of Article 182 of the Cyprus constitution, which
prohibits amendments. Beyond that, it is an accepted principle of
international law that treaties are not subject to unilateral abroga-
tion *(pacta sunt servanda).*[43]

The Turkish view continues by denouncing the Greek Cypriot
majority's policies of "exclusion and oppression" that have alleged-
ly been designed to drive the Turkish minority off the island.
The Turkish Cypriots purport to justify their stern resistance and the
support they are securing from mainland Turkey on the foundation of Article 4 of the Treaty of Guarantee (1960), which states:

In the event of a breach of the provisions of the present
treaty, Greece, Turkey, and the United Kingdom undertake
to consult together with respect to the representations or
measures necessary to ensure observance of those provisions.

Insofar as common or concerted action may not prove
possible, each of the three guaranteeing powers reserves the
right to take action with the sole aim of reestablishing the
state of affairs created by the present Treaty.[44]

In short, the Turkish view is that the Zurich and London treaties
and the 1960 constitution remained valid and, as a minimum for a
settlement, the parties involved should return to the status quo
before 1963. These remained the positions of the two communities during the period 1964—74.

While the conflict has been simmering during the past ten years,
reaching on occasion (twice in 1964 and once in 1967) peak levels

threatening a simultaneous Turkish and Greek intervention in Cyprus that could escalate into a full-scale war between the two countries,[45] efforts have been made to solve the Cyprus problem on at least four levels: international, regional, subregional, and local. Basically these four levels could be more simply divided in two: a) solutions imposed on the Cypriots by outside powers, and b) solutions arrived at by intercommunal negotiations between the two Cypriot ethnic communities.

On the international level of conflict management and resolution efforts, the major focus centers on the activities and initiatives of the United Nations in the Cyprus question. During the 1950s, while the struggle for decolonization was going on in Cyprus, Greece and the Greek Cypriots chose the U.N. as an instrument of policy. Although excluded from the process that brought about the Zurich and London agreements, the U.N. has proved to be a useful echo chamber and world public-opinion forum that generated serious pressures upon the British to relinquish colonial control over the island. The role of the U.N. in the 1960s, the postindependence period for Cyprus, has been considerably more active and decisive than in the 1950s largely because the government of Cyprus placed more trust in the mediating efforts of the international organization, insisting that the Cyprus problem was not a Greek-Turkish dispute to be resolved by NATO.[46] We have already spoken about U.N.F.I.CYP.

The U.N. Secretary-Generals, through their official mediators Sakari S. Tuomioja of Finland and Dr. Galo Plaza of Ecuador, tried to promote a policy of peaceful coexistence and engagement between the two communities, while they recognized the unitary nature of the Cypriot state. They recommended as the most likely path to a permanent solution direct negotiations between the Greek and Turkish Cypriots, with the encouragement (but not intervention) of all outside interested parties. Particular mention should be made of the report on the mediating activities submitted by Dr. Galo Plaza to the Secretary-General in March 1965.[47] This is a document of highly enlightened statesmanship that, with its suggestions of political formulas and structural arrangements and its pervading concern for human welfare, could be an invaluable basis for all resolution efforts. The report, which counseled against persistence

in the pursuit of union or partition and recommended ample safe-
guards of the rights of the Turkish Cypriots in a unitary state, was
accepted by the government of Cyprus but rejected by the government of Turkey and consequently by the leadership of the Turkish
Cypriot community.

To summarize, the approach of the international sector has been
to leave the solution of the problem to the Cypriots alone and to
provide good offices and other mediating and facilitative services,
while discouraging great power and middle power (Great Britain,
Greece, and Turkey) intervention in the internal affairs of the island.

On the regional level, efforts to solve the Cyprus problem have
tended to follow the very direction that the government of Cyprus
had constantly tried to avoid. The predominant elements on this
level have been the efforts of Britain and the United States through
NATO to eliminate the last remaining *casus belli* in the affairs of
Greece and Turkey, regardless of what this might mean for the
fate of Cyprus.[48] As we have indicated, between December 1963
and February 1964 Britain attempted to organize a NATO regional
force to supervise the truce in Cyprus.[49] This would have involved
a three-month renewable NATO-recruited and British-commanded
multinational force of 10,000 men, which would have been placed
under the political guidance of a committee of NATO ambassadors.
Negotiations would have been enhanced through the efforts of an
appointed mediator from a NATO country, other than Greece,
Turkey, Great Britain, or the United States. Turkey and Greece
assented to this plan with some important qualifications. President
Makarios objected and asked instead for a force that would have
been responsible to the U.N. rather than to NATO. This, of course,
was in keeping with the Cypriot policy of strategic nonalignment
and active participation in the Third World movement.

The NATO level activities assumed a far more aggressive and
interventionist nature under the initiative of the United States.
In July 1964, President Lyndon B. Johnson appointed the veteran
diplomat Dean Acheson as a special mediator for Cyprus. Acheson's
view was that the problem should be solved by direct agreement of
Greece and Turkey within the spirit of the NATO alliance. This
meant that the Cypriots, above all Archbishop Makarios, need not
and should not necessarily be consulted. In the last analysis, a

solution would have to be imposed upon the two warring Cypriot communities. Specifically, the plan woven by the aging diplomat would have taken the outward form of *Enosis* of Cyprus with Greece, and, by extension, assured entry of Cyprus into the NATO complex. The Turks would have been pacified with territorial concessions in the form of a sizable sovereign or leased base, extensive guarantees for the Turkish minority, and the development of Turkish cantons in the Greek-controlled portion of Cyprus.[50]

The Greek and Turkish governments initially accepted in principle and quite cautiously the Acheson proposals. President Makarios denounced the plan as a barely disguised form of partition of Cyprus, which was totally unacceptable to the interests of the Greek Cypriot population. Despite difficult odds and unbearable pressures upon the Archbishop, his views somehow managed to withstand the regional-strategic pressures orchestrated by the United States in the framework of the NATO alliance.

Perhaps the most important dimension added by the U.S. to the Cyprus imbroglio has been in the United States' restraining influence over Greece and Turkey to avoid an outbreak of war between them. For example, the U.S. through a series of emissaries and mediators, has continuously counseled prudence and urged a negotiated settlement between Greece and Turkey. George Ball's trip to Cyprus in February 1964, Lyndon Johnson's telegram to Premier Inonu in July 1964 strongly counseling against Turkish intervention in Cyprus, Dean Acheson's mediating efforts in July 1964, and Cyrus Vance's frenzied activity in November 1967 all illustrate this type of activity.

The subregional level focuses on the efforts of Greece and Turkey to safeguard their national interests vis-à-vis Cyprus. Whether one speaks of the pre- or postindependence period of Cyprus (that is, before and after 1960), it would be safe to assume that both Greece and Turkey placed their own general security requirements, their NATO obligations, and their domestic political exigencies on a higher priority than any concern for the welfare of their ethnic brothers in Cyprus.

As we have already pointed out, both Greece and Turkey have attempted to penetrate and control their respective ethnic counterparts in Cyprus, perceiving the two Cypriot communities as clients or, more euphemistically, junior partners. Naturally, Turkey has found it much easier to control the utterly dependent and economically depressed Turkish enclaves. On the contrary, President Makarios and the Greek Cypriot government have proven to be a harder nut to crack, to the point that, particularly in the post-1967 period, one could say that the controlling influence of the Athens government was considerably weakened in Nicosia. This was made abundantly clear in February 1972, when President Makarios ignored a public ultimatum from Athens to drastically restructure his government or resign. He did neither and survived.[51]

It was becoming increasingly clear that in view of the Cypriots' resistance — which was eloquently expressed in the overwhelming popular support enjoyed by President Makarios — and because of the objections voiced by the Soviet Union, NATO could not impose an Acheson type of solution short of using drastic military means. This created political preconditions for a negotiated intercommunal settlement presumably premised not on foreign-strategic interests but on considerations over the welfare and interests of the Cypriots themselves.

This leads us to the local level of settlement efforts through direct negotiations by the two Cypriot communities. We have come full circle, since the objectives and methods of conflict resolution encouraged on the international level have been essentially the same as the strategy of the intercommunal talks. Negotiations were initiated in June 1968 and continued in several phases until mid-1974 between Messers. Clerides and Denktash, who represented the two ethnic communities. At a later stage, two constitutional experts from Greece and Turkey were included to assist the principal negotiators. The special representative of the U.N. Secretary-General in Cyprus attended as well.

The discussions covered many of the constitutional problems raised by the ethnic conflict, and although the content of the negotiations remained secret, informed sources repeatedly intimated that significant progress was being made. At the later stages of the talks, substantive disagreement over the issue of local government was narrowed — the Greek side conceded that considerable decentralization was desirable but also insisted that the jurisdiction and functions of local government should not be such as to create essentially the infrastructure of a communal Turkish state within the unitary state of Cyprus.[52]

We believe that the intercommunal negotiations were the appropriate method of conflict resolution because they provided a channel of direct communication between spokesmen for the two Cypriot ethnic communities. In such a context, misperceptions and misconceptions could be discussed and cleared up, common interests realized, and the bases of agreement identified.[53] The preconditions for a successful strategy of conflict resolution were indeed present in Cyprus and should have been apparent to any perceptive observer of the situation on the island, despite the muted confrontation of the two communities.

The sociological basis for interethnic coexistence and cooperation had not just been historically the feature of life in Cypriot traditional society, but had also survived intact in the ethnically mixed communities of rural Cyprus. The constructive record of the U.N.F.I.CYP. in conflict containment added another useful precondition for conflict resolution. The U.N.F.I.CYP. could be used as an impartial police force to provide the necessary protection and security to all Cypriots once all other armed forces were removed from the scene. If Greek and Turkish military personnel were removed from Cyprus, and the National Guard and Turkish Cypriot fighting units were disbanded, not only the probability of recurrent collisions and explosions would be effectively checked, but also considerable funds would be economized to finance the stationing of a neutral and periodically rotating international force on a semi-permanent basis in Cyprus to act as an arbitrator and observer of a settlement.[54] We think that such a situation would guarantee effectively the security of the Turkish Cypriots so that they could feel free to come out of the self-imposed seclusion of the enclaves and participate in the life of Cyprus. By guaranteeing peace and security a permanent U.N. police force on Cyprus could help create both the practical mechanisms and the psychological climate for ethnic reintegration.

Most important of all, the new directions emerging in the political life of Cyprus and the dynamics of economic development seemed to be working in favor of an accommodation of the conflict. Politically, the growth of moderation and realism had led to the

conclusion that the pursuit of independent statehood was the safest
course for Cyprus. This became official policy when in 1965 the
government of Cyprus formally accepted the recommendations of
U.N. mediator Dr. Galo Plaza who explicitly counseled against
persisting in the pursuit of *Enosis*. In repeated democratic elections,
the Greek Cypriot community had confirmed this policy by casting
their votes overwhelmingly in support of Archbishop Makarios and
his supporters and the feasible solution (that is, independence)
they advocated. This meant that the most fundamental and
uncompromising demand of the Turkish Cypriots had been met and
consequently the way for an accommodation should have been
opened.

Another hopeful indication was the emergence of socially based
political parties that could conceivably meld the ethnic cleavage as
earlier instances of interethnic cooperation in trade unions or in the
cause of Cypriot independence might suggest.[55] The rapid rate of
economic growth and industrial expansion[56] had broadened the
labor market. Turkish Cypriot workers who had remained secluded
and idle in the enclaves could reenter the labor force and become
economically reintegrated into Cypriot society as they had been in
the past. Normal contacts to be resumed in all commercial and
pressed on the Turkish Cypriots by their leaders, was modified or
dropped. The economic reintegration of Cypriot society might also
provide the means of redressing the inequalities in the levels of
economic development of the two communities, thus removing one
of the underlying structural sources of conflict.[57] Indeed by the
early 1970s increasing numbers of Turkish Cypriot workers were
employed in projects of public works, and general economic
exchanges tended to be resumed between the two communities,
although normal economic relations had never been actually se-
vered in the agrarian economy of mixed rural communities.

With these trends in mind, it is plausible to argue that the social
and political context was ripe for a commonly acceptable constitutional formula satisfying the basic needs and long-standing
objections of both sides and setting up the institutional framework
for effective conflict resolution and social reintegration. To meet
these requirements a viable model for Cyprus would have to be
based on independence by ruling out all forms of union and parti-

tion. The institutional setup would have to be premised on decentralization to allow ethnic autonomy and sharing in the central institutions of power to secure the integrated character of the state. The constitutional infrastructure of reintegration could have been established if a number of divisive provisions of the 1960 constitution were amended. For instance, the Greek president and the Turkish vice-president would have to be elected by the entire population of the island. The representation of the Turkish side in Parliament, the bureaucracy and the security forces would have to be analogous to the percentage of Turkish population (eighteen percent) rather than ranging up to thirty or forty percent. Considerable autonomy and self-management would have to be granted to the Turkish communities of the island in conducting their local and broadly cultural affairs (religion, education, and so forth) to reassure them in their desire to preserve their highly valued ethnic identity.[58] International guarantees could have been adopted to oversee and secure the effective operation of this autonomy. The Parliament however would have to be divided into Greek and Turkish caucuses voting separately only on residual matters dealing exclusively with intracommunity affairs. The experience of 1960–63 had amply demonstrated that the entire Parliament would have to vote as a cohesive unit without the requirement for separate majorities of each ethnic caucus on all important legislation.

This was not an inconceivable way in which events could have developed, and Cyprus might have become a model case of a fair resolution of ethnic conflict. Unfortunately, the positive trends outlined above were not allowed to come to fruition. Ethnic dualism has not been the only or even primary cause of conflict in Cyprus. The dynamics of conflict resolution were effectively blocked by outside interference. Every time the intercommunal talks seemed to reach a point of substantial agreement on fundamental issues, the trend was reversed by behind the scenes manipulation of the Turkish Cypriot negotiator by the Turkish government in Ankara.[59] Writing with events since July 1974 in mind, we can assert with considerable certainty that despite its grudging endorsement of the interethnic negotiations, Turkish policy never abandoned the pursuit of partition that was first suggested by Britain in the 1950s and later presented as the official Turkish view on Cyprus to the U.N. mediator in 1965.[60] Underlying this posture was the fact that manipulation of the Cyprus issue in Turkish internal politics had proved to be a convenient diversion of public attention from pressing domestic problems.[61]

In the pursuit of this aim, Turkey was fortified by U.S. policy that has favored some form of partition of Cyprus between Greece and Turkey that would achieve the eradication of a cause of conflict threatening the solidity of the southeastern flank of NATO and the incorporation of Cyprus, a territory with some strategic value,[62] within the boundaries of two members of the Western alliance. This was adequately indicated by U.S. insistence on a settlement of Cyprus within NATO in the 1950s by the Acheson plans promoted during the crisis of the mid-1960s and finally by American acquiesence in if not support for the Turkish invasion and violent partittion of Cyprus in the summer of 1974. Probably the most eloquent indication of American attitudes on the problem of Cyprus is offered by the vote the U.S. cast against the innocuous resolution affirming the independence and sovereignty of Cyprus, passed by the U.N. General Assembly in December 1965.[63]

Greece also was converted to the line of some form of NATO-oriented partition once the military dictatorship rose to power in 1967.[64] The Athens colonels felt that some territorial concessions to Turkey would be desirable in order to satisfy the atavistic aspirations of Greek irredentist nationalism. Apparently such a foreign maneuver was expected to generate some popular sympathy for the repressive military regime; hence, the encouragement and direction of the several moves to unseat President Makarios.

The pattern of intraethnic discord that the Greek military regime encouraged in the ranks of the Greek Cypriot community escalated in the formation of extremist underground armed groups like the National Front (1969–70) and E.O.K.A.-B. (1971–74), which preached a revival of the *Enosis* movement.[65] These developments in turn exacerbated the fears of the Turkish Cypriots and undermined further the efforts at an accommodation of ethnic differences. Deprived of popular sympathy, these campaigns of extreme right-wing subversion and terrorism failed to unseat President Makarios, who won reelection for a third term in 1973. Several documents captured during police operations against E.O.K.A.-B.

terrorism clearly implicated the Greek junta and Greek officers serving in Cyprus. In a now famous letter to the figurehead president of dictatorial Greece, Archbishop Makarios expressed his abhorrence for military regimes and demanded the termination of the disastrous activities of the junta in Cyprus. As political oppression and bankruptcy were reaching their climax in Greece, the junta responded by engineering the coup of 15 July 1974. This coup and the subsequent Turkish invasion have plunged Cyprus into an immense human tragedy: five thousand people have been killed, and three thousand are missing as a result of the fighting in the summer of 1974; one third of the population (about 200,000 people) have become refugees as a consequence of the occupation of northern Cyprus by the Turkish army — about forty percent of the territory of the Republic. A flourishing economy has been ruined and a confident and optimistic society has been overtaken by a sense of desperation and grief. All this and the prospects of recurring explosions so long as things remain as they are make the future appear very bleak and dramatize the enormity and urgency of the problems arising from ethnic conflict — and the responsibilities both of students of politics and political leadership toward coping with these needs.[66]

From the point of view of the future of the ethnic conflict, the most momentous effect of the Turkish invasion is the forceful demographic change imposed on the occupied areas of northern Cyprus. This consists of a policy of moving Turkish settlers (either infiltrators from the south or, according to some reports, colonists from Asia Minor) into Greek villages and towns to occupy the properties of refugee Greek Cypriots.[67] This process of forceful demographic transformation is placed in its proper symbolic context by Turkicizing place names, by destroying monuments of Greek culture, by turning Orthodox churches into mosques, and by erecting statues of Kemal Ataturk in the occupied areas. We cannot forecast what the precise outcome of this will be, but there can be no doubt that it will have a powerful impact on the future pattern of interethnic relations in Cyprus and elsewhere.

Epilogue

Whenever Cyprus has captured the attention of students of politics, it has done so as an international problem, an element in the strategy and power relations in the eastern Mediterranean. What has come to be known as the *Cyprus question,* essentially a left-over of the Eastern question of old, has involved the issue of control over a strategically located island at the threshold of the Near East. We have tried to shift the focus from the international to the do-mestic aspect of conflict in Cyprus by considering the emergence of the ethnic dispute that has dominated the politics of the island for many years.

From a theoretical point of view, we have tried to point at the relation between the workings of social change and the evolution of the ethnic conflict. The most significant finding in this connection is the fact that despite the effort to concentrate on domestic social and political processes, it is ultimately impossible to consider the nature of ethnic conflict in Cyprus without discussing international politics — especially at all those points when instability and strife escalate in the island. This points at the close linkages between the politics of inter- and intraethnic conflict in Cyprus with internation-al power politics in the area. Instability in Cyprus tends to be telescoped and engulf the politics and foreign relations of Greece and Turkey, and through the 1950s and early 1960s British imperial policy in the Middle East as well. All this in turn affects the inter-national equilibrium in a sensitive and fragile geopolitical region. Conversely, conflict and instability in Cyprus are influenced, and domestic developments are often distorted by the attempts of outside powers to shape the political situation in the eastern Mediterranean in their own interest. Through a variety of social and political processes, internal conflict in Cyprus is internationalized and its outcome becomes dependent upon external factors.[68]

External sources have contributed greatly to the stimulation and exacerbation of conflict within Cyprus. Initially British colonial policy and the nationalist influences emanating from Greece and Turkey provided the context and the momentum needed for the escalation of ethnic strife. As NATO implemented Cold War Ameri-can policies nurtured the conflict indirectly, and then more directly in the recent past (early 1970s),[69] they promoted the partition and NATOization of Cyprus. In this phase both Greece and Turkey be-came — willingly and consciously — the channels through which systemic NATO pressures were exercised on Cyprus, a nonmember of the alliance. The close historical, national, and social ties of the island with these two countries ultimately provided the most effective conduits to those who knew how to manipulate these intimate ethnic bonds in order to undermine and subvert the Republic of Cyprus. The contribution that the experience of Cyprus has to make to the comparative study of ethnic conflict concerns primarily the importance of exogenous sources in the creation and intensification of communal antagonism.

Still, the force of this claim rests significantly on the evidence that one can adduce in support of an argument that in the absence of outside pressures ethnic conflict could have been regulated in the context of democratic coexistence and elimination of violent confrontation. A number of indications, possibilities, and trends could be interpreted in this light. Indeed the history of Cyprus is as much one of ethnic diversity and conflict as it is a history of ethnic coexistence. A reading of this history clearly suggests that ethnic conflict may have been equally the result of certain politi-cal choices and political misjudgments within Cyprus as it was the outcome of outside policies. But it is equally clear from the historical record that after the bitter experience of violent conflict, both a maturity of political wills and the direction of social devel-opments were pointing confidently toward conflict resolution.

There is nothing inexorable about ethnic conflict: complete ethnic assimilation and the creation of new unified nationalities is probably unrealistic to expect — and certainly we should not be understood to mean this when we discuss the possibilities of conflict resolution and political reintegration. But this is beside the point: ethnic coexistence based on mutual accommodation of fundamental needs and aspirations has proved possible wherever appropriate motivations could be put to work.[70] What outside interference did in Cyprus was to stifle the motivation for conflict regulation whenever it appeared. As a consequence, Cyprus has never been given the chance to resolve its ethnic and political problems on its own. On the contrary both ethnic conflict and intraethnic dissension have always been effectively manipulated by outside powers to promote their own objectives and designs on Cyprus. In this sense, conflict within Cypriot society provided the needed opportunities for foreign intervention.

The claim that communal separation is the only workable solution to ethnic conflicts and, in the case of Cyprus, that partition is the only alternative to continuing violence appears very much like a self-fulfilling prophecy and conceptually is perhaps not unrelated to the failure of theories of ethnic conflict and political integration to take into account the disruptive effects of foreign interference. Characteristically, the argument for partition is advanced in the case of Cyprus but not in connection with many other ethnically diverse societies ridden with communal problems. Indeed in Cyprus partition could be achieved only at the price of a bloody invasion, a vicious war, and a policy of forced ethnic separation designed to destroy the basis of ethnic coexistence before any other alternative strategies of conflict resolution could be tested: the development of class-based democratic politics to supplant ethnic cleavages, the new loyalties that a development-oriented welfare state could have nurtured, the shared stakes in a developing economy, and a cultural dialogue to replace the antagonism of traditional nationalist symbols and stereotypes with the discovery of common experiences and values. All of these still carry real possibilities for peace and cooperation, and it is for this reason that the fate of Cyprus is all the more tragic.

Notes

1. In preparing this chapter, we benefited from the comments of Simon Simeonides of the Harvard Law School and Daniel P. Tompkins of Swarthmore College.

2. For an analysis of these aspects of the problem, *see* the interpretive essay by Paschalis M. Kitromilides, "Cyprus: The Nature of Ethnic Conflict," in *U.S. Foreign Policy toward Greece and Cyprus,* ed. T. A. Couloumbis and S. M. Hicks (Washington, D.C.: The Center for Mediterranean Studies, 1975), p.83.

3. For the meaning of *millet* and the *millet* system, *see* Bernard Lewis, *The Emergence of Modern Turkey* (London: Oxford University Press, 1968), p.335.

4. For the history of Cyprus as an Ottoman province, *see* Sir George Hill, *A History of Cyprus* (Cambridge, England: Cambridge University Press, 1952), 4: 1–400; Sir Harry C. Luke, *Cyprus under the Turks 1571–1878* (London: Oxford University Press, 1921); Doros Alastos, *Cyprus in History* (London: Zeno Publishers,

1955), pp.234–301.

For the ethnological evolution of the population of Cyprus in this period, *see* Theodore Popadopoullos, *Social and Historical Data on Population 1570–1881* (Nicosia: Cyprus Research Centre, 1965). For the problem of conversions to Islam, *see* the evidence presented in idem, "Recent Islamizations of Rural Population in Cyprus" (in Greek), *Kypriakai Spoudai* 29 (1965): 27–48. *Also see* C. F. Beckingham, "The Turks of Cyprus," *The Journal of the Royal Anthropological Institute* 87, part 2 (July–December 1957): 165–74.

5. For the historical character of the phenomenon of Greek-Turkish symbiosis, *see* the monumental work of Speros Vryonis, Jr., *The Decline of Medieval Hellenism in Asia Minor and the Process of Islamization from the Eleventh to the Fifteenth Century* (Los Angeles: University of California Press, 1971), especially pp.444–97.

6. For a detailed account, *see* D. E. Lee, *Great Britain and the Cyprus Convention Policy of 1878* (Cambridge, Mass.: Harvard Historical Studies, no. 38, 1934).

7. Hill, pp.518–19.

8. For politics under the British, *see* Hill, and Alastos, pp.302–381.

9. For an analysis of this process, *see* Adamantia Pollis, "Systemic Factors and the Failure of Political Integration in Cyprus" (paper presented at the International Studies Association Convention, Washington, D.C., February 1975), pp.14–21.

10. The account of the *Enosis* movement in Hill, pp.488–568, is very detailed but obviously biased and lacks any wider perspective. It should be read in the light of Alastos, pp.330. The best account of the 1931 uprising is still perhaps that by Arnold Toynbee, *Survey of International Affairs 1931* (London: Oxford University Press, 1932), pp.354–94.

11. *See Treaty of Peace with Turkey,* Signed at Lausanne on 24 July 1923, Cmd 1929 (London: H. M. Stationery Office, 1923). Note Article 16 (p. 21) by which Turkey renounces all rights of sovereignty on territories outside her frontiers as specified in the treaty; and Article 20 (p.23) by which Turkey recognizes the annexation of Cyprus by Britain.

12. Developments in Cyprus between 1946–59 are covered in detail in the recent two-volume work of François Crouzet, *Le Conflit de Chypre, 1946–1959* (Brussels: Bruylant, 1973).

13. Ibid., 1: 266–77. For the reactions of the Turkish Cypriots, pp.303–307.

14. Coral Bell, *Survey of International Affairs 1954* (London: Oxford University Press, 1957), pp.173–84. The British attitude was expressed in the refusal of Prime Minister Eden to discuss the future of Cyprus with Greek Prime Minister Papagos and in the statement in the House of Commons by the Minister of State at the Colonial Office Henry Hopkinson that change of sovereignty over Cyprus could not be contemplated. All this could and was interpreted by the Greek government and the Greek Cypriots to mean that a settlement through direct Anglo-Greek diplomacy was not possible. For relevant documents *see* D. Folliot, ed., *Documents on International Affairs 1954* (London: Oxford University Press, 1957), pp.227–42. *See also* Stephen G. Xydis, "Toward Toil and Moil in Cyprus," *The Middle East Journal* 20, no. 1 (Winter 1966): 1–19, for events leading up to the outbreak of the anticolonial struggle in Cyprus.

15. On the E.O.K.A. struggle, *see* Doros Alastos, *Cyprus Guerrilla: Grivas, Makarios, and the British* (London: Heinemann, 1960); and Charles Foley, *Island in Revolt* (London: Longmans, 1962). Crouzet, 2: 481–649, provides the most recent and synthetic account drawing on voluminous documentation.

16. For the theoretical foundation of these views *see* Karl W. Deutsch, *Nationalism and Social Communication* (Cambridge, Mass.: M.I.T. Press, 1953). For a conceptualization of the political implications of socioeconomic change on which the previous discussion is based, *see* idem , "Social Mobilization and Political Development," *The American Political Science Review* 55, no. 3 (September 1961): 493–514.

17. On the precipitation of ethnic conflict by the approach of independence, *see* Cynthia H. Enloe, *Ethnic Conflict and Political Development* (Boston: Little, Brown and Co., 1973), p. 22: "as soon as independence or foreign economic pressures make independence and pooling of scarce resources imperative, institutional expressions of cultural separateness become threats to stability, instead of the assurances of social harmony they once were."

18. *See* Adamantia Pollis, "Intergroup Conflict and British Colonial Policy, The Case of Cyprus," *Comparative Politics* 5, no. 4 (July 1973): 575–99. For the historical origins of this policy, *see* Ronald Robinson and John Gallagher, *Africa and the Victorians* (Garden City: Doubleday, 1968), pp.10–11.

19. Statistics and Research Department, Ministry of Finance, *Statistical Abstract, 1970, no. 16* (Nicosia, Cyprus: Printing Office of the Republic of Cyprus, 1970), p.24.

20. The escalation of conflict in the 1950s has stimulated voluminous writing on the Cyprus question, including many accounts by journalists, official papers, and many pamphlets explaining the respective viewpoints of those involved. The bibliography of primary sources in Crouzet, 2: 1,155—1,166, though incomplete is very useful. Robert Stephens, *Cyprus: A Place of Arms* (London: Pall Mall, 1966), is a useful account by a distinguished journalist with great experience in the politics of the eastern Mediterranean. Important scholarly studies of this phase of the problem of Cyprus are, in addition to Crouzet, Stephen G. Xydis, *Cyprus: Conflict and Conciliation 1954—1958* (Columbus, Ohio: Ohio State University Press, 1967); Leontios Ierodiakonou, *The Cyprus Question* (Stockholm: Almquist and Wiksell, 1971); Pantazis Terlexis, *Diplomacy and Politics of the Cyprus Question* (in Greek) (Athens: Rappas, 1971). The most serious statement of the Turkish point of view is that by Suat Bilge, *Le Conflit de Chypre et les Cypriotes Turcs* (Ankara: Publications de la Faculté des Sciences Politiques de l'Université d'Ankara, 1961). Finally, a valuable source of information and insights is C. Christides, *The Cyprus Question and Greek-Turkish Matters* (in Greek) (Athens: 1967).

21. The pertinent documents appear in Royal Institute of International Affairs, *Documents on International Affairs 1958, 1959,* ed. G. King, *1960,* ed. R. Gott (London: Oxford University Press, 1962, 1963, 1964), pp.376—95, 541—52; 422—27, respectively. The complex diplomacy of the years 1958—60 leading up to the independence of Cyprus is studied in great detail in Stephen G. Xydis, *Cyprus: Reluctant Republic* (The Hague: Mouton, 1973).

22. For the impact of the Cyprus problem on the politics of Greece, *see* Theodore A. Couloumbis, *Greek Political Reaction to American and NATO Influences* (New Haven, Conn.: Yale University Press, 1966), pp.93. For Turkey, *see* Frank Tachau, "The Face of Turkish Nationalism as Reflected in the Cyprus Dispute," *The Middle East Journal* 13, no. 3 (Summer 1959): 262—72. For the British decision to relinquish sovereignty over Cyprus, *see* Naomi Rosenbaum, " Success in Foreign Policy: The British in Cyprus, 1878—1960," *Canadian Journal of Political Science* 3, no. 4 (December 1970): 605—27.

23. For the text of the Treaties of Guarantee and Establish-

ment, *see United Nations Series,* 1960, 382: 3–16. Several pages of Annexes to the Treaty of Establishment follow. The Treaty of Alliance appears in the *United Nations Treaty Series,* 1961, 397: 287–95.

24. The Cyprus constitution is analyzed in Stanley Kyriakides, *Cyprus: Constitutionalism and Crisis Government* (Philadelphia: University of Pennsylvania Press, 1968), pp.53–71.

25. *See* the analysis and evaluation in S. A. de Smith, *The New Commonwealth and Its Constitutions* (London: Stevens, 1964), pp.282–96. Note the characteristic remark on p.285: "Constitutionalism has run riot in harness with communalism."

26. Kyriakides, pp.72–103.

27. Ibid, pp.85–86, for revealing views of Turkish Cypriot deputies.

28. The text of President Makarios's thirteen proposed amendments appears in *International Relations* 2, no. 5 (April 1964): 8–24. *See* Dimitri Bitsios, *Critical Hours* (in Greek) (Athens: 1973), pp.134–37, on the encouragement given to the Archbishop in this initiative by the then British High Commissioner in Cyprus.

29. For accounts of the 1963–64 crisis, *see* Charles Foley, *Legacy of Strife: Cyprus from Rebellion to Civil War* (Baltimore, Md.: Penguin, 1964); Stephens, pp.168–91; Kyriakides, pp.104–134, which is based on detailed primary-source documentation; George S. Harris, *Troubled Alliance: Turkish-American Problems in Historical Perspective, 1945–1971* (Stanford, Calif.: Hoover Institution Press, 1972), pp.105–124, which brings the story up to the 1967 crisis. On U.S. involvement in that crisis, *see* Edward Weintal and Charles Bartlett, *Facing the Brink* (New York: Scribner, 1967), pp.16–36. For relevant documents, *see American Foreign Policy Current Documents 1964* (Department of State Publication 8253, Released August 1967), pp.555–6.

30. Text of the resolution in *19 United Nations Security Council Official Record, Supplement, January–March 1964* (U.N. Doc. S/5575, 1964), pp.102–103. For the appeal and the debates, *see 19 U.N. S.C.O.R.,* Meetings 1094 to 1103 (17 February to 13 March 1964).

31. Detailed accounts on the activities of the U.N.F.I.CYP. are provided in the reports submitted by the U.N. Secretary-General to the Security Council every six months since 1964 and published in the Supplements of the S.C.O.R. (usually in the June and

December issues). An important contribution to the subject is that by Michael Harbottle, *The Impartial Soldier* (London: Oxford University Press, 1970). *See also* James Stegenga, "U.N. Peacekeeping: The Cyprus Venture," *Journal of Peace Research* 7, no. 1 (1970): 1–15.

32. *See* Kemal H. Karpat, "Solution in Cyprus: Federation," *The Cyprus Dilemma: Options for Peace* (New York: Institute for Mediterranean Affairs, 1967), pp.35–54. This essay expressing the Turkish view on Cyprus states that the concentration of the Turkish Cypriot community in certain areas of the island following the 1963–64 breakdown created the geographical basis for a cantonal federation. The author suggests that four Turkish Cypriot and six or seven Greek Cypriot cantons could be formed and united in a federal structure that, he suggests, due to the special needs of Cyprus ought to be tighter than that of Switzerland.

33. *See* "Report of the Secretary-General on the U.N. Operation in Cyprus,"*19 U.N. S.C.O.R., (*Doc S/6102, 12 December 1964, paragraph 32, Supp. October-December 1964), pp.230–31; "Report of the Secretary-General on the U.N. Operation in Cyprus," *20 U.N. S.C.O.P.* (Doc. S/6228, 10 March 1965, paragraphs 53–56, Supp. January–March 1905), pp.118–19.

34. The foreign diplomatic missions to Cyprus and U.N. officials continued to consult with the Turkish Cypriot leadership. Dr. Kuchuk and, after February 1973, Mr. Denktash were considered as the vice-president of the Republic.

35. *See* Clifford Geertz, "The Integrative Revolution: Primordial Sentiments and Civil Politics in the New States," *Old Societies and New States,* ed. Clifford Geertz (New York: Free Press, 1963), pp.105–157.

36. The Turkish insistence on the partition of Cyprus in the guise of geographical separation of the two communities was formally reiterated to the U.N. mediator. *See* "Report of the United Nations Mediator on Cyprus to the Secretary-General," *20 U.N. S.C.O.R.* (Doc. S/6253, 26 March 1965, paragraph: 73–75, 97–98, 107–109, Supp. January–March 1965), pp.199–253.

37. For details, *see* Pollis, pp.31–34.

38. A very good recent study of the legal aspects of the disputes over Cyprus in their political context is Thomas Ehrlich, *Cyprus 1958–1967* (London: Oxford University Press, 1974).

39. Xydis, *Cyprus: Reluctant Republic,* ch. 11, pp.420, for

the reservations of Archbishop Makarios concerning the agreements and the pressures exerted on him by the Greek government.

40. For the full arguments of the government of Cyprus concerning the Treaty of Guarantee, *see 19 U.N.S.C.O.R..'* 109th Meeting (27 February 1964), pp.15—21. *see also* the Charter of the United Nations, Articles 2 (1), 2 (4), and 103, all of which can be invoked against the validity of the Treaty of Guarantee. This treaty also contravenes Article 53 of the 1969 Vienna Convention on the Law of Treaties.

41. *20 U.N. General Assembly Official Records,* 1402d Plenary Meeting, 18 December 1965, pp.2—11. The vote on this resolution was 47 for, 5 against, 54 abstaining. Text of Resolution 2077 in *20 U.N. G.A.O.R., Annexes,* 3:13.

42. *See* Greek Cypriot official views as outlined in the "Report by the U.N. Mediator on Cyprus to the Secretary General," paragraphs 92—93.

43. For a fuller statement of Turkish arguments, *see 19 U.N. S.C.O.R.,* 1045th Meeting, 18 February 1964, pp.34—40.

44. *U.N. Treaty Series,* 382: 6.

45. The unfolding of the conflict in the 1960s has not yet formed the object of scholarly studies comparable to those that analyze events in the 1950s. For general surveys, *see* Christides, pp.249—300; Kyriakides, pp.135—170; Linda B. Miller, *Cyprus, The Law and Politics of Civil Strife,* Occasional Papers in International Affairs (Cambridge, Mass.: Harvard University, Center for International Affairs, 1968).

46. The involvement of the United Nations in the Cyprus problem and the discussion of the issue in the Security Council and General Assembly repeatedly since 1964 is covered regularly in successive volumes of the *U.N. Monthly Chronicle.*

47. For full citation, *see* note 36 above. For the substantive proposals of the mediator, note in particular paragraphs 132—48 on the issues of independence, self-determination, and international peace; 149—57 on the structure of the state, and 158—65 on the protection of the individual and minority rights.

48. The involvement of NATO in the 1963—64 crisis is assessed in Philip Windsor, "NATO and the Cyprus Crisis," *Adelphi Papers, no. 14* (London: Institute of Strategic Studies, 1964).

49. For the relevant document, *see American Foreign Policy*

Current Documents 1964, pp.556–57.

50. For an official U.S. assessment of the Cyprus problem, *see* George Ball, "The Responsibilities of a Global Power," *Department of State Bulletin* 51 (1964): 476–77. For Acheson's own account of his activities, *see* Dean Acheson, "Cyprus: The Anatomy of the Problem," *Chicago Bar Record* 46, no. 8 (May 1965):349.

51. For an excellent analysis of the relations between the governments of Greece and Cyprus in the period 1960–72, *see* the essay by Alexander G. Xydis, "The Psychological Complex," in *Makarios and his Allies* (in Greek), ed. A. G. Xydis, Sp. Linardatos, and K. Chadjiargyris (Athens: Gutenberg, 1972), pp.11–40.

52. *See* C. A. Theodoulou, "Quelques aspects de la crise chypriote actuelle," *Politique Etrangere* 37, no. 2 (1972): 221–33. Agreement was repeatedly reported as being very close at hand, but in all those occasions the following pattern would recur in the behavior of the Turkish side: the Turkish Cypriot negotiator would fly to Ankara to brief the Turkish government on the progress of the talks; upon his return to Cyprus, however, the Turkish views would be invariably announced as hardened and the previous points of agreements discarded. This systematic subversion of all agreements reached in intra-Cypriot negotiations by Ankara was last manifested in the rejection of an agreement over the operation of Nicosia International Airport, after the abortive resumption of talks in January 1975. *See* The New York *Times*, 24 January 1975, p.3, and 1 February 1975, p.2.

53. For the social-psychological dynamics of such situations and the importance of direct communication for the resolution of conflict, *see* John W. Burton, *Conflict and Communication: The Use of Controlled Communication in International Relations* (London: Macmillan, 1969). *See also* Herbert C. Kelman's evaluation of this work, "The Problem-Solving Workshop in Conflict Resolution," in *Communication in International Politics,* ed. Richard L. Merritt (Urbana, Ill.: University of Illinois Press, 1972), pp.168–204. For an argument that by the late 1960s the Cyprus conflict was becoming a problem of misperception, *see* John W. Burton, *World Society* (Cambridge: Cambridge University Press, 1972), pp.55–59, 68–69, 75–77.

54. It should be added here that the government of Cyprus had repeatedly argued for demilitarization of the island in the context of a settlement. *See*, for instance, the "Report of the U.N.

Mediator," paragraph 92.

55. The emergence of political parties and electoral politics in their social context are examined in Paschalis M. Kitromilides, *Patterns of Politics in Cyprus* (thesis, Wesleyan University, 1972). *See also* Peter Loizos, *The Greek Gift: Politics in a Cypriot Village* (Oxford: Blackwell, 1975), pp.235–88.

56. The best sources on economic planning and development in Cyprus are *The Second Five-Year Plan, 1967–1971* and *The Third Five-Year Plan, 1972–1976,* both prepared by the Planning Bureau of the Republic of Cyprus and containing all the relevant statistical information on achievements, targets, and problems in the economic development of Cyprus. The performance of Cyprus can be best appreciated in a comparative perspective as presented in the special report on economic development published in *The UNESCO Courier,* February 1970 (23d year), pp.22–23; in a survey of 69 developing countries, Cyprus is classified in the category of those with both the highest growth rate and per capita income in the decade of the 1960s.

57. *See* Stahis Panagides, "Communal Conflict and Economic Considerations: The Case of Cyprus," *Journal of Peace Research* 5, (1968): 133–45.

58. According to the 1960 Constitution, such matters were to be administered by the Communal Chambers. *See* Constitution of Cyprus, Part V, Articles 86–111, in *Constitutions of Nations,* ed. A. T. Peaslee (The Hague: Nijhoff, 1968), 3: 170–78. In his amendments in 1963, President Makarios proposed the abolition of the Greek Communal Chamber and the delegation of its functions to the Ministry of Education for reasons of increased governmental efficiency. He stated however that the Turkish Cypriot community was free to retain its Communal Chamber.

59. *See* note 52 above.

60. *See* note 36 above. For an informative survey of the views of the various political parties of Turkey on Cyprus, *see* Ferenc Vali, *Bridge across the Bosporus: The Foreign Policy of Turkey* (Baltimore, Md.: Johns Hopkins Press, 1971), pp.78–99.

61. *See* Richard D. Robinson, *The First Turkish Republic* (Cambridge, Mass.: Harvard University Press, 1965), p.188. For the manipulation of the public's sensitivity over Cyprus in Turkish domestic politics, *see* idem, pp.99–114, 358–64.

62. The following view is revealing as to how Cyprus is per-

ceived in certain American quarters: "As a center of operations directed toward the Soviet bloc — presuming overflight rights with Turkey — Cyprus has great potential. Moscow is only 1,500 air miles from Cyprus airstrips; Baku, the Soviet oil center on the Caspian Sea, lies only 1,000 miles away; Rostov, a main industrial center on the Don River, is 900 miles distant; Sverdlovsk, a center of Soviet heavy industry, is situated at a distance of 2,000 miles. In fact, Batum, the nearest point in the Soviet Union from Cyprus, is only 830 miles away, and the nearest city in the Soviet bloc, the Bulgarian city of Akhtopol, is a mere 550 air miles. Cyprus thus occupies a peculiarly strategic location as an air base." T. W. Adams, *A.K.E.L.: The Communist Party of Cyprus* (Standord, Calif.: Hoover Institution Press, 1971), p.87.

63. The study of U.S. policy toward Cyprus has been placed on an entirely new basis by the research of Van Coufoudakis, who has presented convincing arguments and documentation supporting a view of a continuity of American policy since the 1950s in pursuit of the partition of Cyprus as the ideal solution from the vantage point of American interest. *See* Van Coufoudakis, "United States Foreign Policy and the Cyprus Question: A Case Study in Cold War Diplomacy" (paper presented at the 16th Annual Convention of the International Studies Association, Washington, D.C., 22 February 1975).

64. More correctly it can be said that Greece agreed to cooperate in undermining the independence of Cyprus already under the governments that came to power after the fall of the Papandreou government in 1965. For an incisive critique, *see* Christides, pp.9—122. On the policy of the Greek military junta toward Cyprus, *see* Alexander G. Xydis, "The Military Regime's Foreign Policy," *Greece Under Military Rule*, ed. Richard Clogg and George Yannopoulos (New York: Basic Books, 1972) pp.191—209. A strand of radical opinion tends to attribute the advent of the military dictatorship in Greece to the increasing urgency felt by NATO and the U.S. to quell the independent stands taken by the Papandreou government in opposing the partition of Cyprus. *See* Andreas Papandreou, *Democracy at Gunpoint: The Greek Front* (Garden City, N.Y.: Doubleday, 1970), pp.129—41; and Constantine Tsoucalas, *The Greek Tragedy* (London: Penguin, 1969) pp.153—65, 189—91.

65. For the sociological character and social bases of this movement, *see* Peter Loizos, "The Progress of Greek Nationalism in Cyprus, 1878—1970," in *Choice and Change: Essays in Honour of*

Lucy Mair, ed. J. Davis (L.S.E. Monographs on Social Anthropology, no. 50, 1974), pp.114–33; Kyriacos Markides, "Social Change and the Rise and Decline of Social Movements: The Case of Cyprus," *American Ethnologist* 1, no.2 (May 1974): 304–330.

66. The fullest account of these developments yet available is that by Laurence Stern, "Bitter Lessons: How We Failed in Cyprus," *Foreign Policy* 19 (Summer 1975): 34–78.

67. The New York *Times,* 2 November 1974, pp.1, 7; idem, 17 January 1975, p.8; idem, 10 February 1975, p.10, and idem 3 July 1975, p.2. On the pressures on the Greek Cypriots to leave the occupied area, *see* The Manchester *Guardian Weekly,* 1 March 1975.

68. This and the following paragraph draw on the conceptualizations advanced in James N. Rosenau, ed., *International Aspects of Civil Strife* (Princeton, N.J.: Princeton University Press, 1964), pp.1–44; and idem, *The Scientific Study of Foreign Policy* (New York: Free Press, 1971), pp.307–338.

69. Increasing indications of covert American involvement, destabilizing activities, and encouragement of local subversion in Cyprus are becoming available. *See* Stern, for some hints in this direction.

70. *See* Eric Nordlinger, *Conflict Regulation in Divided Societies,* Occasional Papers in International Affairs, no. 29 (Cambridge, Mass.: Center for International Affairs, Harvard University, 1972).

The Afro-Saxons

Ali A. Mazrui

Before the end of this century there will probably be more black people who speak the English language as their native tongue than there will be British people. Already black Americans alone, who speak the language as a first language, are nearly the equivalent of half the population of Great Britain. In addition there are a few more million black speakers of the language scattered round the Caribbean and the northern fringes of South America. Within the African continent, the only black native speakers of the English language so far are members of the ruling community of Liberia, descended from black Americans, and a few in places like Sierra Leone. But at least as important a phenomenon is the growing number of educated African families using English as the language of the home. A number of African children, especially in West Africa but increasingly in East Africa, are growing up bilingual in English and their own African language because their parents are highly educated and therefore speak English to each other.

It is these considerations that make it likely that by the end of the twentieth century there will be more black native speakers of the English language than there are speakers of it in the British Isles. An Afro-Saxon population, linguistically influential, would have truly come into being. Yet this kind of situation has its tensions. The Anglo-Saxons, liberal in some spheres but racially exclusive in their history, have tended to create complexes among those they have ruled or dominated. And where English conquers the black man as effectively as he was once conquered by the Anglo-Saxon race, tensions between dignity and linguistic rationality are unavoidable.

James Baldwin, one of the most gifted black users of the English language living today, illustrates this point. Baldwin once wrote an article on how he stopped hating Shakespeare. He admitted that part of his hate of Shakespeare as such was originally the phenomenon of turning away from "that monstrous achievement with a kind of sick envy." In Baldwin's most anti-English days, he condemned Shakespeare for his chauvinism ("This England" indeed!). But his most important area of revulsion against Shakespeare was in connection with his being a black man condemned to being a native speaker of the English language, and in his case to writing in that language.

Some of the irritation came from the characters created by Shakespeare himself. Baldwin mentions how some Jews have, at times, been bitterly resentful of Shylock. Baldwin, in turn, as a black man, was bitter about Caliban and dubious about Othello.

Baldwin's quarrel with the English language was that it did not reflect any of his experience. But when one day he found himself in a non-English-speaking situation, having to think and speak in French, Baldwin began to see Shakespeare and the English language in a new light.

> If the language was not my own, it might be the fault of the language; but it might also be my fault. Perhaps the language was not my own because I have never attempted to use it, had only learnt to imitate it. If this were so, then it might

be made to bear the burden of my experience if I could find the stamina to challenge it, and me, to such a test.[1]

Baldwin found support for this possibility from two mighty witnesses — his black ancestors, who had evolved the sorrow songs, the blues and jazz, and created an entirely new idiom in an over-whelmingly hostile place; but Baldwin also found support from Shakespeare, whom he now regarded as the last bawdy writer in the English language.

> Shakespeare's bawdiness became very important to me since bawdiness was one of the elements of jazz and revealed a tremendous, loving, and realistic respect for the body, and that ineffable force which the body contains, which Americans have mostly lost, which I had experienced only among Ne-groes, and of which I had been taught to be ashamed.[2]

The language with which Baldwin had grown up had certainly not been the King's English. It had been the English of the black man in the New World.

> An immense experience had forged this language, it had been (and remains) one of the tools of the people's survival, and it revealed expectations which no white American could easily entertain.[3]

What ought to be grasped here, in addition, is that the bawdi-ness of Shakespeare was intended for public performance. In Shake-speare and in drama at large we, therefore, have that important link between the literature of oral utterance and the literature of the written word. The character of Falstaff was indeed written by Shakespeare, but it had to be made to live on the stage. The writing of a play before its performance would be alien to indigenous East African tradition; but the performance of the play on the stage could reestablish a link with East Africa's dramatic experience. Much of the poetry of Africa was indistinguishable from song — it was intended for recitation in a collective context, rather than for the private enjoyment of one individual lover of poetry retreating to an isolated spot for solitary indulgence.

The mighty lines of Shakespeare were not primarily intended for solitary indulgence either. They were intended for the throbbing spontaneity of Elizabethans, reminiscent in their very sense of involvement with the performance and hearty assimilation into the mood of the moment of audiences in Africa, black America, and the West Indies.

Yet because Shakespeare wrote his plays, the question of identity was important. There were plays by Shakespeare, whereas much of African oral literature is a literature without authors. The African experience is a collective heritage, modified and augmented, sometimes diluted, as it passes from person to person, from generation to generation. But the heritage of Shakespeare, precisely because he wrote the plays and made them bear his name, has individualized the genius. It has pinpointed the fountain of creativity. And with that focusing there has emerged a whole branch of knowledge known as *Shakespeare studies,* ranging from minute discussion of original editions of certain plays to discussions connected with the biographical details of the author.

Yet in the case of Shakespeare, there is, at least, one residual link with the kind of literature where authorship retains an element of uncertainty. Disputes have persistently erupted every century as to whether Shakespeare's plays were indeed written by Shakespeare. Disputes as to whether he was the front man for dramatic exercises written by Bacon or Christopher Marlowe have periodically animated the scholarly world. There are those who, echoing traditional African attitudes, have argued that it did not matter who had written *Hamlet;* the play was a collective inheritance. Shakespeare's plays might just as well have been, according to this school, plays without authors or plays by an anonymous contributor to English civilization.

In short, the written word and, in the case of music the written notes, have so far been indispensable both in preserving the details of what was originally created and, often, in preserving knowledge about authorships. The two forms of preservation are, of course, interrelated. A written record on its own that at the Globe theater a play called *Hamlet* was performed, authored by William Shakespeare, would not be enough if the play then became transmitted from generation to generation by memory. Much of the structure would change, the outlines of the characters could be transformed, the whole exercise might become radically different. A play transmitted by word of mouth from generation to generation, from the sixteenth century, would hardly survive intact by the time it was being enacted from memory at the National Theatre in Kampala. The written word, then, becomes important both in determining authorship and in preserving that which was actually authored.

And precisely because the written word is a method of conservation, it also helps to stabilize a language. Ideas that are not reduced to writing can be very perishable indeed. Where is the complete wealth of Africa's wisdom over the centuries? Africa must have had great philosophers, great mystics, even great eccentrics all trying out new ideas. But much of that old intellectual activity has simply been lost to us. Yes, Africa does indeed have oral tradition. Some of Africa's wisdom has been transmitted, from generation to generation, by word of mouth. But oral tradition tends overwhelmingly to be the transmission of consensus rather than heresy, of accepted ideas rather than innovative, intellectual deviations. In Africa's history, many of the latter kind of ideas, which might indeed have commanded acceptance one or two generations later had they been preserved in writing, died very early because they were never so recorded. Ancient radicalism did not find the conserving blessing of the written word.

Among the things that change very fast when there is no widespread tradition of writing is, quite simply, language itself. Swahili has had a written tradition for two or three centuries, but it has not been very widespread. One consequence of this is the fact that the Swahili of the 1950s differs more from the Swahili of the 1970s than the English of the 1850s differs from the English of the 1970s. English has changed less rapidly partly because of the conserving influence of a literate culture on the language as a whole. It is true that literacy in the early part of the nineteenth century in England was far from universal. But the literate section of the community had become so big, and its impact on the rest of the population so great, that much of the language of the other classes of nineteenth-century England has survived with little change to the 1970s.

But there are also disadvantages in the preservation of all aspects of language. The disadvantages might lie partly in consolidating, and deepening, even those aspects of the language that need to be changed. One of the least explored of these aspects is metaphor. Metaphor accumulates certain associations and, if the language undergoes relatively little change, that wealth of associations may be impossible to dissipate should this ever become desirable.

Black Metaphor and English Semantics

This is what brings us to residual racism in English metaphor on matters connected with white and black. In the correspondence columns of the monthly magazine *Africa Report* was a bitter complaint from a Tanzanian living in the United States who was critical of President Nyerere's regime. The Tanzanian complained that articles published about his country tended to "whitewash" the regime and its failings. I have sometimes caught myself saying that one of "the blackest stains" on Nyerere's career was his decision to let his former ambassador in Washington, Othman Sherrif, be taken to Zanzibar, probably to his death.

In such a context, a different metaphor could be used if one thought of it soon enough. But how much of a choice in synonyms is there to discuss blackmail? Or something sold on the black market?

Most of the time when these words are used, we are not connecting them with any racist tradition that associates black with evil and white with goodness. The metaphor is so much part of the English language, beautifully integrated, ready for use unconsciously in a spontaneous flow. In the metaphor of the English language black has repeatedly, and in a variety of contexts, decidedly negative connotations. White has ambivalent connotations but, more often, favorable ones. The connotations have been so stabilized that users of the language are unconscious of those wider links with racist traditions. But does not the unconsciousness make the situation worse than ever?

It would not matter if English continued to be the language of the English people. But precisely because it is the most eligible candidate for universality, and also because black native speakers of the language are on their way toward becoming more numerous than the inhabitants of the British Isles, the case for a gradual diversification of English metaphor in the area of color becomes important for

African writers. They need not change the word *blackmail* into *whitemail*, or *black market* into *white* or *brown market*; but a new consciousness of the residual racism of the English language and new imaginative coinings of alternative metaphors, at least within African versions of the English language, would help to improve the credentials of the English language as an African medium. In accepting the English language as their own, black people should not accept passively and uncritically. There may be a case for the deracialization of the English language.

As a starting point in such an endeavor, we should at least be aware of the broad negative connotations that the metaphor of blackness has assumed in the English language. There is, first, the association of blackness with evil; second, there is the association of blackness with void and emptiness; third, there is the association of blackness with death. These three areas of negative assoication have, in fact, multiple subassociations. The association with death, for example, also makes black the color of grief. Conversely, if war is death, white becomes the color of peace. The white dove becomes the messenger of reconciliation.

But let us take each of these three broad negative connotations in turn: black is evil, black is void, black is death. In some ways, most deeply structured into the language is the notion that black is evil. To some extent the difficulty has its origins in the European-ization of Christianity. As Christianity became a religion whose chief champions were white people, angels gradually became white and the devil became black.

The biblical heritage of the West profoundly influenced meta-phorical usages in more popular literature. With regard to the English language, the Bible and Shakespeare might well be the greatest single contributors to popular metaphor. From the point of view of the association of black with evil, nothing has captured it more sharply than Blake's poem *The Little Black Boy*. The poem exclaims with a startling revelation of this whole universe of metaphor: "And I am black but O My soul is white."

John Bunyan and other religious writers also have suggestions about washing a black man, or an Ethiopian, white as a way of con-ferring upon him salvation. But John Dryden puts limitations on the degree of blackness that is admissible in heaven, as well as on the degree of whiteness that could ever deserve hell. To John Dryden the agony of purgatory is the predicament of he who is "too black for heaven, and yet too white for hell."

Next to the Bible, it is Shakespeare who has had the greatest single impact on the metaphorical evolution of the English language. Problems, therefore, arise when African literary figures, and even African heads of state, find themselves imbibing the Shakespearean idiom.

President Julius Nyerere has even had to confront the ominous task of translating the Bard into Swahili. Nyerere has translated *Julius Caesar* and *The Merchant of Venice,* both of which include metaphors of negative association of blackness. *The Merchant of Venice,* a play partly concerned with racial or religious consciousness, contains references to black people and customs of color. But there is also a very explicit association of the dark complexion with the devil in the play. Portia had had to deal with earlier suitors but also among those who had wanted her was the prince of Morocco. She notes the importance of his dark complexion, even if his entire behavior is saintly. Blake may be satisfied that a black boy may be black but yet have a white soul. Portia had different ideas about the black-skinned prince interested in her.

> If he have the condition of a saint and the complexion of a
> devil, I had rather he should shrive me than wive me.[4]

Mwalimu Julius Nyerere had to grapple with this racialistic insinuation in order to render it into Swahili. He decided to translate "complexion of a devil" to "face of a devil."

Milton Obote, Nyerere's friend and former president of Uganda, was perhaps even more consistent in his admiration of John Milton. The devil portrayed by Milton in *Paradise Lost* had, at least in the initial phases of the rebellion, a heroic stature. Satan had rebelled against the tyrannical omnipotence of God. He had rebelled against the tradition of kneeling to pray, of flattering the Almighty with grand epithet, and of singing hymns in His praise. Until he rebelled, Satan, like all angels was, of course, white. Obote at school and at Makerere College in Uganda admired Satan as a symbol of rebellion against total tyranny. Indeed, Obote adopted the first name of

Milton in honor of the author of *Paradise Lost.*

When Satan and his followers were driven out of Heaven into the great deep, they found themselves lying on the burning lake of hell. John Milton's epithet for hell is "Black Gehenna." From being a white angel, Satan was becoming a black devil. We might almost say that this heroic figure portrayed by Milton, and admired by Obote, was the first black person in eternity. And God had sentenced him from the start to a life of perpetual hell.

Related to the whole tradition of identifying blackness with the devil and whiteness with the angels are the metaphors of shepherds, flocks, sheep, and lambs in the figurative language of Christianity. "The Lord is my shepherd," but what is the Lord to do with the black sheep of Africa?

We are back to the color prejudices of Christianity and of the English language: the sheep and their wool, which is usually white. The black sheep of the family is the deviant, sometimes the wicked, exception.

From blackness and its association with evil there is an easy transition to blackness and death. Sir Patrick Renison, then governor of Kenya, defiantly resisting pressures to release Jomo Kenyatta, bracketed these two associations of darkness and death in his very denunciation of Kenyatta. He called Kenyatta, "Leader into darkness and into death."

The concentration of darkness in the middle of the night carries ominous suggestions of danger and evil. The black cat is often interpreted in this tradition of metaphor as an omen of bad luck. The worst luck was death, and the worst omen impending death.

Alfred Tennyson described a grave as "the gross blackness underneath."[5] The black band round the arm at funerals, the black suit that the dead man is sometimes supposed to wear, the black dress the widow is expected to use — all the cumulative associations of blackness with death. Even in translating *Julius Caesar,* Mwalimu Julius Nyerere had to translate the phrase by Octavious, "Our black sentence." This was the sentence of death passed by the counter-conspirators against those who might have been implicated in the assassination of Caesar.

As for the association of blackness with the void, this has given rise to a number of subassociations ranging from emptiness, ignorance, and primitiveness to sheer depth. The Dark Ages are dark both because we do not know very much about them and because there is a presumption of barbarism and primitivism to them.

It is partly because of these preconceptions concerning emptiness and barbarity that many African nationalists, black as they were in color, objected to Africa being described as "a dark continent." Why were these dark people indignant that their ancestoral land mass should bear the title of *dark continent*? Precisely because their initiation into the connotations of the English language had sensitized them to the negative implications of such a description of Africa.

Darkness as emptiness and barbarity certainly influenced Hugh Trevor-Roper in his dismissal of the concept of African history as being meaningless. In his own infamous words:

> Perhaps, in the future, there will be some African history. . . but at present there is none: there is only the history of the Europeans in Africa. The rest is darkness. . .and darkness is not a subject of history.[6]

Darkness as a characterization of Africa's past is thus resisted by the darkest of all peoples in color — the African nationalists themselves south of the Sahara. The connotations of the English language, with all its cumulation of negative associations in relation to blackness and darkness, are preeminently to blame for these anomalies.

Black Identity and Linguistic Reform

The starting point of black aesthetics must, therefore, be not only the black power motto "Black is Beautiful," but also the insistence that black is neither evil, emptiness, nor death. The Christian symbolism of the black soul, of the black devil, and of the black armband at a funeral might need to be transformed in the pursuit of new aesthetics for the black man.

Resorting to symbolism from African traditions could help gradually to provide alternative metaphors for African English. Death certainly can be as legitimately portrayed by whiteness, if African traditions of body-painting are involved, as by blackness. In the third dimension of Islamic tradition, the dead body is covered in white cloth. And a completely white cloth could be ominously reminiscent of what the Waswahili call *sanda,* the white material that is the last apparel of man.

Of course, there are occasions when African customs themselves equate blackness with negative connotations. But these anomalies are present even in the English language. The simile "deathly white" is perfect English, if one remembers that a white man, when he is dead and no longer has blood flowing in his veins, becomes indeed, at last, really white. The white man only manages to live up to his name when he dies.

The reform of the English language for African purposes has to include an awareness of these issues. Black aesthetics has to rescue blackness and darkness from the stifling weight of negative metaphor.

What emerges from this analysis are three interrelated processes of linguistic reform for the black man's English. The most ambitious of the proposals for reform would amount to the de-Anglicization of the English language. The logic of the universalization of English must lead to its de-Anglicization.

A more modest ambition among linguistic reformers is not the de-Anglicization of the English language but the deracialization. The adoption of the language as the official language of African states is certainly one step in that direction. Another is precisely that effort to rescue the concept of blackness from Satan's embrace.

The third process that flows on logically from the partial de-Anglicization and deracialization of the English language is the more positive aspiration to Africanize it. African writers have a special role to play in experimenting with usages more appropriate to the African experience. Those of their books that find their way into the new systems of education in African countries may help the trend toward the Africanization of English. African fiction in English produced in West Africa is already well on the way toward this kind of commitment. The characters in the novels of Chinua Achebe do not use the Queen's English. They use credible English. As a conscious artist Achebe has himself illustrated how he has sought artistic credibility by maintaining contact with the world of simile and metaphor in West Africa. In his novel *Arrow of God,* the chief priest is telling one of his sons why it is necessary to send him to the mission school:

> I want one of my sons to join these people and be my eyes
> there. If there is nothing in it you will come back. But if there
> is something there you will bring home my share. The world
> is like a Mask, dancing. If you want to see it well you do not
> stand in one place. My spirit tells me that those who do not
> befriend the white man today will be saying *had we known* to-
> morrow.[7]

Achebe himself revels not only in the distinctiveness of West
African English but also in the very fact that writers like him are not
native to the language. He feels inclined to the view that the very
fact of not being native to the language, at least for the time being,
would put the stamp of distinctiveness on African usage.

> So my answer to the question, Can an African ever learn
> English well enough to be able to use it effectively in creative
> writing?, is certainly yes. If on the other hand you ask: Can he
> ever learn to use it like a native speaker? I should say, I hope
> not. It is neither necessary nor desirable for him to be able
> to do so.[8]

Achebe captures the essence of combining the Africanization of the
English language with a continuing commitment to the role of
English as a world language. Achebe's formulation would be well
within our conception of a subfederation of Anglophone cultures,
each sector of the English-speaking world maintaining its own
distinctiveness without departing so far from mutual intelligibility as
to render the language no longer useful as a universal currency. To
use Achebe's words:

> The African writer should aim to use English in a way that
> brings out his message best without altering the language to
> the extent that its value as a medium of international exchange
> will be lost. He should aim at fashioning out of English which
> is at once universal and able to carry his own experience. . . .
> But it will have to be a new English, still in full communion

with its ancestral home but altered to suit its new African surroundings.[9]

The work of the African writer in the English language would be in vain if the educational system were rebelling against English. In Asia, English is to some extent on the defensive. In Malaysia, since the Federation, there has been a strong desire to make all communities speak Malay, and the ambition has been pursued to make Malay not only a compulsory subject in all the schools but also finally the sole official language of the country.

In India, a similar tendency is observable to reduce the areas of education that are covered by English and increase the utilization of Hindi for primary education in at least some parts of the country. It has been estimated that within forty years one-third of the urban population and one-fifteenth of the rural population may become literate in English, but that literacy in Hindi may be equal to that in English for people in the towns and five times as great in the country. The greatest growth in literacy, so it is estimated, will be in indigenous Indian languages. In fact, literacy in languages other than both Hindi and English by the year 2000 could account for more than half the total literates in India. The concept of Indo-Saxons is more remote than the concept of Afro-Saxons.

Certainly on the linguistic front the African situation in education contrasts starkly with the Asian. There is less of a push in Africa to promote indigenous languages as media for literacy, though some attempts in that direction are under way in Tanzania. There is also less linguistic nationalism generally in Africa than has been observable in places like Malaysia, India, and Bangladesh. The African situation is characterized by an expanding utilization of English; whereas in Asia there is a declining utilization of English. African governments are introducing English at an earlier phase in the educational pyramid than the British themselves had done. As Geoffrey Moorehouse once stated:

On both sides of Africa, moreover, in Ghana and Nigeria, in Uganda and Kenya, the spread of education has led to an increased demand for English at a primary level. The remarkable thing is that English has not been rejected as a symbol of colonialism; it has rather been adopted as a politically neutral language beyond the reproaches of tribalism. It is also a more attractive proposition in Africa because comparatively few Africans are completely literate in the vernacular tongues and even in the languages of regional communication; Hausa and Swahili, which are spoken by millions, are only read and written by thousands.[10]

It is these considerations favoring the growing ascendancy of the English language among black people that continue to assert the likelihood of an expanding population of Afro-Saxons.

Winston Churchill once wrote a mammoth three-volume study entitled *A History of the English-Speaking Peoples.* Churchill lived at a time when the English-speaking peoples were overwhelmingly white, and he was basically right about the Anglo-Saxons. A future Churchillian historian writing a similar study might have to pause and reflect whether the English-speaking peoples did not include a population of Afro-Saxons greater in number than the population of Australia, New Zealand, and even Great Britain, each taken on its own.

Those who speak the tongue that Shakespeare spoke will by the end of the twentieth century include the descendants of Julius K. Nyerere, president of Tanzania and translator into Swahili of Shakespeare. Those holding the faith and morals that Milton held might be deemed to include the descendants of A. Milton Obote, former president of Uganda. The Afro-Saxons are not only here to stay, but they are probably here to multiply as well.

Notes

1. James Baldwin, "Why I Stopped Hating Shakespeare," *Insight, no.11* (Ibadan: British High Commission, 1964), pp.14–15.

2. Ibid.

3. Ibid.

4. *The Merchant of Venice,* Act I, Scene 2, lines 151–53.

5. *Supposed Confessions of a Second-Rate Sensitive Mind,* Conclusion.

6. Opening lecture of the series on "The Rise of Christian Europe," broadcast by Hugh Trevor-Roper and reprinted in *The Listener,* 28 November 1963, p.871.

7. Chinua Achebe, "English and the African Writer," *Transition* (Kampala), 4, no. 18 (1965): 29–30.

8. Ibid.

9. Ibid.

10. Geoffrey Moorehouse, "Tongue Ties," Manchester *Guardian Weekly,* 16 July 1964, p.5. The estimates of likely proportions of literacy among Indian languages are also from Moorhouse's two articles in the Manchester *Guardian Weekly* in that year.

Linguistic Nationlism and
India's National Development

Ajit Kumar Sharma

Language is the main instrument of intercommunication in a civilized society. Inevitably, in a modern community the question of a linguistic medium becomes important to the country's political organization and development. In the conduct of legislative bodies, in the day-to-day dealings with citizens by administrative agencies, in the dispensation of justice, in the system of education, in industry, trade, and commerce, in practically in all segments of a modern government, the state must tackle the problem of linguistic consistency. Apart from this practical aspect of language barriers within a political community, language serves as an emotional rallying point and as an integrating tool in nation building.

India is a subcontinent extending over a million square miles. Its recorded history encompasses five millennia during which cultural patterns of one sort or another have successively flourished in this land. With an area almost equal to the European continent without Russia, a population forming one-seventh of the human race, and a geographical position turning it into a meeting ground throughout history for people of diverse racial and demographic origins, it is hardly surprising that there should be a multiplicity and variety in its forms of speech.

Grievson's linguistic survey of India had put the total number of languages at 872.[1] This number, however, is to be taken with reservation. India is not exactly a babel of tongues with hundreds of languages. "The real language situation in India is important not because of that cry of the ignorant that India is a babel of tongues with hundreds of languages. India, as everyone who looks round can see, has significantly few languages considering its vast size, and these are intimately allied to each other. India has also one dominant and widespread language which, with its variations, covers a vast area. . . ."[2]

The outstanding feature of the linguistic landscape of India is the existance of over a dozen different languages, each spoken by large numbers of people. These languages are prevalent in the compact linguistic regions of the country, each with a history and literary tradition going back over many centuries. These provincial or regional languages are "ancient languages, each tied up inextricably with the life and culture and ideas of the masses as well as the upper classes."[3] Some of these are spoken by as large, or even a larger, number of people than the speakers of some of the advanced languages of the West. In point of its growth and the number of speakers claimed by each of the major Indian languages, the position of size and growth is indicated by the following table, compiled from the 1951 and 1961 censuses.

Language	1951 (in millions)	1961 (in millions)
1. Hindi or Hindusthani	150.0	206.3
2. Telegu	33.0	37.7
3. Bengali	25.0	33.9
4. Marathi	27.0	33.3
5. Tamil	27.0	30.6
6. Gujrati	16.0	20.3
7. Kannada	15.0	17.4

8. Malayalam	13.0	17.0
9. Oriya	13.0	15.6
10.Punjabi	–	11.0
11.Assamese	5.0	6.8
12.Kashmiri	–	2.0
13.Sindhi	–	1.4

The multilingual pattern as indicated, however, should be considered in the context of a large measure of similarity and affinity among all these languages. This kinship reflects a common cultural inheritance that underscores the linguistic variety existing among Indian languages: Sanskrit.

These great and ancient languages, potentially the richest in the world, have suffered a long period of disuse and neglect. As a consequence, they are like "vessels which have been put out of use for years together and on which time has deposited rust. Words of these languages remained unused for the last 300 years or so, which were also the years of continuous development of the modern world, that is, of science, technology, agriculture, and industry. In this whole period India was retarded in politics and also in the use of her languages and these two things go together."[4]

During the more than hundred years of British rule, these languages were cut away from all significant levels of activity, both government and private, and the English language gradually came to supersede them in the work, activities, and thought processes of the higher intelligentsia of all the linguistic regions. English, in time, became the sole means of communication throughout India of all persons holding positions of authority or prominence in private and public life.[5] In completing such a process of linguistic revolution, the British government was no doubt assisted by many Indian leaders who associated English with a promise of modernization and liberation. English thus became the most important medium of communication in the upper sector of national life. A state of cultural havoc, then, was produced by linguistically alienating the educated class and rendering them unable to lead a national regeneration.

The resurgence of India, in the true sense, began in 1915 when Mahatma Gandhi appeared on the scene. Gandhi was the most powerful exponent of a new policy to reestablish the people's lan-

guages and develop a common national language as an instrument of
revolution. He openly charged that it was "not the English themselves but our own English-knowing men who have enslaved India."[6]
In his address at the opening of the Banaras Hindu University in
February 1916, denouncing the role of English as an instrument of
slavery, he declared: "The charge against us is that we have no
initiative. How can we have any, if we are to devote precious years
of our life to the mastery of a foreign language? . . . But suppose
that we had been receiving during the past fifty years education
through our vernaculars, what should we have today? We should
have today a free India, we should have our educated men, not as
if they were foreigners in their own land but speaking to the heart
of the nation."[7] Gandhi's crusade against English was actually an
attack on the English-speaking educated elite, who, forming a caste
by themselves, constituted a vested interest in administration and
education.

As the national movement gathered force, the need of language
for national identity was brought out vividly. Under Gandhi's influence Indian leaders accepted Hindusthani as the symbol of the
national struggle for freedom. Since then the program of encouragement for regional languages as the instrument of mass communication cum political participation and to Hindusthani as the common
Indian language for interregional communication became an integral part of politics of Indian nationalism. The most significant
step in its language policy was taken by the Indian National Congress
when, in 1920, it revised its constitution and provided for the reorganization of its provincial organization on a linguistic basis.

In 1934 the constitution of the Indian National Congress, for
the first time, gave official recognition to Hindusthani and installed
it as the language of proceedings of the congress and its committees.
Following the constitutional reforms brought about by the British
government, the Indian National Congress assumed power in the
provincial governments in 1937. Until then the congress had been
the spearhead of a language policy on a nonofficial level. Once
governmental power came to its hands, the need of a policy of the
state in regard to language was urgently felt. Jawaharlal Nehru initiated such a policy by formulating a set of suggestions, with Mahatma Gandhi's endorsement, as its basis:

1. One public work should be carried on and the state education should be given in the language of each linguistic area. This language should be the dominant language in that area. These Indian languages, to be recognized officially for this purpose, are Hindusthani (both Hindi and Urdu), Bengali, Gujrati, Marathi, Tamil, Telegu, Kannada, Malayalam, Oriya, Assamese, Sindi, and to some aspect Parshi and Punjabi.
2. Hindusthani (both Hindi and Urdu scripts) will be recognized as the all-India Language. As such it will be open to any person throughout India to address a court or public office in the Hindusthani (either script) without any obligation to give a copy in another script or language.
3. The policy governing state's education should be that education is to be given in the language of the student. In each linguistic area education from the primary to the university stage will be given in the language of the province. In the non-Hindusthani speaking areas, basic Hindusthani should be taught in the secondary stage. Provision for teaching foreign language as well as classical language should be made in the secondary schools.[8]

While formulating the above policy, Nehru specifically stated that English could not develop into an all-India language, known by millions.

The congressional governments in the provinces generally accepted Nehru's formulations and initiated a vigorous program for development of their repective languages as well as a national language during their short term of office from 1937 to 1939.

Meanwhile the pressure to replace English with their own mother tongue was mounting. In 1937, Punjab and Calcutta universities permitted the use of regional languages in the matriculation (entrance) examination. Pointing to the writing on the wall, Sir Philip Hartog, chairman of the Simon Commission's Education Committee, warned at the time that as the entrance examination went, so would go all language policy in Indian education.[9]

By the time India became independent in 1947, the fundamental deficiency that had afflicted her people throughout the colonial past was corrected. India possessed a national state and its people could now establish a political system that would accommodate the country's social diversity and generate forces promoting unification and advancement. Ideals set in the course of the national freedom movement had now to be translated into action. The problem of language was one of the first to be tackled in the process of nation building. Freedom was won after a long struggle by the masses, particularly the lower-middle class and the peasantry. For thirty years they had spoken Hindusthani for national purposes and the regional language for provincial purposes. It was, therefore, a natural desire on the part of the people to see their languages given their due place and honor.

Political consolidation of the nation is intimately connected with cultural regeneration. Immediately after independence, Gandhi reminded the new government of the danger inherent in the continued dominance of English in the management of the state. His plea was "for banishing the English language as a cultural usurper."[10] He also warned that unless the government took care, the English language was likely to usurp the place of Hindusthani, doing infinite harm to millions of Indians who would never be able to understand English. For him any delay in the installation of the Indian languages in administration and education would be harmful to the nation. Already the old controversy as to whether Hindusthani or Hindi should be the interprovincial speech was revived by the postpartition communal situation in the country. Gandhi wanted the provincial government to make the desired reform immediately, without waiting for the solution of the controversy on the interprovincial medium. He feared that this "wholly unnecessary controversy was likely to be the door, through which English may enter to the eternal disgrace of India."[11] The University Education Commission under the chairmanship of Dr. S. Radhakrishnan, analyzing different facets of the language problem, also came to the conclusion that English could not occupy the place of state language as in the past. Giving its verdict against English, the commission said: "Use of English as such divides the people into two nations, the few who govern and the many who are governed, the one unable to take the language of the other, and mutually uncomprehending. This is negation of democracy."[12]

The administration of independent India passed into the hands of the English educated elite with no inclination to part with their privilege. When Gandhi succumbed to bullets on 30 January 1948, the formidable challenge to the vested interest of English was removed from the national scene. Though Prime Minister Nehru was personally committed to the replacement of English by a national language, his government showed lack of will to implement the language policy that he himself had initiated in 1937. In an article in 1949, Jawaharlal Nehru, writing "not as the Prime Minister but as an author," expressed his dilemma. "In India, we are rightly committed to the growth of our great provincial languages. At the same time we must have an all-India language. This cannot be English or any other foreign language, although I believe that English, both because of its world position and the present widespread knowledge of it in India is bound to play an important part in our future activities. The only all-India language that is possible is Hindi or Hindusthani or whatever it is called."[13]

In 1948, a linguistic provinces commission appointed by the Constituent Assembly of India reported that on the question of national language the evidence was somewhat divided. The minority favored the retention of English, having Hindi take the place of English, while the majority favored the mother tongue as the regional language with Hindi as a second language for interprovincial purposes and English as a third language for foreign business and commerce.

Inside the Constituent Assembly the debate on the national language raised a Hindi-Hindusthani controversy, signifying two divergent political approaches to a national question. Those who stood for a Hindu-oriented nationalism wanted Sanskrit-based Hindi. Those who favored a composite-cultures based nationalism supported Hindusthani. In this debate Hindi emerged the victor. The preeminence of Hindi, which according to Dr. S.K. Chatterjee was "the result not of propaganda in recent times but as the final transformation of a tradition which began with beginnings of Hindu history and culture," was thus established.[14]

The constitution declared Hindi in Devanagari script as the official language of the union. It provided for the use of Hindi as (a) the official language of the Union; (b) the medium of expression for all the elements of the composite culture of India; (c) the official language for communication between one state and another and between a state and the union; and (d) as an alternative official language of a state along with one or more of its regional languages. It was also provided that for fifteen years from the commencement of the constitution (that is, till January 1965), the English language "shall continue to be used for all the official purposes of the union for which it was being used immediately before such commencement " (article 343:2).

As far as the regional language was concerned, the constitution permitted the legislature of a state to adopt either one or more of the languages spoken in the state or Hindi as its official language. Until such steps were taken by the legislature, English would continue to be used for official purposes of that state. No transitional period for changeover from English to regional languages in the states was prescribed by the constitution as it was in the case of the union.

Further, Parliament was empowered to provide, by law, for the use of English for specific purposes after the above deadline of 1965. Thus English was treated as the outgoing official language and Hindi as the incoming one. The constitution visualized progressive extension of the use of Hindi and contemplated that the use of English would begin to be restricted, eventually to be replaced entirely by Hindi. While providing for the language policy, the Constituent Assembly avoided a decision on the national language in favor of a declaration of an official language. Another significant feature of this policy was the retention of English, though only for a transitional period. As Nirad C. Chaudhury stated: "The really significant feature of the language provision of the constitution is not the recognition of Hindi as heir-presumptive to English. The crucial enactment is the maintenance of English for fifteen years, only with a contingent claim for an Indian language."[15]

When these formal provisions were made in the constitution, the immediate question was how to implement them. It was a formidable task for the Indian political authorities at both the federal and state levels. The democratic structure of politics, the federal form of polity, and the plural basis of the Indian society added complications. To cross all these barriers there was, no doubt, available a dominant political instrument in the Congress party that controlled governments of the center as well as in the states. But, for about two decades after independence the Congress did not provide a unifying structure of leadership. The ruling party, consisting of a relatively loose coalition of diverse groups, leaders, and orientations, tended more to reflect the difficulties of implementing the language provisions than to offer a single-minded direction for solving them.[16]

By retaining the colonial language for a transitional period of fifteen years, the constitution makers sought to smooth the switch over from English to Hindi. This very arrangement later produced a climate to the best advantage of those who calculated great dangers from the emergence of a unifying people's language in the country.

The opposition to Hindi came at first from the urban educated elite of Madras and Bengal, where the spread of English education was more rapid and widespread than in other parts of the country. The upper castes in both these provinces, especially the Brahmans with their long tradition of learning, were the first to turn to English and thus occupy a dominant position in the social, economic, and political life.

English education enabled southern Indians not only to secure a much larger share in the central services than their strength in the total population of the country would seem to justify, but also to get employment as teachers, journalists, lawyers, doctors, and engineers outside their own provinces. "Till the advent of independence a significant proportion of teachers of English language and literature in the universities and colleges in north India came from Madras and Bengal."[17] After the independence of India, when the middle class in other parts of the country, more particularly the enterprising Punjabi and Sindhi Hindus, took to English education zealously in order to rehabilitate themselves in the central government services, the army of English supporters increased its strength.

A year after the promulgation of the constitution, the first five-year plan of India's development was started, and a new economic power structure came to dictate the entire course of subsequent economic development. In the framework of the mixed economy that was developed, the alliance between the top bureaucracy and big business under the political umbrella of ministers was institutionalized. All this meant "absolute economic leadership and control over the nation's economy by the Minister-Top Bureaucrat-Big Business power elite, absorbing into their fold the elite economists, statisticians, scientists, engineers, and so forth, as their advisors."[18]

This initiation of this planning process provided the most powerful stimulus for intellectual activities inside the country. Apart from massive mobilization of intellect by the planning commission, the different ministries and other government agencies, as well as foreign and Indian business houses, there has been a luxurious growth of higher training and research centers. "Most lively and creative participation of the intellectuals in the planning process is being achieved through the organization of committees, conferences, consultations, workshops, seminars, and so forth, involving sizable amounts of travel inside and outside the country. Foreign intellectual participation in the planning process has been equally important, if not more."[19]

By 1956 the ruling party in India set up a Socialist pattern of society to be achieved through accelerated development of rapid industrialization and expansion of the public sector. The golden age of the power elite was thus ushered in. Because of this the importance of English gained more emphasis as an instrument of modernization and scientific development. The prime minister of India also repeatedly stressed the importance of English as a language of science and technology. The upper-class sector had meanwhile strengthened its base in the process, with English serving them as a handy and coveted instrument. All over the country the power elite, comprising the upper classes and upper castes, constituted itself as a great defender of English. As a direct outcome of the process of economic development, a grand alliance was forged between the urban-upper and middle classed and the rural-upper gentry, both acquiring a vested interest in English education.

There were two significant parallel movements in the country: the retention of English directed by C. Rajagopalachari,[20] an astute Brahman politician of Madras who had been the last governor general of India and the first Indian to occupy the high office; and the removal of English, led by Dr. Rammonohar Lohia,[21] a younger intellectual and Socialist leader, who zealously wished to develop the Indian languages as Gandhi had wanted in the preindependence period. The former demanded gradual replacement of English by Hindi, an extension of the fifteen-year limit in the constitution and a national status for English, and finally insisted on an amendment to the constitution to make English the only official language. The latter countered the English resistance movement by demanding immediate banishment of English from public use and maintaining Hindi and other regional languages in their respective spheres.

Both these movements had a great impact on the course of national development. Rajagopalachari succeeded to a great extent in mobilizing the non-Hindi upper-middle-class conservative forces into one common platform, while Lohia provided a radical program for the lower-middle class and rural people to regenerate the people's language. Through his "banish English" strategy, Lohia sought to attack the very foundation of the feudal ruling class. According to him, the root cause of India's national degeneration is the inferiority complex bred by the use of the English language by the ruling class. "The ruling class carries out the daily oppressions over the people with the weapon of English language. They speak in a language which the masses do not know. The peasants, workers, agricultural laborers, shopkeepers, clerks, and such other illiterate masses thereby develop an inferiority complex. This is the root cause of India's degeneration."[22]

Confronted with these two powerful movements, the leaders in the government took the path of least resistance and preferred inaction. No doubt there were certain official endeavors to develop Hindi as the official language and to extend its scope of use, but in view of the government's equivocal stand on the language policy the cause of Hindi as well as the regional language suffered. Such a flexible attitude actually created a situation that, instead of clarifying and resolving the real issue between Hindi and English, succeeded only in raising artificial and poisonous controversy among different languages of India.

Avoiding a decisive stand on the issue, Prime Minister Nehru suggested a line of action, which, in effect, meant a reversal of the constitutional direction on language policy. In a declaration in the Parliament he said: "I suggest two things. First, there must be no imposition. Second, for an indefinite period — I do not know how

long – I would have English as an associate additional language
which can be used for official purposes. I would have it so not mainly because of the existing facilities, but because I do not wish the
people of the non-Hindi areas to feel that certain advantages are
denied to them, being forced to correspond in Hindi. They can
correspond in English. I would have English as an alternate language
as long as the people require it and I would leave the decision not
to the Hindi-knowing people, but to the non-Hindi knowing
people."[23]

The prime minister's suggestion assured the course of events in
the subsequent period. By 1963 the government brought in an
official bill in Parliament "to remove a restriction which had been
placed by the constitution on the use of English after 1965."[24]

The deaths of Prime Minister Nehru and his successor, Lal
Bahadur Shastri, and of Rammonohar Lohia, created a sharp decline in the ruling congress party's strength and a tremendous rise
in the influence of political leadership at state levels. The general
election of 1967 broke the monopoly of the ruling party by depriv-
ing it of power in several states together with narrowing its majority in Parliament. Taking political advantage of this emerging situation, Rajagopalachari renewed his pressure on the government to
give a legal basis to Nehru's assurance. This was done by amending
the Official Language Act "to provide for the continuation of English in addition to Hindi for all official purposes of the union and for
transaction of business in Parliament till the legislatures of all non-
Hindi states agree to its discontinuance and till a resolution to this
effect was passed by Parliament."[25]

The passage of this amendment clearly established bilingualism,
with Hindi and English as equal partners, for the central government
and it conferred on the constituent states a veto power on the
language policy. In political terms, the English-speaking classes in
all the regions finally secured their equality, which, in fact, in the
context of widespread illiteracy in the country as a whole, meant
a more equal status for them.

In the federal structure of India, the major regional languages
are recognized by the constitution. That the boundaries should be
demarcated on linguistic basis had already been accepted during the
national freedom struggle. The linguistic redistribution of the units

of the federation was necessary for the process of nation building. In 1956 the states' boundaries were reorganized, largely on the basis of language, for the administration of education and for the working of courts, legislatures, governmental machinery, and democratic institutions.

Following linguistic reorganization, each state declared its own official or state language. As the different regional languages became the media of administration, it was imperative that these were also made the media of education. But, as in the case of the union official language, the problem of education was the problem of replacing English by the regional languages, especially in the higher stages of learning.

The first education commission of free India, rejecting the case for continuance of English medium in higher education, said that the country "paid a heavy price for learning through English in the past. It affected originality of thought and development of literature in the mother tongue." Recommending a policy for regional language as the medium of university education, it further asserted that "both from the point of view of education and general welfare of a democratic community, it is essential that their study should be through the instrumentality of their regional language. Education in the regional language will not only be necessary for their provincial activities, but it will also enable them to enrich their literature and to develop their culture."[26]

Examining different aspects of the problem, the education commission (1964–66) appointed by the government of India emphasized that the development of the Indian languages was "both urgent and essential for the development of the Indian people and as a way of bringing together the elite and the masses."[27]

Since the regional language "can make scientific and technical knowledge more easily accessible to people in their own languages and thus help in the progress of industrialization, urgent steps were recommended to the universities to change the medium from English to regional languages. The Emotional Integration Committee, appointed by the government of India, also felt that the use of the regional languages on the media of education was a matter of "profound importance for national integration."[28] As a follow-up action, the government provided all universities with financial assistance to implement the regional language medium. The change-over program was adopted by all universities.

The national policy covers (a) the development of Indian languages and literatures as an essential part of educational and cultural development; (b) implementation of a three-language formula at the secondary stage of education, which means the study of the regional language, Hindi, and English; (c) promotion of the development of Hindi as the link for the nation, Sanskrit as the source of cultural unity, and English as the international link language to keep pace with world knowledge of science and technology.

Enforcement of the language policy with respect to education is, of course, not as easy as it appears. The university elite resisted the progress of making the regional language the medium of instruction and examination. A conference of vice-chancellors of all universities in the country convened by the union government in 1967, while "affirming its conviction that energetic development of Indian languages and literature is vital for the promotion of higher education and of national culture generally"[29] and endorsing the statement of the education minister for a program of changeover from English to the regional language medium, they stressed that "the importance of English should be fully recognized and adequate arrangements for its study made at the undergraduate level."[30] Despite the recognition of the importance of regional languages, preeminence of English continues in the sphere of education.

The long evolution of the language policy in India underscores the dilemma faced by a nation escaping from long colonial rule in the task of building itself on the basis of self-reliance. It indicates the difficulty in crossing hurdles put on the road of national development by the vested interest created by the language of foreign domination. In his own style Prime Minister Nehru described this national dilemma: "I have said I am partial to English. But I am also partial to the masses of this country. I cannot forget that we have to carry 400 million people, and we cannot carry them psychologically, emotionally, or practically in any way except through their language. It is no good forgetting that it is the non-English speaking who will decide the fate of India, because they are the vast majority in this country." In the framework of democratic political structure of India this "vast majority" has been trying to establish itself, yet, at every step it has had to dash against the rock of partiality to English. In the particular context of the planned economic development of India, this partiality has further increased. In the upper sector of national life, a cosmopolitan class, consisting of the English elite intelligentsia, has grown. But in the current Indian context, this intelligentsia is cosmopolitan not out of fullness of spirit but out of rootlessness. He not it is alienated from its own society. Through its English medium it looks to inspiration from elsewhere and is cut off from the path of self-reliance. Such cosmopolitanism integrates directly and separately to a world center, snapping the intermediate link of a nation. The national center just does not exist culturally or intellectually. This has added a new dimension to India's language problem in terms of nation building and making the leadership at the local level compatible with the need for cohesive political and administrative leadership at the national level can be removed only through a new language policy that integrates the regional with the national language — not through the vehicle of a foreign language.

Notes

1. Census Report of India, 1961. (Family-wise strength of languages: Austric 30, Karen 11, Man 2, Tibeto-chinese 241, Dravidian 46, Indo-European 519, and Unclassified 23).

2. Jawaharlal Nehru, *The Question of Language* (Congress Political and Economic Studies, no. 5, 1937), pp.1–2. In a foreword to this booklet, Mahatma Gandhi endorsed Nehru's views. Jawaharlal Nehru later became free India's first prime minister.

3. Jawaharlal Nehru's article quoted in *Mainstream,* 11 May 1963.

4. Dr. Rammonohar Lohia, "English and People's Language in India," *Mankind* 4, no. 5 (December 1959).

5. Report of the Official Language Commission, 1956.

6. Cited in the speeches and writings of Annie Besant, *The India That Shall Be* (Madras: Theosophical Publishing House, 1940), p.249.

7. Tendulkar, ed., *Mahatma,* 8 vols. (New Delhi: Ministry of Information and Broadcasting, 1960–63), 1:221.

8. J. Nehru, *The Question of Language.*

9. Selig S. Harrison, *India: The Most Dangerous Decades* (Princeton, N.J.: Princeton University Press, 1960).

10. Mahatma Gandhi, "Take Care," editorial in the *Harijan*, 21 September 1947, as taken from *Mahatma*, vol. 8.

11. *Mahatma*, 8:154.

12. University Education Commission Report, p.316.

13. *The Question of Language* (*Hindusthan Standard* [Calcutta], 13 February 1949). Nehru begins the article in the following words: "I am writing this article not as Prime Minister but as an author and as a person interested in the question of language because of its political and, unfortunately, communal aspects."

14. Dr. S. K. Chatterjee, *Hindi and the Role of Midland Speech in Indian History* (*Hindusthan Standard* [Calcutta] 7 August 1949). Dr. Chatterjee is an internationally reputed scholar and linguist.

15. Nirod C. Chaudhury, "The Question of Language for the Million," *Statesman*, 26 January 1952.

16. J. Dasgupta, *Language Conflict and National Development* (New York: Oxford University Press, 1970), p.150.

17. Dr. B. M. Bhatia, "South's Opposition to Hindi," *Statesman*, 12 February 1968.

18. B. V. Krishnamurthy, "Power Elite Planning for People's Welfare," *Socialist Digest* 1 (March 1968).

19. Ibid.

20. C. Rajagopalachari was one of the most respected leaders of India. As the first prime minister of the Madras province he had introduced Hindi as a compulsory language in the schools. Explaining his attitude to Hindi he wrote (*Thought*, 18 August 1956): "Some people think that my objection to making Hindi the 'official' language of India is contrary to the views I held and enforced when I was in charge of the Madras government in 1937. Let me make it clear that even now I am, as before I was, for Hindi being made an important and compulsory part of the students' curriculum all over India."

21. Dr. Rammonohar Lohia has explained his views in his article on language, *see* note 4 above.

22. "English and the People's Languages in India," *Mankind* 4, no. 5 (1959).

23. Prime Minister Nehru's speech in the House of the People, 7 August 1959, *Nehru's Speeches* (New Delhi: Publications Division of the Ministry of Information and Broadcasting, 1959).

24. Prime Minister's speech, 24 April 1963, *Hindusthan Standard*, 25 April 1963.

25. *Statesman*, 28 November 1967.

26. Report of the University Education Commission, Government of India, 1949. Chairman of this commission was Dr. S. Radhakrishnan, who later became the President of India.

27. Report of the Education Commission (1964–66), p. 13.

28. Ibid.

29. Ibid.

30. Recommendations of the Vice-Chancellors' Conference convened by the Ministry of Education and the University Grants Commission, September 1967.

CONTRIBUTORS

Walker Connor is Professor of Political Science at State University College at Brockport, New York. He has authored books and articles on Ethnicity and Development.

Theodore A. Couloumbis is Professor of International Relations at The American University. He has authored books and articles on International Relations and Greece and Cyprus.

Irving Louis Horowitz is Professor of Sociology and Political Science at Rutgers University. He is director of Studies in Comparative Development and editor-in-chief of *Transaction/Society.* The essay in this volume is from a larger, ongoing effort, the first fruits of which were published as *Israeli Ecstasies/ Jewish Agonies.*

Paschalis M. Kitromilides is a graduate of Pancyprian Gymnasium. He served in the Cyprus National Guard before coming to the United States on a Fulbright Scholarship. Currently, he is a teaching fellow in the Department of Government at Harvard University.

Ali A. Mazrui is Professor of Political Science and Head of the Department at Makerere University, Uganda. He has published several books and articles on Africa.

Gustav Morf is a psychiatrist in Montreal, Canada. He has worked as consultant psychiatrist at St. Vincent de Paul Penitentiary. He also has authored books and articles on political movements in Quebec.

Hamid Mowlana is Professor of International Communication and Relations and Director of Program in International Communication at The American University. He has authored several books, is editor of three scholarly journals, and has contributed to numerous books and anthologies on communication, sociology, and international politics.

J.K. Obatala is Professor of Black Studies at California State University, Long Beach. He has authored numerous articles on black consciousness.

Teresa Rakowska-Harmstone is Professor of Political Science, Carleton University, Canada. She has authored *Russia and Nationalism in Soviet Central Asia; the Case of Tadzhikistan*

(Johns Hopkins, 1970); and authored and coauthored articles
and books on the Soviet Union.

Ann Elizabeth Robinson is a communication specialist who has
worked with ethnic groups and has done field work in Jamaica
and the United States.

Abdul Aziz Said is Professor of International Relations, The American University. He has authored several books and articles on
various aspects of world politics.

Ajit Kumar Sharma is Professor of Political Science at Gauhati University, India, and President of A.S.S.A.M. Political Science
Association.

Luiz R. Simmons is a Washington attorney. He has authored several
books and articles on subcultures, youth, narcotics, foreign
policy, and American politics.

Nikolaos A. Stavrou is Associate Professor of Political Science,
Howard University. He has authored books and articles on
Yugoslavia and Eastern Europe.

INDEX